# African Voices
# of the Global Past

# African Voices
# of the Global Past

*1500 to the Present*

## TREVOR R. GETZ

*Editor*

**WESTVIEW PRESS**

*A Member of the Perseus Books Group*

Westview Press was founded in 1975 in Boulder, Colorado, by notable publisher and intellectual Fred Praeger. Westview Press continues to publish scholarly titles and high-quality undergraduate- and graduate-level textbooks in core social science disciplines. With books developed, written, and edited with the needs of serious nonfiction readers, professors, and students in mind, Westview Press honors its long history of publishing books that matter.

Find us on the World Wide Web at www.westviewpress.com.

Every effort has been made to secure required permissions for all text, images, maps, and other art reprinted in this volume.
Westview Press books are available at special discounts for bulk purchases in the United States by corporations, institutions, and other organizations. For more information, please contact the Special Markets Department at the Perseus Books Group, 2300 Chestnut Street, Suite 200, Philadelphia, PA 19103, or call (800) 810-4145, ext. 5000, or e-mail special.markets@perseusbooks.com.

Designed by Jeff Williams

Library of Congress Cataloging-in-Publication Data
African voices of the global past : 1500 to the present / Trevor R. Getz, editor.
    pages cm.
    Includes bibliographical references and index.
    ISBN 978-0-8133-4787-5 (pbk.) — ISBN 978-0-8133-4788-2 (e-book) 1. Africa—History. 2. History, Modern. 3. Industrial revolution—Africa. 4. Slave trade—History. 5. Africa—Colonization—History. 6. World War, 1914-1918—Africa. 7. World War, 1939-1945—Africa. 8. Africa—History—Autonomy and independence movements. 9. Feminism—Africa. I. Getz, Trevor R., author, editor of compilation.

DT26.A47 2013
960—dc23
                                                                2013000935

PB ISBN: 978-0-8133-4787-5 (alk. paper)
EBOOK ISBN: 978-0-8133-4788-2 (ebook)

10 9 8 7 6 5 4 3 2 1

FOR A. ADU BOAHEN AND JOSEPH C. MILLER,
TWO GREAT HISTORIANS OF AFRICA

# Contents

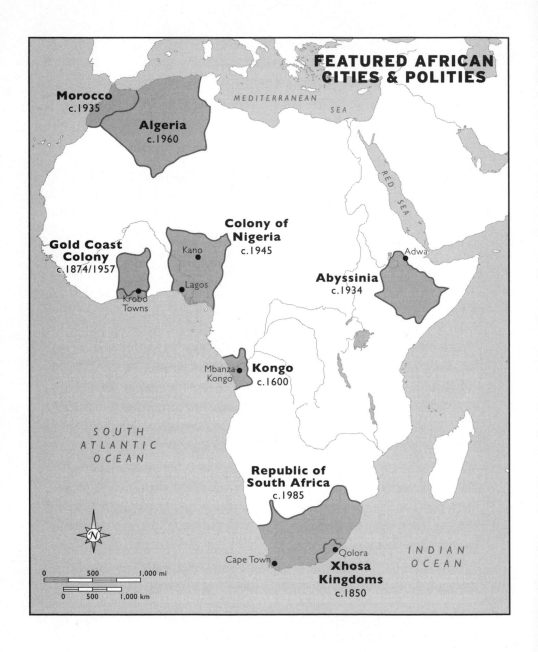

FEATURED AFRICAN
CITIES & POLITIES

MEDITERRANEAN SEA

Morocco
c.1935

Algeria
c.1960

RED SEA

Gold Coast
Colony
c.1874/1957

Colony of
Nigeria
c.1945

Kano

Lagos

Krobo
Towns

Adwa

Abyssinia
c.1934

Mbanza
Kongo

Kongo
c.1600

SOUTH
ATLANTIC
OCEAN

Republic of
South Africa
c.1985

Qolora

Cape Town

Xhosa
Kingdoms
c.1850

INDIAN
OCEAN

0    500    1,000 mi

0    500    1,000 km

# Introduction

Over the past several decades, world history has become a major paradigm through which the past is taught. Through cooperation and debate, world historians since the 1960s have been able to create a shared narrative of the human past. Their work has connected regional experiences and individual histories by revealing the networks, systems, and exchanges that connected us to one another. Thus far, however, they have been less successful in exploring that global past from the perspectives of the people who experienced it. In other words, while events affecting all regions of the world have made their way into world history pedagogy, nonwestern populations' experiences and understandings of these events still remain hidden. This is especially true of the African experience of the last 1,500 years. In general, world historians have discussed Africans largely as the objects of other people's plans and actions rather than as humans with their own perspectives and ability to tell their own stories. For example, world historians have recognized the roles played by the Atlantic slave trade, colonialism, and the industrialization in the impoverishment of African communities. However, they have not really communicated an understanding of the parts that Africans themselves played in these global trends nor an appreciation for their experiences and the art, language, and writing they produced to express their perspectives on such trends.

## OUR PHILOSOPHY

Yet this need not be the case. Scholars of and from Africa have developed the skills and scholarship to bring African understandings of events—in

Africa and elsewhere—to world history students everywhere. Whereas Africa was once considered a "dark" or "silent" continent that produced no historical evidence, we now know that historians just weren't looking hard enough. Indeed, there exists a wealth of oral, written, archaeological, and visual sources from the African past, many of them produced by—and conveying the perspectives and authentic experiences of—Africans themselves.

*African Voices of the Global Past* is the first textbook specifically designed as a world history companion that concentrates on retelling many of the important episodes in the global past (c.1500–present) from African points of view. In this volume, the events and trends discussed are of global significance: the Atlantic slave system, the industrial revolution, formal colonialism, World Wars I and II, decolonization, and the struggle for women's rights and opportunities. But these historical events were also important experiences for Africans, who participated in them in various ways. In many instances Africans were not the protagonists and, at first glance, seem not to have been key players. Yet despite the fact that none of these historical events would have occurred the way they did but for the actions of Africans, such events are typically taught in ways that minimize Africans' roles. Moreover, these events are just the tip of the iceberg. Africans had important parts in numerous other world history episodes not covered in this volume due to space limitations: the globalization of Islam and Christianity, the cold war, and the Arab Spring are just a few examples.

Given the roles that Africans played in the global past, it is of value to all of us to see these events and trends as Africans understood them. The key to this book is the focus on African *perspectives*. The views presented here represent an attempt not just to talk about what happened to Africans, or even how they experienced global trends and episodes, but also to discuss the ways in which Africans talked and wrote about and *perceived* these events and trends. Hence the chapters in this book focus on *primary sources* written by Africans. Most of the authors, too, are citizens of Africa (South Africa, Nigeria) or are of Afro-Caribbean descent. Together, we believe that it is valuable to learn not just about the connections among us and the roles that Africans played but also about the ways that Africans in these periods responded intellectually, artistically, and spiritually to the world in which they lived.

## NAVIGATING THE BOOK

This book is designed to cover six episodes or themes of the global past that are commonly discussed in the world history classroom. The chapters are arranged chronologically, encompassing the Atlantic slave trade/system, which began in the fifteenth century; decolonization; and the feminist struggles of the late twentieth century.

Each chapter begins with a section headed "Global Context" in which the featured global event or trend is introduced. This portion of the chapter is meant to connect Africa to other parts of the globe by situating it within the networks, systems, and exchanges of ideas, people, and things that characterized the period in question (e.g., trade, exploration voyages, intellectual movements, the rise and fall of empires, and war). The second section of each chapter, titled "African Experiences," focuses on social history—an exploration of the ways in which daily life, work, home and family, and relationship patterns changed for African individuals and communities. In some chapters, the author emphasizes a specific region of Africa—for example, the Atlantic seaboard of the continent (Chapter 1), Ethiopia (Chapter 3), Nigeria (Chapter 4), and Morocco (Chapter 6)—whereas Chapters 2 and 5 are broader in focus. The final section of each chapter features a discussion of "African Perspectives." In this section, the authors focus on primary sources in the process of analyzing the ways in which Africans thought, talked, and represented the themes discussed in the chapter. These sources include stories, newspaper articles, poems, speeches, police reports, diaries, and photographs.

At the end of each chapter is a series of questions that will help you to think about the roles and perspectives of Africans. The authors hope that these questions will lead you to think deeply and extensively about the African and global past and our relationship to it. If we succeed in this respect, you may wish to read the books listed in "Further Readings," a short guide to additional resources that concludes each chapter.

Finally, thank you to the reviewers whose valuable comments helped make this a more helpful book for their classrooms: Patience Essah, Auburn University; Alan Karras, University of California, Berkeley; Maxim Matusevich, Seton Hall University; Matt Carotenuto, St. Lawrence University; and Cymone Fourshey, Susquehanna University.

—*Trevor Getz*

# I

# Naming and Framing a Crime Against Humanity

*African Voices of the Transatlantic*
*Slave System, ca. 1500–1900*

Kwasi Konadu

## GLOBAL CONTEXT

The purpose of this chapter is to enlarge our understanding of Africa in the era of the transatlantic slave system, to draw attention to African experiences during that period, and, finally, to explore how Africans themselves interpreted the process of transatlantic slaving through their own ways of making sense of the world. Beginning in the late fifteenth century, this global system of commerce reached its height in the eighteenth century, having grown out of Africa's earlier connections with the globe through long-standing trans-Saharan, Mediterranean, Red Sea, and Indian Ocean trade.[1] Owing to the endurance of Africa's historic relations with Eurasia through these trade networks, transatlantic commerce and human trafficking would surpass rather than replace them, even as the global economy gradually shifted from the Indian Ocean world in the east to the Atlantic Ocean world in the Western Hemisphere.

Since the beginnings of the transatlantic slave system in the fifteenth century, enslavement has been the focus of an enormous number of books, pamphlets, and articles, making it a topic that college students in African or African American history courses anticipate and to which African (American) history is often reduced. Yet, despite this mountain of "slave trade" literature, a cruel irony of the transatlantic system is that its documentation tells us very little about those who suffered the most—the Africans. Thus my aim is to reveal in those documents of repression the humanity of the people being repressed. While we have a far greater quantity of sources and therefore know much more about African lives under the transatlantic system than about the enslavement of Africans across the Sahara desert or the Indian Ocean, excavating those lives is not an easy task. Indeed, the sheer terror and violence of the transatlantic system not only attacked the bodies and humanity of Africans caught in its grasp, it also transformed these individuals in terms of the numbers representing them etched on ledgers and in log books, thereby subjecting them to the violence of abstraction.

Where can we search for Africans' perspectives and accounts of their experiences in this system? While much can be learned about African lives from the numeric data and observations recorded by European slaving companies and their agents, we must move beyond the statistics that silenced African voices during the transatlantic era, for the silences of the past continue to stubbornly shape our present understandings about racism, pervasive stereotypes about Africa and Africans and those in its diasporas, and the meaning of the transatlantic slave system as a crime against African humanity. A synthesis such as this chapter, which looks at central themes in the African experience of the transatlantic slave system, cannot fully address these important contemporary issues. However, as an examination of transatlantic slaving through African eyes and experiences, it can provide an integral perspective on these issues and on the study of the transatlantic slave system itself.

## Naming and Framing a Crime Against Humanity

The historical events discussed in this chapter are usually referred to as the "Atlantic slave trade" or "African slave trade." I have instead chosen to use the phrase "transatlantic slave system" to emphasize the systemic reach of transatlantic slaving, which extended well beyond commerce, encompassing the culture and ecology of African communities as well. The naming of this historical process is not a purely academic issue. Many African societies have long known what western scholars have begun to suspect: that words themselves have power, and that their meaning is situational. In other words, names and labels can affect how we perceive a person, place, or historical process.

The first word we must examine in the name of this set of experiences is "slave." For most of us, the first image that comes to mind when we hear or read this term is that of an enslaved African. Indeed, many of us still view Africans principally as (former) "slaves," rather than as humans first. Historically, however, the word "slave" derives from the Greek term *sklavos* (referring to the large number of Slavic peoples under captivity) and the Latin *sclavus* (meaning both "Slav" [Slavic] and "slave"). Our own racialized contemporary vision of the slave as African is packed with more than five centuries of indelible images very different from those of the Greeks or Romans: "blackness" as a synonym for "Africans" and as the demonic opposite of a Judeo-Christian "whiteness," and pejorative ideas of Africans and their worldwide descendants as barbarous, idolatrous, and without beauty and intelligence. It is only recently that some scholars have begun to define these humans under captivity as "enslaved Africans"—a phrase that more accurately underscores their condition within the transatlantic slave system than does the crude and intellectually violent word "slaves."

My decision to use the phrase "transatlantic slave system" rather than the more commonly employed "slave trade," "African slave trade," and even "transatlantic slave trade" is also important. For one thing, the term "trade" embedded in each of these labels conceals the violence of the system: the raids, captures, escapes, and uprisings, the incarcerations at coastal ports, the languishing of men, women, and children in the holds of ships, the disease, suffering and death on those one-way Atlantic crossings, commodification, the lives of laboring. The term "trade" conjures up an image of an exchange of commodities for other commodities or capital, and little of this straightforward arithmetic occurred, though it was certainly a part of the process of converting Africans into property or chattel. Moreover, combining either "slave" or "African" with "trade" only leads us once again into the trap of equating "slave" with "African," making them interchangeable terms with equivalent meanings. Nor is the use of "African" strictly accurate. So much of the trafficking in enslaved Africans revolved around European capital, and within this system African labor created a great deal of wealth and industries for the benefit of European and neo-European societies (i.e., the colonies and then, later, the nations established by Europeans in the Americas). Thus some critics might suggest that we refer instead to "European slave trade." That argument does have weight and can be applied in many cases, but it is similarly insufficient. Substituting one homogenization (i.e., "Africans sold other Africans") for another (i.e., "Europeans bought and enslaved Africans") does little to get the full story right. For example, this simplification would make it difficult to understand the experiences of powerful merchants of mixed African and European parentage and of both genders who were active players in the transatlantic slave system but, according to their own accounts, were neither "African" nor "European."[2]

There is one additional danger of homogenizing and oversimplifying this system as African. For far too long, the sound bite that "Africans" sold or enslaved other "Africans"—or, Africans sold their "brothers and sisters"—has rolled almost effortlessly off the tongues of scholars, students, and the general public. In most historical instances, members of distinct and sometimes partnering African societies, even those linked by clan affiliations, viewed others not as "Africans" (in the sense of a shared, continental identity) but, rather, as specific cultural groups—that is, as individuals of "foreign" or captive origins, criminals, war captives, and vulnerable people who could become enslaved. To cast a wide net of inhumanity upon all Africans by suggesting that "Africans sold Africans" reaffirms the violence of homogenization and reduces historical processes that shifted according to time, place, and people to a simple matter-of-fact statement. In much the same way that Christian Europeans sold their war captives to Muslims and did not see this transaction as putting their "countrymen" into slavery, some Africans exchanged members of other groups without viewing those destined for export as fellow "Africans." In cases involving the kidnapping and pawning of kin on account of debt, the kidnapped or pawned individual was usually seized by force and without the consent of the debtor; sometimes, the debtor (usually a male) would also be seized, put in chains, and exported from his homeland. It should be noted that the institution of pawning (using valuables or individuals as collateral for credit and the establishment of trust) contributed only a small number of captive Africans to the transatlantic system inasmuch as pawns, in the form of gold or humans, guaranteed a loan and theoretically prevented one from being arbitrarily seized and sold on account of a defaulting debtor. In many of the slaving regions in Africa, however, there were few valuables (in the eyes of Europeans) other than people, and European merchants and their agents almost always preferred to trade in humans. In short, the mechanisms through which Africans found themselves as captives defy homogenization and should temper our urge to reduce the matter of transatlantic slaving to African depravity.

How we define a subject such as international slaving and thus frame it is a crucial part of the process by which we restore the humanity not only of those millions of Africans who violently died under its systemic weight but also of their descendants who still suffer in a racialized global order made possible in part by the transatlantic slave system. Indeed, one meaningful way to hold accountable the transatlantic slave system—including its institutional and individual beneficiaries—for its crimes against African humanity is to tell its human story on both sides of the Atlantic. For we now know quite a bit about the intricacies of the transatlantic slave system.

However, we know comparatively little about the enslaved Africans who were brought to the Americas and those who remained in Africa and in some state of captivity. In Africa and in the Americas, those who were literate or became so under captivity left us a few autobiographical accounts of their experiences (whereas many of the untapped sources for the era of the transatlantic slave system remain archived in African and African diasporic art, song, ritual, and memory). Accordingly, the next section of this chapter surveys the experiences of those enslaved Africans, bringing out patterns and overarching themes across wide geographical areas while providing specifics that make those patterns and themes more tangible.

## AFRICAN EXPERIENCES

*The Origins of the Transatlantic Slave System*

The transatlantic slave system was an outgrowth and expansion of prior commercial systems centered on the Mediterranean region from the Atlantic to western Asia. These systems connected Europe, western and southern Asia, and northeast and North Africa, including those areas of interior Africa where captives were carried across the Sahara by Arab-Muslim merchants to coastal ports. By the early thirteenth century, Italian (specifically Genoese and Venetian) merchants had already established slaving ports using captive "Slavs" and other peoples to produce sugar for export within a commercial system that stretched from the Atlantic, through the Mediterranean, and to the Black Sea (in and around the Crimean peninsula). On the Atlantic end of this network the Iberian nations of Portugal and Spain, after the former and then the latter rose from under Arab-African Islamic rule, were aided by the Italian model of plantation slavery and soon extended the network to islands off the northwest and west central African coast in the 1400s. Portugal and Spain dominated the transatlantic slave system until the mid-seventeenth century, and Britain and Portugal would continue that dominance until the early nineteenth century, when the British made international slavery illegal. The Portuguese and Spaniards would control the trafficking in captive Africans until Cuba and Brazil abolished the system of transatlantic slaving in 1886 and 1888, respectively.

The *Reconquista*—the centuries-long Christian retaking of the Iberian peninsula from Islamic control—set the stage for the transatlantic slave system. Through this process, the Portuguese expelled their Muslim overlords almost two centuries sooner than the Spaniards, acquired some essential nautical knowledge and technologies through Muslim scholars (who obtained their know-how from as far as China), added cannons to their vessels, and established plantations off the coasts of western Africa (e.g., Madeira islands and São Tomé) while raiding African communities for captives. By the fifteenth century, these African captives were increasingly replacing the "Slavs" and other captives in Portugal, Spain, and France. These early African captives were victims of Portuguese slaving voyages as well as of Arab slaving across the Sahara and through north African ports in Morocco, Tunisia, and Libya. This Africanization of the trade in enslaved humans reached a new level in the late fifteenth century when the Ottoman Turks captured Constantinople (what is now Istanbul, capital of present-day Turkey) and diverted the flow of eastern Mediterranean and Black sea captives, including Christian Europeans sold by their countrymen, from the northern Mediterranean to the lands of Islam. The production of Christian Europe's sugar by enslaved labor and the sources of such labor then shifted west toward the Atlantic, eventually stretching from northwest to west central Africa in the late fifteenth and sixteenth centuries.

In the 1440s, the first recorded group of African captives from the West African region of Senegambia reached the capital of Portugal. Upon arrival, naked and terrified, they were paraded through the streets of Lisbon as a "barbaric" spectacle to be gawked at by onlookers. A century later, enslaved Africans were commonplace in Portugal. Captive Africans in Lisbon, one of the largest cities in sixteenth-century Europe, are estimated to have accounted for 10 percent of that city's population. The first enslaved Africans destined for the Americas left from such cities as Lisbon and Seville, Spain. Once in the Americas, their skills and labor were utilized on plantations, in mining operations, and at urban enslavement sites. By the end of the seventeenth century, Africans had almost fully replaced enslaved Amerindians (from various societies) and indentured white laborers (many of whom became planters) as the primary source of labor in the Americas for the production and exportation of sugar, rum, molasses, tobacco, coffee, cotton, indigo, precious metals and minerals, luxury items, and, indeed, some of the very irons used in their physical bondage. These so-called saltwater Africans brought with them not only their experience with large-scale agriculture (especially root crops and rice) and their iron-working and textile skills but also some immunity against certain parasitic diseases, such as malaria. With only a small number of exceptions, these captive Africans did not return to their homelands to recount their experiences or observations. Theirs was a one-way voyage—first as captives, then as commodities packed below and above slave vessels' decks, and finally as valuable yet often uncontrollable property.

*Experiencing the "Middle Passage"*

As noted, sources providing African perspectives on the Atlantic crossing from Africa to the Americas are very few in number. Africans traveled this "middle passage" on vessels that made multiple crossings, each time adding another thick layer of blood, sweat, urine, excrement, uneaten food, and death to the lower decks. The upper decks of these vessels were also encrusted with similar matter resulting from the floggings of captives who refused to dance, jump, or sing. Ultimately, they served as platforms from which some captives jumped or were forcibly thrown overboard. In *The Slave Ship: A Human History*, maritime historian Marcus Rediker describes the sheer violence and terror on board the slave vessel, at once a machine of death, a social institution, and a vehicle that prepared the enslaved for the continued terror to be experienced once their sea-bound journey ended. His apt summation of the slave ship's preparatory role is worth quoting at length.

> The slave ship had not only delivered millions of [African] people to slavery, it had prepared them for it. Literal preparation included readying the bodies for sale by the crew: shaving and cutting the hair of the men, using caustics to hide sores, dying gray hair black, and rubbing down torsos with palm oil. Preparations also included subjection to the discipline of enslavement. Captives experienced the "white master" and his unchecked power and terror, as well as that of his "overseers," the mate, boatswain, or sailor. They experienced the use of violence to hold together a social order in which they outnumbered their captors by ten to one or more. They ate communally and lived in extreme barrack-like circumstances. They did not yet work in the backbreaking, soul-killing ways of the plantation, but labor many of them did, from domestic toil to forced sex work, from pumping the ship to setting the sails. It must also be noted that in preparing the captives for slavery, the experience of the slave ship also helped to prepare them to resist slavery.[3]

Historians have amassed a total of 388 recorded cases of enslaved African uprisings on board vessels close to African waters or en route to the Americas.[4] One African region, the area from Senegambia to the Ivory Coast, accounted for 42 percent of such revolts but contributed only about 12 percent of the total number of recorded captives who found themselves under the transatlantic slave system. By contrast, west central Africa accounted for more than 45 percent of all the (recorded) captives embarked for the Americas but experienced only 11 percent of the revolts, supporting European slavers' belief that such captives were less likely to resist.

Resistance to enslavement took place not just aboard ship but also when captives caught sight of a slaver or raiding party or realized that a visit to the European fort would be the last time they saw their relatives or smelled the aroma of locally prepared foods. Africans' responses to capture and enslavement included attacks on European forts, and at least sixty-one recorded attacks on ships were carried out by land-based Africans in the seventeenth and eighteenth centuries. Africans also built fortresses, fortified towns, resettled in hard-to-find places, transformed habitats and the ways in which they occupied land, diverted rivers, and burned down European factories. In addition, they employed young men in militias to protect and defend communities. Africans also used medicinal plants for camouflage, ritual cleansing, and protection as well as poisonous plants and thorny trees and bushes for general resistance. A variety of resistive strategies led to rising costs for the slavers—costs that, in turn, factored into the decline of the transatlantic slave system. In short, enslaved and potentially enslaved peoples employed protective, offensive, and defensive strategies irrespective of their origins in Africa, including resistance to capture and deportation. Such resistance, however, was interlinked with accommodation to, and participation in, the slave system—regardless of whether the captivity occurred on the African coast or on board slave vessels en route to foreign lands.

### The Shape and Scale of the Transatlantic Slave System

The captives and vessels that constituted the middle passage were part of a transatlantic slave system that was linked to the spread of sugar cane production. In fact, the earlier westward movement of slaving and sugar production across eastern Asia into the Mediterranean and southern Europe, and then on to coastal Africa and the Americas, came full circle to the Pacific in the nineteenth century.[5] In the Caribbean basin, sugar and slavery also started in the east—specifically, in Barbados—and then moved westward throughout the region. These movements of people and the sugary products that came to define slave societies in the Americas were supported by two distinct yet mutually reinforcing sets of prevailing winds and ocean currents—in the north Atlantic and the south Atlantic—that created two sub-slaving systems within the broader transatlantic world. The north Atlantic currents turned clockwise north of the equator, and thus this sub-slaving system was based in Europe and North America. Most captives taken into this system were procured north of the Congo River (in what is now the Democratic Republic of Congo) and shipped primarily to the Caribbean and North America and, in some cases, to the South American ports of Buenos Aires and Montevideo. The British, especially after the mid-seventeenth century, dominated this north Atlantic system. The southern system, by contrast, was largely controlled by the Portuguese (whether in Brazil or Portugal). In this latter system, the Atlantic currents turned counter-clockwise and the traffic in captive Africans was based primarily in Brazil. The source of captives for the south Atlantic market was chiefly west central Africa, with relatively smaller numbers coming from the bights of Benin and Biafra and southeast Africa (e.g., Mozambique), especially during the nineteenth century. Southeast Africa was linked to both sub-slaving systems, demonstrating that the trade winds and ocean currents did shape where captive Africans were drawn and where they landed. In another sense, however, the multiple movements of Africans transcended wind and water. On the whole, the north and south Atlantic slaving sub-systems shared much in common, ultimately forming a transatlantic system driven by demand and greed—as evidenced by the increasing number and price of captive Africans, and the increasing quantity of the sugar they produced, between the fifteenth and nineteenth centuries.

Over the course of those four centuries, approximately 13 to 15 million Africans living across a broad swathe of the continent from Senegambia to west central and southeast Africa embarked for the Americas, but only about 50,000 went to Europe (see Map 1.1). These numbers are still being debated, however, and any set of numbers attempting to quantify an acknowledged

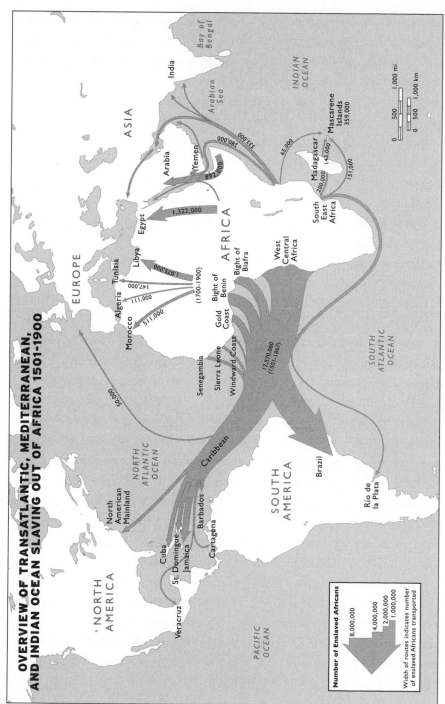

**OVERVIEW OF TRANSATLANTIC, MEDITERRANEAN, AND INDIAN OCEAN SLAVING OUT OF AFRICA 1501–1900**

ASIA

*Bay of Bengal*

India

*Arabian Sea*

INDIAN OCEAN

Arabia

Yemen

533,000

280,000

65,000

Mascarene Islands 359,000

Madagascar

143,000

200,000

151,000

South East Africa

EUROPE

Egypt 1,322,000

892,000

AFRICA

Libya

Tunisia

147,000

1,075,000

111,000

Algeria

(1700–1900)

Bight of Benin

Bight of Biafra

West Central Africa

115,000

Morocco

Gold Coast

Senegambia

Sierra Leone

Windward Coast

12,570,000 (1501–1867)

*SOUTH ATLANTIC OCEAN*

50,000

*NORTH ATLANTIC OCEAN*

Caribbean

Brazil

Rio de la Plata

SOUTH AMERICA

North American Mainland

Barbados

Cartagena

Cuba

St. Domingue

Jamaica

Veracruz

NORTH AMERICA

*PACIFIC OCEAN*

1,000 mi

500

1,000 km

500

**Number of Enslaved Africans**

8,000,000

4,000,000

2,000,000

1,000,000

Width of routes indicates number of enslaved Africans transported

Map 1.1

crime against (African) humanity must be digested with caution. For in-stance, how, in the absence of verifiable records or recollections, do we cal-culate the human cost to Africa? We cannot quantify such factors as disease, abortions, suicides, mortality in the quest for captives and after their capture, or unscrupulous merchants who discarded or undercounted captives to evade fees levied upon them. Even the most sophisticated transatlantic stud-ies cannot and do not account for these factors; rather, their economic and statistical models focus, almost religiously, on volume, prices, supply, cargo, expenses, profits, losses, competition, and partnership without much atten-tion to the qualitative, human dimensions of their African subjects. Yet the numbers do have a place, for they tell us something significant about long-term patterns.

Recent scholarship suggests the vast majority of outbound Africans left their homelands in six major coastal regions: the territory between Senegam-bia and the Ivory Coast (Côte d'Ivoire), the Gold Coast, the Bight of Benin, the Bight of Biafra, west central Africa, and southeast Africa. However, re-gions of embarkation should not necessarily be conflated with regions or ports of origin: many captive Africans were drawn from political and, at times, religious areas wider and more inland than the major coastal ports—some traveling hundreds of miles to the coast on foot. We can certainly imagine thousands of captive families and friends in and around the vast west central African region being led through forests, over rocky pathways, and across river water to the Atlantic, since this region accounted for about 45 percent of all recorded Africans who left for the Americas.

As for points of debarkation, the relatively early start of the Portuguese in establishing sugar plantations off the African coasts and in Brazil, and the equally early importation of captive Africans to Portugal and to the Americas along the south Atlantic currents, meant that Brazil and the Caribbean were major destinations for enslaved Africans. Brazil received a large number of captives; almost the same percentage who had left west cen-tral Africa landed in the Caribbean, giving this region and South America (including Brazil) close to 95 percent of the approximately 13 million cap-tives who landed in the Americas. But the Caribbean was also shaped by peoples and cultures other than those of west central Africa. Indeed, the

Gold Coast and the Bight of Biafra were the only two other regions to contribute more than a million Africans in shaping the Caribbean basin. It may
surprise readers that of the recorded 13 million Africans who reached the
Americas as captives, perhaps no more than 4 percent landed in North
America, entering the colonies through a limited number of major ports in
Georgia, South Carolina, Virginia, Maryland, and southern Louisiana as
well as in northeastern cities such as New York and Boston.

The vast set of statistical data analyzed by historians such as Joseph Inikori
and David Eltis reveal something else about the African experience under
the transatlantic slave system: almost two-thirds of the captives were adult
males and 15 to 20 percent were children, most of whom came in the eighteenth and first half of the nineteenth century, especially from west central
Africa.[6] In the nineteenth century as a whole, about half of the captives from
west central Africa were children. Surprisingly, mortality rates were highest
in the Bight of Biafra, which, unlike west central Africa, had little history of
kingdoms or centralized political structures and entered the transatlantic
slave system as late as the late seventeenth century.[7] It is likely that these mortality rates were linked to high morbidity rates, which in turn were related to
poor diet: captives were being fed (uncooked) starchy and "foreign" foods (e.g.,
cassava, corn, and rice) that were inconsistent with their indigenous diets. In
fact, the major cause of morbidity during the Atlantic crossings was gastroin-
testinal disease.[8] In other words, the rate of sickness and possibly the fre-
quency of death boiled down to what these captive Africans ate and how
much clean water they received. African deaths were recorded (if records were
kept at all) with a skull symbol, and the bodies were thrown overboard without ceremony. (In contrast, seamen's deaths were recorded with a cross and
the bodies were thrown overboard after a Christian-like ceremony.) The data
we have from the European companies, merchants, and bankers who organized and profited the most from the transatlantic slave system are quite silent
on fundamental and still-debated questions, such as how to pragmatically
redress the system's impact on African societies and their descendants and
why this international enslavement happened in the first place.

Why did the transatlantic slave system happen? The short answer has to do with the greed and pleasure of European colonists and their homeland supporters, who voraciously sought the cheapest labor for the production of and satisfaction of demands for sugar, rum, tobacco, and coffee. This quest for pleasurable stimulants unleashed European "free market" forces unto the world, creating a slave-based globalization and peaking during the period referred to as the European age of "enlightenment." The spread of the enlightenment ideals of freedom and reason across Europe and North America in the eighteenth century during the same time that human trafficking increased within a European-managed transatlantic slave system is just one of several contradictions of the era—a contradiction exacerbated by the fact that those "free market" forces needed both skilled and unskilled labor to meet growing demands. A range of people, both African and European, participated in this system, though at different levels, but always with dire consequences for African societies.

A number of factors contributed to enslavement on the African side of the equation, including drought, famine, debt, warfare, raiding, and kidnapping or pawning. The drought, clearly beyond Africans' control, influenced the outcome of causative factors such as warfare and the raiding of villages, and other human-determined causative factors existed in African societies prior to European involvement to varying degrees. But there is little doubt that the availability of European capital in Africa drove the exponential growth of firearms for use in raids or wars—an outcome that not only further harmed those most affected by drought and famine nut also increased levels of debt and pawning. This capital was brought in by bankers, captains and crew members, merchant-banking families, and insurance companies from Portugal, Spain, France, Britain, the Netherlands, Germany, Sweden, and the European societies of the Americas.

## AFRICAN PERSPECTIVES ON THE TRANSATLANTIC SLAVE SYSTEM

As rare as they are, records of African perspectives on the transatlantic slave system can be found in at least two major slaving regions in west central and

West Africa. These two regions represent geographic bookends, since the vast majority of captive Africans departed their homelands from the four-thousand-mile coastline between these two regions. The African "voices" presented in this section have in some cases been muffled or altered by the historical recorder or editor in the source material and will be edited here only for clarity and with minimal analysis to facilitate the reading of each perspective in context.

## Context and the Gold Coast

By lumping together Senegambia, Sierra Leone, and the Windward coast under the broader West African region called the "Upper Guinea coast," we find that there are six major slaving regions along the approximately four thousand miles of African coastline from Senegal to Angola. The Gold Coast (present-day Ghana) is one of these, its trade name reflecting Europeans' interest in the precious metal. It became the third-largest slaving region in West Africa. Exporting about 1.2 million captive Africans between 1600 and 1850, the Gold Coast, as its name suggests, was an early and competitive magnet for all the major and minor European slaving nations and their respective trading companies. Chartered by the European states, these national trading companies were given a monopoly over those states' trading interests in the region. To these companies, captive Africans were human cargo irrespective of their cultural origin or their importance in the society from which they came. Companies such as the Dutch West Indies Company and the Royal African Company of England emerged in the late sixteenth and early seventeenth centuries, having been officially sanctioned by their governments. Private European ships, however, often circumvented the monopolies of national trading companies and conducted a substantial part of the enslavement commerce.

Whether employed by national companies or private ones, the Portuguese merchants and sailors who encountered the Gold Coast found communities—the most important of which were Akan societies—with sophisticated cultural knowledge and commercial skills developed over centuries of local and regional trade. The Portuguese and Europeans who followed remained largely on the Gold Coast littoral and knew very little about the interior. Thus, the coastal ports of embarkation were significant contact points between European nationals and Akan (and other indigenous) societies. However, although the coastal towns grew in population and in commerce, the greater parts of the Gold Coast population lived in large towns and villages of the interior. Here, a trade network known as the Akani dominated the gold trade between the hinterland and the coast. In the seventeenth century, the western and central Gold Coast trade was controlled by the state known as Denkyira in the interior, whereas in the east of the region it was dominated by Akyem and Akwamu. Meanwhile, merchants, porters, interpreters, and slavers from coastal settlements such as Accra, Kormantin, Elmina, Cape Coast, and Anomabu became inextricably bound to the movement of goods and captive people between the interior and the transatlantic slave system. By the mid-eighteenth century, both Akwamu and the Akani network collapsed, and Denkyira and Akyem came under the rule of the growing Asante state. After this time, the commerce in European goods (including firearms) and captive Africans was firmly controlled by the Asante in the interior and by their Fante trading partners on the coast. More than a half-million souls—almost half the Gold Coast's total exported captive population—departed the Gold Coast between 1750 and 1800.

The Asante Empire spent much of the eighteenth century—the height of the transatlantic slave system—extending its vast dominion and incorporating new territories and resources, including the men paid as tribute by conquered states. These war captives were political assets, for they had cash, labor, and tributary value. However, Asante wars of expansion contributed less than is commonly thought to the half-million Gold Coast captives exported in the second half of the eighteenth century, for there was little Asante warfare between 1760 and 1800. The Asante economy was not built around the exportation of captive peoples, although firearms and gunpowder procured from European merchants facilitated Asante's military innovations and territorial expansion. Moreover, a significant number of eighteenth-century captives acquired by war or trade were not exported to the Americas but, rather, were incorporated into commoner families, contributing to the demographic and economic expansion of the agrarian village system. In other words, many non-Asante captives were assimilated after a generation or two into the Asante social order. For the Asante, several categories of servile labor existed: *akoa* (subject), *domum* (captive), *odonko* (captive person from northern Ghana), *akyere* (often condemned criminals and captives intended for sacrifice), and *awowa* (person pledged or given as surety for the debt of a kin). These categories of servile labor and status, as well as their changing meaning over time, must be distinguished because grouping such social identities together under "internal African slavery" would do little to clarify the relationship between domestic captivity and the demands of the transatlantic slave system.

If the Asante wars of expansion are not to blame for the increase in the export of captives from the Gold Coast in the late eighteenth century, how are we to account for the departure of at least 1.2 million Africans through Gold Coast ports? The answer can be found in Europe. Compared to the major European slaving nations, Gold Coast societies were significantly less able to exploit the transatlantic slave system, in that they lacked key industries and their port cities were built primarily for fishing, salt, and commerce in goods rather than human beings. Within Europe, by contrast, the transatlantic slave system spawned the development of British port cities like London, Bristol, and Liverpool. The growth of these cities drove demand for stimulants such as coffee and sugar, provided the financial capital to create and satisfy even more demand, and funded the increasing Portuguese, Dutch, British, French, Swedish, Danish, and German (Brandenburger) presence on the Gold Coast during the eighteenth century. These outcomes in turn transformed domestic forms of servile labor on the Gold Coast to feed the transatlantic slave system, while suppressing local economic activities. Writing at the peak of the transatlantic slave system in the eighteenth century, Gold Coast captive Ottobah Kobina Cugoano argued quite accurately: "If there were no buyers there would be no sellers."[9] In short, some Gold Coast farmers, merchants, and rulers became sellers of the enslaved, but they did so in an early capitalist system that was out of their control—a system in which they, too, were exploited, receiving cheap linen and metals in exchange for commodified humans.

*Gold Coast Captive Perspectives*

At the height of the transatlantic slave system in the eighteenth century, more than 6.5 million captive Africans left their homelands for the Americas. It is not surprising, then, that nearly all first-person accounts by (once) captive Africans appeared during that century. Even these are only a very limited set of documents. Africans who were literate, who became literate under captivity, or who had their accounts transcribed were few in number. In many instances their accounts emerged after they had won or received their freedom, often after a long period of enslavement and usually as part of a religious conversion or an abolitionist cause. Nonetheless, among their key themes are their departures from Africa. These departures often occurred during warfare, when they were kidnapped by slave raiders, or after they were torn from their homes and families as a result of their own or a relative's debt. These mechanisms of enslavement and the various positions in society from which a range of captives were drawn, including the Africans' experiences under the transatlantic slave system, take center stage in the following passages.

We begin with Belinda (Royall), so named by her owner Isaac Royall, one of wealthiest Loyalists in eighteenth-century Massachusetts. Although there is some debate about who aided Belinda in crafting her account and whether her transcriber embellished some of its content, we know about Belinda's early life from a few versions of a petition she presented to the General Court of Massachusetts in 1783. Perhaps her transcriber took some creative license with the seventy-year-old Belinda's words, or possibly her memory of events that occurred when she left the Gold Coast at twelve years of age was less than precise. Nevertheless, we can be assured that the content of Belinda's account, including this first-person description of her youth in Africa, was not fictional.[10]

> Seventy years have rolled away since, on the banks of Rio da Valta [Volta River], I received my existence. The Mountains, covered with spicy forests; the vallies [valleys], loaded, with the richest fruits. . . . Before I had twelve years enjoyed the fragrance of my native groves, and before I had realised that

Europeans placed their happiness in yellow dust [gold], wherein I carelessly marked my infant footsteps, even when in a sacred grove . . . a band of white men, driving many Africans before them in chains, rushed into the hallowed shades.

Could the tears, the sighs, the supplications from tortured parental affections, have blunted the keen edge of avarice, I might have been rescued from that agony which thousands of my country's children have experienced. . . . I was ravished from the bosom of my country. . . . Scenes which imagination never conceived—of a floating world—the supporting monsters of the deep, and the familiar meetings of billows and clouds, strove, but in vain, to divert melancholy attention from three hundred Africans in chains, suffering the most excruciating torments;—some, however, rejoicing that the pangs of death ensured them freedom. Once more my eyes were blessed with a continent . . . only to know that my doom was slavery, from which death alone could emancipate me.

The laws had rendered me incapable of receiving property [in Massachusetts]; and though I was a free, moral agent, accountable for my own actions, yet I was never a moment at my own disposal. One of his [Isaac Royall's] meanest servants robbed me of my innocence by force, and at an age when my youth should have been my security from pollution. Fifty years were my faithful hands compelled to ignoble servitude, for the benefit of a cruel, ungrateful master, until [he fled and died. . . . My face is now marked with the furrows of time and my frame feebly bending under the oppression of years; while, by the law of the land, I am denied the enjoyment of one morsel of that immense wealth, a part whereof hath been accumulated by my own industry, and the whole augmented by my labour.[11]

The court ruled in Belinda's favor for what amounted to reparations for her years of slave labor, although she received only a few years' pension from the estate of Isaac Royall. Following another successful petition in 1787, we learn nothing more about Belinda or her daughter Prine.

At the time of Belinda's embarkation in the 1720s, another captive, though not originally from the Gold Coast, embarked through a Gold Coast port and found himself on a Dutch slaving vessel to Barbados. That male captive was James Albert Ukawsaw Gronniosaw, who came from Bornu in what is now northeastern Nigeria. He was exported to the Americas and eventually freed and relocated to England, where he composed his biography (published in 1772) around the age of sixty. In that account, which is heavily shaped by his conversion to Christianity, Gronniosaw tells us about his capture in great detail and includes a brief mention of his Atlantic journey:

[One day,] a merchant from the *Gold Coast* (the third city in GUINEA) [who] traded with the inhabitants of our country in ivory &c. . . . he expressed vast concern for me, and said, if my parents would part with me for a little while, and let him take me home with him. . . . He told me that if I would go with him I should see houses with wings to them walk upon the water, and should also see the white folks; and that he had many sons of my age, which should be my companions; and he added to all this that he would bring me safe back again soon. . . . When my dear mother saw that I was willing to leave them, she spoke to my father and grandfather and the rest of my relations, who all agreed that I should accompany the merchant to the Gold Coast. . . . [If] I could have known when I left my friends and country that I should never return to them again[,] my misery on that occasion would have been inexpressible. . . .

I had a very unhappy and discontented journey. . . . I cannot recollect how long we were in going from BOURNOU to the GOLD COAST; but as there is no shipping nearer to BOURNOU than that City, it was tedious in travelling so far by land, being upwards of a thousand miles. . . . I was soon inform'd that their King imagined that I was sent by my father as a spy, and would make such discoveries at my return home that would enable them to make war with the greater advantage to ourselves; and for these reasons he had resolved I should never return to my native country. . . . [Eventually, the king said] he would not kill me, and that I should not go home, but be sold for a slave. . . .

A few days after[,] a Dutch ship came into the harbour, and they carried me on board, in hopes that the Captain would purchase me. As they went, I heard them agree, that, if they could not sell me *then*, they would throw me overboard. . . . [A]s soon as ever I saw the Dutch Captain, I ran to him, and put my arms round him, and said, "father, save me." . . . And though he did not understand my language, . . . he bought me *for two yards of check*, which is of more value *there*, than in England. . . . I was exceedingly sea-sick at first; but when I became more accustom'd to the sea, it wore off. My master's ship was bound for Barbadoes [Barbados]. When we came there, . . . I was sold for fifty dollars.[12]

Another Gold Coast captive who followed a route very similar to Gronniosaw was Venture Smith, born around 1729. Smith was kidnapped and taken to the British fort at Anomabu on the Gold Coast and transported to Barbados around 1737, but he relocated to New York and, eventually, to Rhode Island. Smith purchased his own and his family's freedom at age thirty-six but narrated his story at age sixty-nine. In the passage that follows, Smith recalls the series of events leading up to his deportation as a child. His account begins with his capture by a slave raiding party and the death of his father, who was killed before his eyes:

The army of the enemy was large, I should suppose consisting of about six thousand men. Their leader was called Baukurre. After destroying the old prince [Smith's father], they decamped and immediately marched towards the sea, lying to the west, taking with them myself and the women prisoners. . . . All the march I had very hard tasks imposed on me, which I must perform on pain of punishment. I was obliged to carry on my head a large flat stone used for grinding our corn, weighing, as I should suppose, as much as twenty-five pounds; besides victuals, mat and cooking utensils. Though I was pretty large and stout of my age, yet these burdens were very grievous to me, being only six years and a half old.

The invaders then [captured another community of peoples] . . . and moved on their way towards the sea. . . . They then went on to the next district, which was contiguous to the sea, called in Africa, Anamaboo [Anomabu]. The enemies' provisions were then almost spent, as well as their strength. The inhabitants . . . attacked them, and took enemy, prisoners, flocks and all their effects. I was then taken a second time. All of us were then put into the castle and kept for market. On a certain time, I and other prisoners were put on board a canoe, under our master, and rowed away to a vessel belonging to Rhode Island. . . . While we were going to the vessel, our master told us to appear to the best possible advantage for sale. I was bought on board by one Robertson Mumford, steward of said vessel, for four gallons of rum and a piece of calico, and called VENTURE, on account of his having purchased me with his own private venture. Thus I came by my name. All the slaves that were bought for that vessel's cargo were two hundred and sixty. AFTER all the business was ended on the coast of Africa, the ship sailed from thence to Barbadoes. After an ordinary passage, except great mortality by the small pox, which broke out on board, we arrived at the island of Barbadoes; but when we reached it, there were found, out of the two hundred and sixty that sailed from Africa, not more than two hundred alive. These were all sold, except myself and three more, to the planters there. The vessel then sailed for Rhode Island.[13]

As in the case of Venture Smith, other Gold Coast captives found themselves in a predicament regardless of their social standing in local society. From the same port of Anomabu, William Unsah Sessarakoo (also possibly known as William Ansa Sasraku), a "young prince of Annamaboe," was duplicitously enslaved and, like Smith, sold to a planter in Barbados around 1744. However, unlike the previous Gold Coast captives, Sessarakoo was not only liberated in 1749 but managed to return to his family on the Gold Coast a few years later. In the passage that follows, Sessarakoo (or more likely his biographer) recounts the way he actually left the Gold Coast, thinking he was bound for England to be educated:

Under [a] happy Delusion he [Sessarakoo] compleated his Voyage from the Road of *Annamaboe*, to *Bridge-Town* in *Barbadoes*. When the Captain had sold him, and he was put into a Boat to be carried to his Master, he thought he was going on board the Ship that was to carry him to *England*. But what Language can express his Surprize, when from the rough Usage that he met with from two Slaves that were in the Boat, he had no Room left him to doubt that his Condition was the same with theirs? . . .

He saw numbers in the like Condition, from a Variety of Accidents, but none of them in any Degree comparable to that which had brought this heavy Lot upon him. He was ashamed however to shew less Courage than the rest, or not to oppose Misfortune with equal Steadiness of Mind; he resolved therefore to bear, tho' he could not be reconciled to his Fate, and to sustain without complaining a Calamity it was out of his Power to remove. In this sad State his Innocence afforded him the only Consolation; . . . it rather heightened than abated his other good Qualities, which gained him universal Esteem, while in the low State of a Slave.[14]

The next Gold Coast captive, reportedly also a Fante, was Ottobah Kobina Cugoano, who was kidnapped around the age of thirteen and sent to Cape Coast Castle. He was then shipped to Grenada and, finally, like a number of other freed captives, to England in 1772. It was here that he published his account at age thirty. In the following excerpt, Cugoano relates his capture and experience on board the slave vessel:

I WAS early snatched away from my native country, with about eighteen or twenty more boys and girls, as we were playing in a field. We lived but a few days' journey from the coast where we were kidnapped, and as we were decoyed and drove along, we were soon conducted to a factory, and from thence, in the fashionable way of traffic, consigned to Grenada. Perhaps it may not be amiss to give a few remarks, as some account of myself, in this transposition of captivity.

I was born in the city of Agimaque, on the coast of Fantyn; my father was a companion to the chief in that part of the country of Fantee, and when the old king died I was left in his house with his family; soon after[,] I was sent for by his nephew, Ambro Accasa, who succeeded the old king in the chiefdom of that part of Fantee, known by the name of Agimaque and Assince. . . . [Captured by a group of armed individuals,] [s]ome of us attempted, in vain, to run away, but pistols and cutlasses were soon introduced, threatening, that if we offered to stir, we should all lie dead on the spot. . . . Next day we travelled on, and in the evening came to a town, where I saw several white people, which made me afraid that they would eat me, according to our notion, as children, in the inland parts of the country. . . . I saw many of my miserable countrymen chained two and two, some handcuffed, and some with their hands tied behind. We were conducted along by a guard, and when we arrived at the castle, I asked my guide what I was brought there for, he told me to learn the ways of the *browfow* [Twi: *oborofo,* "white people" in common parlance], that is, the white-faced people. I saw him take a gun, a piece of cloth, and some lead for me, and then he told me that he must now leave me there, and went off. This made me cry bitterly, but I was soon conducted to a prison, for three days, where I heard the groans and cries of many, and saw some of my fellow-captives. But when a vessel arrived to conduct us away to the ship, it was a most horrible scene; there was nothing to be heard but the rattling of chains, smacking of whips, and the groans and cries of our fellow-men. . . . When we were put into the ship, we saw several black merchants coming on board, but we were all drove into our holes. . . . [A] plan was concerted amongst us, . . . but we were betrayed by one of our own countrywomen, who slept with some of the headmen of the ship, for it was common for the dirty filthy sailors to take the African women and lie upon their bodies; but the men were chained and pent up in holes.[15]

Despite the British abolition of transatlantic slaving in the early nineteenth century, international and domestic forms of slaving continued unabated. Though the Gold Coast then became a very marginal participant, the story of Asante captives John Joseph and his unnamed sister shows that Gold Coast captives were still being exported to the Americas from this region or an adjacent one into the mid-nineteenth century. Here, Joseph recounts his journey and the continued terror experienced in North America:

I, JOHN JOSEPH, the subject of this narrative, am a native of Ashantee [Asante], in Western Africa. I was born of respectable parents, my father being a distinguished Chief. . . . When I was about three years of age, my father engaged in a deadly war with one of the [local Gold Coast societies], and in an unsuccessful encounter with the enemy he was completely routed, and a great many of our tribe taken prisoners. The enemy ransacked my father's habitation, and savagely dragged me and my beloved sister, from the arms of a dear distracted mother. We were then taken to the coast, together with three hundred prisoners of war, where we were put on board a slave ship, sent to New Orleans, in the state of Louisina [Louisiana], South America [southern United States], and there sold as slaves. I was bought at the public auction, by one Mr. Johnstone, a cotton planter, in New Orleans. I was then put by him in the calaboosh, or prison (a place for keeping slaves when they are brought from Africa, and also runaway slaves.) I was kept there until I was old enough to work, when I was placed on a cotton plantation. My occupation there was to press the cotton, under the superintendence of what is called the negro-driver, who often punished me very severely for the least fault, in a most cruel and inhuman manner. . . . After my inhuman punishment, I was heavily laden with chains by night, to prevent any possibility of my escape from this den of horrors, and on one ocasion[occasion] on my remonstrating with my cruel persecutor he struct me a blow on the mouth with the butt end of his whip which knocked out three of my front teeth.[16]

Joseph was later resold to slaveholders in South Carolina and Virginia. Eventually he escaped to England in 1843, converted to Christianity, and then related his account. What became of his sister he does not say, and we do not know.

### Context and West Central Africa

The coastline of west central Africa stretches is approximately 1,200 miles long, stretching from the island of Fernando Po (Bioko) to the south of Benguela in present-day Angola. This section focuses on the two major slaving regions in west central Africa: Kôngo and Ndongo (Angola). Like the Gold Coast, west central African societies such as the Kingdom of Kôngo had early encounters with the Portuguese in the late fifteenth century. However, the disparate nature of those encounters would shape the two African regions' histories in totally different ways. The Kôngo-Angola region fell under the sway of Catholicism and early Portuguese slaving and colonization via the Portuguese colonial states in Luanda and Benguela, whereas the Gold Coast resisted Christianization and remained a small-scale net importer of captives (from neighboring peoples) until the mid-seventeenth century. But like the Gold Coast, the Kingdom of Kôngo enjoyed an early history of economic prosperity quite some time before the Portuguese arrived on its coastline. The economies of west central Africa, which relied on the trading of cloth, copper, shell, and iron goods—and the use of currencies made from these commodities—were not wholly dependent on domestic forms of servile labor or slave trading, though the region had extensive commercial markets that could have been used for slave trading, and captive laborers were indeed present in the area.

West central African societies prior to the arrival of the Portuguese valued people above property and goods—though in some cases subjugated peoples with a captive ancestry or "foreign" origins, as well as those under the patronage of another, risked exportation when their patron or holder had to settle a debt or purchase desired European goods. The Portuguese entry into the region was highly transformative, however. A few decades after the Portuguese arrived on the coast of Kôngo in 1483, their influence and colonization on the coast reached as far as the Kôngo capital of Mbanza Kôngo (renamed São Salvador) and, later, Angola. This influence had two related consequences. First, the system of various-sized independent communities and large states in the region became (more) stratified as the transatlantic slave system grew and as the number of predatory groups and "big men" (what historian Joseph Miller calls "warlords")[17] increased to facilitate the workings of that system. Second, societies using captive laborers, whether war captives or subjugated persons who had been "inherited," turned into slave raiding and slave trading societies. Some societies without a centralized political system were transformed into slave trading communities, and some slave raiding societies became trading societies indirectly linked to the transatlantic slave system. In northwestern Angola, the Imbangala state of Kasanje (ca. 1620–1912), for instance, became a major supplier of European goods to the new series of slave "frontiers" in the east as well as a key supplier of captured Africans destined for the Atlantic coast of Angola in the west and eventually to the Americas. In both Angola and the Kôngo, the transatlantic slave system made it possible to exchange people (captive criminals, kidnap victims, and individuals secured from the interior) for political power in the form of imported European goods and guns—a process that widened the cycle of violence involved in the importation of captives from the interior and of guns from the Atlantic coast. Those "big men" of local origin, including so-called Luso-Africans of mixed African-Portuguese parentage and *prazeros* warlords (Portuguese settlers with large estates worked by enslaved Africans who had been secured through slave raiding), were dependent on credit extended from the Atlantic—credit that allowed them to buy guns and captive Africans. Indeed, if capital was the catalyst for the transatlantic slave system, credit was the driving force that kept the system in motion.

If the major human actors in the drama of the transatlantic slave system in west central Africa were suppliers and buyers from Portugal, Brazil, Britain, and the Kôngo-Angola region, the key nonhuman factors were disease, malnutrition, drought (which facilitated the capturing and selling of enslaved Africans), and the very organization and violence of the transatlantic system. Though both Luso-Africans and droughts (accompanied by malnutrition) were much less common on the Gold Coast, in the Kôngo-Angola region they sustained a European system in which wealth was created (in a gold-and-silver-based capitalist economy) by transforming Africans into captives and captives into precious metals. The latter, in turn, found their way to Europe in exchange for goods. As one early-eighteenth-century British slave ship captain was instructed, "turn your whole Cargoe of Goods and Negroes into Gold," for these "Negroes" were "a perishable commodity" and "the Portugueze [*sic*] chiefly [brought] Gold from Brazil to purchase their Negroes."[18] Viewed from this capitalist perspective, the high mortality among and violence toward African captives (as well as potential captives) was a low business risk for European merchants, investors, insurance companies, and the wealthy among them. Moreover, as historian Marcus Rediker has argued, the violence of the transatlantic slave system was central to the rise and movement of global capitalism.[19] Meanwhile, the impact on west central African societies was enormous: transatlantic slaving altered sex ratios and led to depopulation, created social hierarchies and political fragmentation, introduced new forms of domestic enslavement, and encouraged materialist values in societies that valued people above all.[20]

*West Central African Perspectives*

In the Kôngo-Angola region, very few first-person accounts exist for those who were enslaved. For this region, there is no Olaudah Equiano—the eighteenth-century "Igbo" African whose account of his capture, Atlantic crossing, life in North America, and freedom and involvement in abolitionist movement in Britain remains a staple literature. However, we do have internal accounts by rulers who participated in the transatlantic slave system in the Kingdom of Kôngo and in Angola during the sixteenth and seventeenth centuries. These perspectives, plus a brief account by one captive who made the Atlantic crossing to Cartagena (Columbia), complement those shared by Gold Coast captives and enlarge our understanding of the human toll taken by the transatlantic slave system.

We begin with several excerpts from the voluminous letters of Nzinga Mbemba (Afonso I, ruler of Kôngo, ca. 1509–1542), the first and perhaps most reputed promoter of Christianity and Europeanization in the Kôngo. After the death of Afonso's father Nzinga Nkuwu in 1509, a power struggle ensued between Afonso and his "half-brother" Mpanzu a Kitima. With Portuguese military support, Afonso and his supporters defeated what he called "our enemies" and developed a special relationship with the Portuguese crown and certain Portuguese merchants and clergymen stationed in the Kôngo thereafter. The following passages from his extensive writings focus on the transatlantic slave system. In a letter to Manuel I, king of Portugal (dated October 5, 1514), Afonso or his clerk wrote the following:[21]

> Then there arrived in our kingdom a ship of Gonçalo Rodrigues which had gone to Mina [Gold Coast] and had come for [two Portuguese Catholic] fathers, who had been here a long time. We therefore sent them away and gave each of them, and Gonçalo Rodrigues, 1500 manilhas [copper bracelets used as currency] and 150 slaves.
>
> [After the arrival of some Portuguese priests] . . . we gave them [money] so that they all began to deal in buying and selling. We [told them] . . . if they were to buy some slaves, they should not purchase any women. . . . Yet notwithstanding they began to fill the houses with whores, in such a fashion

that Father Pero Fernandes impregnated a woman in his house and she gave birth to a mulatto. . . .

[W]e sent a letter to your Highness and another to Queen Dona Leonor—and with our relatives we sent 700 manilhas, many slaves, parrots, animals, and civet cats. . . . [E]ach of them [masons] already had bought from 15 to 20 slaves. . . . Those masons left, and took as many slaves and goods as they had, and no more than three remained here. We dispatched the said ship promptly and sent 200 manilhas and 60 slaves to Fernão de Melo, aside from those we gave to his servants; and we sent our nephew Pedro Afonso on the ship, with a letter to your highness in which we gave an account of affairs here, and sent your Highness 200 manilhas and certain slaves, so that Pedro Afonso could take them to Portugal and buy us some clothes there. . . . [In] the large ship and the caravel we sent two of our nephews, with our son Dom Francisco—and 500 slaves for both ships, with 30 extra slaves, so that if some of the 500 slaves died their number could be made up from the 30. . . .

And Dom Pedro took 190 slaves—that is 100 of ours and 90 for your Highness—to make up for those who had remained here because they were too thin. With him went all our nephews, and he was to convey our obedience to the Pope. . . . Some priests came . . . and they all began to buy slaves— in spite of the fact that Your Highness' instructions forbade it. And then we posted our own decree that no one was to buy slaves except the factor.

In another letter from Afonso to João III (dated July 6, 1526), Afonso talked about the destruction of his kingdom at the hands of the Portuguese nationals he had invited to live in Kôngo:[22]

Your Highness should know how our Kingdom is being lost in so many ways that it is convenient to provide for the necessary remedy, since this is caused by the excessive freedom given by your factors and officials to the men and merchants who are allowed to come to this Kingdom and set up shops with goods and many things which have been prohibited by us. . . . And we cannot reckon how great the damage is, since the mentioned merchants are taking every day our natives, sons of the land and the sons of our noblemen and vassals and our relatives, because the thieves and men of bad conscience grab them wishing to have the things and wares of this Kingdom which they are ambitious of; they grab them and get them to be sold; and so great, sir[,] is the corruption and licentiousness that our country is being completely depopulated.... [I]t is our will that in these kingdoms there should not be any trade of slaves or outlet for them.

In October 1526, Afonso again wrote to João III, king of Portugal, complaining of the ways in which imported European goods have created a predatory environment among his people:

Moreover, in our kingdoms there is another great inconvenience which is of little service to God, and this is that many of our people, keenly desirous as they are of the wares and things of your kingdoms, which are brought her by your people, and in order to satisfy their voracious appetite, seize many of our people, freed and exempt men; and very often it happens that they kidnap nobleman and the sons of noblemen, and our relatives, and take them to be sold to the white men who are in our kingdoms; and for this purpose they have concealed them; and others are brought during the night so that they might not be recognized.[23]

And as soon as they are taken by the white men they are immediately ironed and branded with fire, and [then] they are carried to be embarked....

And to avoid such a great evil we passed a law so that any white man living in our Kingdoms and wanting to purchase goods in any way should first inform three of our noblemen and officials of our court whom we rely upon in this matter.... [I]f cleared by them [the appointed noblemen and officials] there will be no further doubt nor embargo for them to be taken and embarked. But if the white men do not comply with it they will lose the aforementioned goods [i.e., enslaved peoples]. And if we do them this favor and concession it is for the part Your Highness has in it, since we know that it is in your service too that these goods are taken from our kingdom.

Judging from these letters, the internal decline of independent Kôngo began during Afonso's reign. Its disintegration accelerated after his death as the country dissolved into warring factions seeking the throne. This situation came to a head when Kôngo-Portuguese relations deteriorated as a result of the Portuguese invasion of Angola in the 1620s, followed by a crippling civil war after the death of anti-Portuguese ruler Garcia II (r. 1641–1661)—an outcome that led to further internal squabbling. The Portuguese invasion of Angola brought another important ruler into the picture—Njinga Mbande of Ndongo and Matamba—and the complex alliances between the Portuguese and Africans, especially rulers such as Njinga, sustained Portuguese influence in its coastal enclaves, while extending that sway into the interior through such alliances.[24] Born around 1582 in the Kingdom of Ndongo, Njinga was the eldest child of King Mbandi Ngola (whose name was the source of name "Angola"). After claiming the throne in the wake of her brother's suicide in 1624, Njinga, like Afonso, was also Christianized (baptized as Ana de Sousa) and engaged in the transatlantic slave system in competition with other local rulers. In an early letter to the Portuguese commander in eastern Angola (dated March 3, 1625), Njinga wrote:

> I will give you an account of how as I was sending some slaves to the market of Bumba Aquiçanzo: Aire came out with his army, and robbed me of thirty slaves of those I had sent[.] I sought satisfaction against my vassal [and] my army met with nine men who were with the Tiger [a Portuguese field commander] in the land, and putting upon these nine who went to meet my army outside of Pedra [(a fortress),] it pleased God that they were defeated by mine where I brought back six alive. . . . Your Grace, send me a hair net and four yards of gram for a cover, and a bedspread of montaria, and good wine, and a arroba of wax from Vellas, and a half dozen Indian colored cloths and two or three table cloths of Rendas, some red, blue and wine-colored rubies, and a sun hat of blue velvet, or the one that you wear, and 100 folios of paper.[25]

In another letter to the Governor General of Angola (dated December 13, 1655), Njinga wrote the following words in the context of peace treaty negotiations beginning in 1626 with the Portuguese:

> I have complained so much to the past governors, who have always promised to return my sister [captured by the Portuguese in battle], to which end I

have given infinite slaves and done thousands of banzos [trading goods], and she was never returned but after wars were made to disquiet me and make me always go about as Jaga [Imbangala; fierce warriors used as mercenaries by Njinga and the Portuguese], using tyrannies, some as not allowing children, this being the style of quilombo [military encampment], and other ceremonies, with [which] I have completely given up. . . . [26]

Concerning the two hundred slaves which Your Lordship asks for the ransom of my sister D. Barbora [Kijunji], it is a very rigorous price, I have given the slaves which Your Lordship already must know, to past governors and ambassadors, outside mimos and secretaries and servants of your house, and many residents, that already today I feel tricked. That which our Lordship wishes me to give would be 130 slaves, the 100 I will send when my sister [is] in Embaca [Mbaka; a Portuguese fort].

Near the end of her life, Njinga wrote a letter (dated June 15, 1660) to Antonio de Olivderia de Cadornega, resident historian and slave dealer in Angola, about runaway captives. In it, she responded to the claim that she harbors them:

The letter which your grace wrote to me concerning your runaway people which my people sold or stole, this is said by people who wish ill to the peace and Christianity, because if your grace could ask all the Pumbeiros [agents dispatched by merchants to acquired inland captives] of the whites who come to my Court with the goods of their masters to trade, your grace would know that the blacks of your grace are so backward that when we sell slaves to them, they inform us that the slaves were well watched over and captured; they say of them that they are villains[,] they send free slaves to do your service to say to Your Grace that in this my banza [capital town] many old free women fled to me as the said people say; of the newer people: If they were here they could make diligent [inquiries concerning the "slave" status of those offered for sale].[27]

By the time of Njinga's death in 1663, more captive Africans had departed the Kôngo-Angola region than had departed the Gold Coast throughout the period 1440–1820. Many of these captives endured a terrible journey from the interior to the ports of west central Africa, but that experience did not—and could not—prepare them for the violence and fear they experienced upon embarking for the Americas. In the following account of a journey across the Atlantic in 1659, Jose Monzolo, an enslaved African from the Kingdom of Kôngo residing in Cartagena, focused on a widespread belief among captive Africans from Senegambia to Angola:

> When they left their own country, they believed that the Spanish [or another European slaving nation], whom they called whites, brought them to kill them and to make the flags for the ships from their remains, for when they were red it was from the blood of the Moors [Africans], and desperately fearing this many threw themselves in the sea on the voyage.[28]

For the captives who arrived in the Americas, the terror only continued. Even those who remained on the African continent witnessed the intensification of local forms of enslavement that eventually transformed, in the late nineteenth century, into an extractive colonial economy based on cash crops (e.g., coffee, cocoa, oil palm), natural resources (e.g., timber, bauxite, gold, diamond), low-paid contract and migrant laborers, and taxation systems that funded the colonial state. Thus, the termination of domestic slavery by European colonists only brought African labor within the European currency-based world economy, where many became bound to slavery by another name.[29]

## QUESTIONS

1. Describe the ways in which Africans became synonymous with the ideas of "slave" and the "slave trade." What are some useful ways to talk about the "slave trade"?

2. What were the key mechanisms and forces, both local and international, that led to the capture, enslavement, and exportation of enslaved Africans from Senegambia to Angola?

3. What significant cultural or socioeconomic ideas, themes, or perspectives about the eighteenth-century Gold Coast and the transatlantic slave system

can we draw from the accounts of Belinda (Royall), James Gronniosaw, Venture Smith, William Sessarakoo, Ottobah Cugoano, and John Joseph?

4. What significant cultural or socioeconomic ideas, themes, or perspectives about sixteenth- and seventeenth-century west central Africa and the transatlantic slave system can we draw from the accounts of Nzinga Mbemba (Afonso I), Njinga Mbande, and Jose Monzolo?

5. How might the transatlantic slave system and the Americas have looked then and today if the enslaved labor force between 1500 and 1900 was predominantly European and not African?

## FURTHER READINGS

Berlin, Ira. *Many Thousands Gone: The First Two Centuries of Slavery in North America.* Cambridge, MA: Belknap Press of Harvard University Press, 1998.

Barry, Boubacar. *Senegambia and the Atlantic Slave Trade.* New York: Cambridge University Press, 1998.

Eltis, David, and David Richardson. *Atlas of the Transatlantic Slave Trade.* New Haven: Yale University Press, 2011.

Inikori, Joseph E. "Ideology Versus the Tyranny of Paradigm: Historians and the Impact of the Atlantic Slave Trade on African Societies." *African Economic History* 22 (1994): 37–58.

Inikori, Joseph E., and Stanley L. Engerman, eds. *The Atlantic Slave Trade: Effects on Economies, Societies, and Peoples in Africa, the Americas, and Europe.* Durham, NC: Duke University Press, 1992.

Miller, Joseph C. *Way of Death: Merchant Capitalism and the Angolan Slave Trade, 1730–1830.* Madison: University of Wisconsin Press, 1988.

Rediker, Marcus. *The Slave Ship: A Human History.* New York: Penguin, 2007.

Smallwood, Stephanie. *Saltwater Slavery: A Middle Passage from Africa to American Diaspora.* Cambridge, MA: Harvard University Press, 2007.

Thornton, John K. *Africa and Africans in the Making of the Atlantic World, 1400–1800.* New York: Cambridge University Press, 1998.

## NOTES

1. On Indian Ocean and trans-Saharan commerce in Africa and world history, see, respectively, Edward A. Alpers, *East Africa and the Indian Ocean* (Princeton: Markus Wiener Publishers, 2009), and Ralph A. Austin, *Trans-Saharan Africa in World History*

(New York: Oxford University Press, 2010).

2. For more on these powerful merchants and other individuals of mixed parentage, see Peter Mark, *"Portuguese" Style and Luso-African Identity: Precolonial Senegambia, Sixteenth–Nineteenth Centuries* (Bloomington: Indiana University Press, 2003), and George E. Brooks, *Eurafricans in Western Africa: Commerce, Social Status, Gender, and Religious Observance from the Sixteenth to the Eighteenth Century* (Athens: Ohio University Press, 2003).

3. Marcus Rediker, *The Slave Ship: A Human History* (New York: Penguin, 2007), p. 350.

4. David Eltis, *The Rise of African Slavery in the Americas* (New York: Cambridge University Press, 2000), p. 171; Stephen D. Behrendt, David Eltis, and David Richardson, "The Costs of Coercion: African Agency in the Pre-modern Atlantic World," *Economic History Review* 54, no. 3 (2001): 455, 459, 464.

5. The governments of certain Pacific nations have sought compensation from Britain and France for slave labor. See, for instance, David Fickling, "Pacific Islands Appeal to UK for 'Slave Voyages' Compensation," *The Guardian*, April 13, 2004.

6. See Joseph Inikori, Africans and the Industrial Revolution in England: *A Study in International Trade and Development* (New York: Cambridge University Press, 2002); David Eltis, *The Rise of African Slavery in the Americas* (New York: Cambridge University Press, 2000), and David Eltis (with David Richardson), *Atlas of the Transatlantic Slave Trade* (New Haven: Yale University Press, 2011).

7. The most significant account of the Bight of Biafra and the transatlantic slave system is G. Ugo Nwokeji's *The Slave Trade and Culture in the Bight of Biafra: An African Society in the Atlantic World* (New York: Cambridge University Press, 2010).

8. Stephen D. Behrendt, David Eltis, David Richardson, "The Costs of Coercion: African Agency in the Pre-Modern Atlantic World," *Economic History Review* 54, no. 3 (2001): 461.

9. Ottobah Kobina Cugoano, "Narrative of the Enslavement of Ottobah Cugoano, a Native of Africa; published by himself, in the Year 1787," in Thomas Fisher, ed., *The Negro's Memorial, or, Abolitionist's Catechism by an Abolitionist* (London: Hatchard and Co., and J. and A. Arch, 1825), p. 126.

10. In the extant sources, Belinda was consistently referred to as an "African" rather than by the more common term "Negroe," implying North American birth.

11. "The Complaint of Belinda, an African," *The Weekly Miscellany* 2, no. 35 (Sherborne) (September 1, 1783): 207–208. See also Roy E. Finkenbine, "Belinda's Petition: Reparations for Slavery in Revolutionary Massachusetts," *William and Mary Quarterly* 64, no. 1 (3rd series) (2007): 95–104.

12. James Albert Ukawsaw Gronniosaw, *A Narrative of the Most Remarkable Particulars in the Life of James Albert Ukawsaw Gronniosaw, an African Prince, as Related by Himself* (Bath, Eng.: W. Gye, 1770), pp. 4–10.

13. Venture Smith, *A Narrative of the Life and Adventures of Venture, a Native of Africa, But Resident Above Sixty Years in the United States of America. Related by Himself* (New London: Printed for the Author, 1798), pp. 10–13.

14. William Ansah Sessarakoo, *The Royal African: or, Memoirs of the Young Prince of Annamaboe* . . . (London: W. Reeve, G. Woodfall, and J. Barnes, 1750), pp. 42–44. Readers should note that the authorship of this account is in question, for it contains very little on Sessarakoo's life; in fact, "The Royal African" is a novel based on Sessarakoo's presence in mid-eighteenth century England. They should also note that Sessarakoo was the son of powerful Fante merchant and de facto ruler John Corrantee, whose well-known dealings and scuffles with the Royal African Company of England and the French are a large part of what led to Sessarakoo's enslavement and his return home.

15. Cugoano, "Narrative of the Enslavement," pp. 120–124.

16. John Joseph, *The Life and Sufferings of John Joseph, a Native of Ashantee, in Western Africa* . . . (Wellington: Printed for John Joseph by J. Greedy, 1848), p. 4.

17. See Joseph C. Miller, *Way of Death: Merchant Capitalism and the Angolan Slave Trade, 1730–1830* (Madison: University of Wisconsin Press, 1988).

18. Quoted in David Eltis and David Richardson, *Atlas of the Transatlantic Slave Trade* (New Haven: Yale University Press, 2011), p. 68.

19. Rediker, *The Slave Ship: A Human History.*

20. On these matters, readers can consult Eltis and Richardson, *Atlas of the Transatlantic Slave Trade*; Miller, *Way of Death*; Joseph E. Inikori, "Ideology Versus the Tyranny of Paradigm: Historians and the Impact of the Atlantic Slave Trade on African Societies," *African Economic History* 22 (1994): 37–58; John Thornton, "Demography and History in the Kingdom of Kongo, 1550–1750," *Journal of African History* 18 (1977): 507–530; and John Thornton, "The Slave Trade in Eighteenth Century Angola: Effects on Demographic Structures," *Canadian Journal of African Studies* 14, no. 3 (1980): 417–428.

21. Antonio Brasio, ed., *Monumenta Missionaria Africana* (hereafter, *MMA*), vol. 1, first series, 15 vols. (Lisbon, Agéncia Geral do Ultramar, 1952–1988), pp. 295–317.

22. *MMA*, vol. 1, pp. 470–471.

23. *MMA*, vol. 1, p. 489.

24. For more on the Portuguese presence on the Angolan coast and its hinterlands, see Roquinaldo Ferreira, *Cross-Cultural Exchange in the Atlantic World: Angola and Brazil During the Era of the Slave Trade* (New York: Cambridge University Press, 2012), and José C. Curto, "Experiences of Enslavement in West Central Africa," *Histoire sociale/Social History* 41, no. 82 (2008): 381–415.

25. Queen Njinga to Bento Banha Cardoso, March 3, 1625, quoted in Fernão de Sousa to Gonçalo de Sousa and his brothers (ca. 1630), in Beatrix Heintze, ed., Fontes

para a história de Angola do século XVII, *vol. 1* (Wiesbaden, 1985–1988), pp. 244–245.

26. *MMA*, vol. 11, pp. 524–528.

27. *MMA*, vol. 12, p. 289.

28. Quoted in John Thornton, "Cannibals, Witches, and Slave Traders in the Atlantic World," *William and Mary Quarterly* 60, no. 2 (2003): 273.

29. Miller, *Way of Death*, pp. 690–692.

# 2

# Prophetesses and "Native Capitalists"

*African Voices of the Industrial Revolution,*
*ca. 1760–1880*

Trevor R. Getz

## GLOBAL CONTEXT

The purpose of this chapter is to present the industrial revolution as an episode in which Africans participated, to understand Africans' experiences during this period, and, finally, to look at the industrial revolution through their eyes.

We do not usually think of Africans and industrialization together. Instead, we often conceptualize Africa as part of the third (or developing) world and therefore as excluded from the kinds of technologies that come to mind when we think about industrialization—factories, mass transportation, high-rise buildings. This dominant characterization of Africa as being nonindustrialized isn't entirely accurate either historically or in the present, although certainly industrialization came later to most of Africa than to places like Britain, northwestern Europe, and the northeastern United States. These areas were the earliest locations of a series of changes that we refer to as industrial revolutions. Britain, especially, was the site of the so-called first industrial revolution, usually dated to the late eighteenth century.

In this chapter I argue, however, that the first industrial revolution—like all industrial revolutions since—involved social, economic, and political changes much wider than those experienced just by factory workers in big cities. In fact, during the eighteenth and nineteenth centuries the lifestyles and life experiences of many Africans changed because of the industrial revolution. These changes mirrored transformations taking place in Britain, although they had their own unique character as well.

*The First Industrial Revolution*

To discuss the origins and experiences of the industrial revolution, we need to understand when it occurred. This is not as easy as it may seem. Industrialization was not a single, simple event but, rather, a series of processes that built on each other, including changes in energy use, technology, production and productivity, rural and urban lifestyles, economics, and social systems. The first of these changes was probably really an agricultural revolution, which arguably began in Britain with the importation of new food crops from the Americas in the early sixteenth century and was later accelerated by the enclosure of land into large private fields throughout the eighteenth century. This transformation was facilitated by new technologies such as the Rotherham plough introduced in 1730 and the threshing machines developed in the 1780s. The transition to coal-powered steam engines largely took place in Britain between 1750 and 1850, although industry may already have developed before this using water and wind power.[1] (The windmill and waterwheel were in increasing use in eighteenth-century Britain for sawing wood, grinding grain, and powering simple machines, for example.) Historian Eric Hobsbawm has argued that the social and economic changes of the industrial revolution did not actually occur on a mass scale in the first decades of the nineteenth century.[2] Social developments included urbanization and the factory system as well as changes in rural lifestyles and work regimes.

All of these transformations were intertwined. The influx of calories and materials of the agricultural revolution helped support a greater population density. New techniques for harnessing wind and water made factories possible, and later coal and petroleum products increased mechanical production even more.

Although these changes generally took place in rural areas before urban ones, the industrial revolution in Britain drove the development of urbanization. The transformation of land from subsistence production by peasants to surplus production for the benefit of large landowners, and the subsequent enclosure of croplands into large tracts in which to raise sheep for the wool industry, drove many rural-dwellers into cities. Initially, this movement created a great social transformation by which former peasant-farmers, and especially women, became piece-workers or other informal wage-earning workers while remaining in the country. Over time, however, it also drove many former peasants into the cities, where increasingly dense populations had to learn to work together in large factories and live together in crowded tenements. Their lives as a "working class" were quite different from those of their rural ancestors. They tried to keep many rituals and cultural artifacts of their rural lives alive, of course. Thus, for instance, the urban pub was a re-creation of the village public house—a place to gather, sing old songs, and discuss the day's activities. Nevertheless, industrial workers' lives were oriented around the factory workplace. Their daily rhythms became reoriented toward the work shift, and over time the nuclear family with its wage-earning head-of-household replaced the extended family as the principal unit of social and economic organization. Industrial factories employed the principles of task segregation and the assembly line, giving each worker a single, repetitive task to carry out throughout the day—and the idea of each individual as a "working" or "consuming" cog in the wheel of society slowly spread into popular culture. So, too, did the idea of a segregation of tasks at home, such that men and women had different jobs in the family as well as in the factory. Working and living conditions for the working class were generally difficult during the first industrial revolution, although the new technological economy did open up some opportunities to the skilled or lucky.

At the same time, the power of the rural aristocracy in Britain slowly declined. The nobility were gradually replaced by a new class called the bourgeoisie, whose power was tied to wealth rather than to social status or noble titles. In the Britain of the first industrial revolution, members of this social class gained political power in the parliament, formulating laws and regulations that favored their factories and financial concerns such as ensuring protection for private property and making the circulation and investment of money easier. They also gained social power, including the ability to define how people of "status" should act—for example, regarding the duties of the father as family head, the proper behavior for a lady, and rigid notions of the "working" and "middle" classes. We tend now to call these "Victorian values," referring to the late-nineteenth-century reign of Queen Victoria, but in fact they began to emerge at least a century earlier. By sponsoring intellectuals and artists, this new class promoted a cultural system that reinforced its own values within society and, eventually, around the world.

What was the first industrial revolution in Britain like as an actual experience? Not surprisingly, the written sources we have for this period were written by people from groups who tended to be literate—upper- or middle-class urban men, in most cases. However, historians have recently discovered new written and visual sources and read existing sources in new ways that tell us more about the experiences of other groups in this period. Indeed, new histories have emerged showing the experiences of male and female factory and mine workers as well as farm workers, immigrant groups, and children. These historians' interpretations of such sources suggest that despite the general social transformations described above, there was no "single" experience of the industrial revolution, even if we look only at British society. This point is important to the findings of the present chapter, as I discuss below.

The chronology of the first industrial revolution continues to be debated, as does its geographic scope. Almost all experts agree that the transformations specific to industrialization seem to have occurred in Britain first. For this reason, attempts to understand the causes and origins of the first industrial revolution have largely focused on Britain's exceptionality. Some scholars have suggested, for example, that Britain's laws, finances, and social organization were uniquely friendly to scientific innovation and the development of industry. Others have contended that its geographic characteristics—easy water-borne transportation, few mountains, accessible coal deposits—were especially well-suited to industrialization. Some of these arguments were introduced decades ago and have persisted, while others were rapidly or eventually refuted.[3]

Not all attempts to understand the origins of the first industrial revolution have focused on Britain alone, however. Parts of continental Europe—especially the Netherlands and Belgium—underwent similar if more muted processes during the same period, and some historians have argued that trade between Britain and its European neighbors helped to finance and stimulate the development of industry in this period. Other scholars have looked beyond Europe. For instance, historians Kenneth Pomeranz and Eric Williams have consideredthe important role that Britain's colonies played. They point out that British (as well as foreign-flagged) ships in the era leading up to and including the industrial revolution carried vast amounts of resources to Britain from its colonies and trading partners in the Americas, Africa, and Asia. These resources helped to feed, clothe, and employ British workers. In addition, British shipping and investors profited from carrying resources, currency, and even humans between these different regions of the world.[4] Another historian who has written on the global origins of the British industrial revolution is Robin Blackburn, who argues that the wealth produced by the Atlantic slave trade, in particular, funded innovation and economic development in Britain. Blackburn draws a connection between profits from the slave trade and the growth of banks like Barclays Bank. He also suggests that merchants involved in the slave trade used their money to endow universities such as Oxford and Cambridge, to modernize agriculture on their estates, and to invest in steam engines and cotton manufacturing.[5]

The research of these historians indicates that the first industrial revolution, though centered in Britain, involved societies and individuals in many other parts of the world. Thus, to truly comprehend the human experiences and perspectives associated with the first industrial revolution, we must not only study the networks and systems connecting the many regions of the world but also look beyond Britain to the people of the world—including Africa—who were linked into the trade networks of this period.

## AFRICAN EXPERIENCES

### Africans and the Global Industrial Economy

Economic historian David Landes suggests that one or more distinct industrial revolutions have taken place since the first industrial revolution in Britain.[6] These subsequent industrial revolutions differ from the first in place as well as in time. The term "second industrial revolution," for example, usually refers to industrial development in late-nineteenth- and early-twentieth-century western Europe, the northeastern United States, and Japan. And some scholars use the term "third industrial revolution" to talk about changes in East and South Asia in the late twentieth century. Through these processes, the kinds of transformations that first took place in Britain have spread to new regions of the world.

Africa's role in the second and subsequent industrial revolutions is widely recognized, but its importance in the first industrial revolution is sometimes forgotten. One researcher who has pointed this out is Nigerian scholar Joseph Inikori. In his book *Africans and the Industrial Revolution in England*, Inikori argues that Africans made massive contributions to Britain's industrial revolution and that the labor of enslaved Africans in the Americas was key to producing both food and raw materials to fuel the industrial revolution. Inikori writes that "[t]he gold, sugar, cotton, coffee, and other plantation crops produced in Brazil and the Caribbean were produced entirely by Africans and their descendants. The rice, tobacco, and above all, the cotton produced in the South of the United States were produced by Africans."[7] Moreover, he points out that despite suffering huge losses of manpower and productivity due to the Atlantic slave trade, the Africans who remained in Africa "managed to produce some strategic raw materials, such as gum and palm oil, for British industries during the period." In conclusion, he says, "the contribution of Africans was central to the origin of the Industrial Revolution in England."[8]

Africans thus played a major role in the first industrial revolution. But as a number of scholars have argued, industrialization also greatly affected Africa and Africans. One of the earliest scholarly texts to place African experiences in the context of the first industrial revolution was the Afro-Caribbean scholar Walter Rodney's 1972 work *How Europe Underdeveloped Africa*. In this book, Rodney argued that the cumulative effects of the Atlantic slave trade and the industrial revolution both robbed Africa of its human and natural resources and suppressed its economic productivity.[9] Rodney was just the first of many economists, historians, and other researchers to suggest that global industrialization had an overall negative impact on Africa, inasmuch as Africa has historically produced raw materials but consumed finished products and most of the profit from this trade has thus ended up in the industrialized nations of Europe, North America, and, increasingly, Asia. In short, global industrialization has exacerbated poverty and caused massive environmental damage in Africa and has been a major enabling factor in the conquest and colonial rule of African states by outsiders.

Ironically, these processes occurred alongside the decline of the Atlantic slave trade. By the early nineteenth century, the transatlantic slave trade had affected African coastal communities from Senegambia all the way down the west coast of Africa as well as southeastern Africa (today's Mozambique) and, arguably, deep into the interior as well. Europeans began to abolish slave trade in the late eighteenth and nineteenth centuries, beginning with Denmark in 1792 and gradually spreading throughout Europe, including Britain in 1807. Although abolition was arguably a moral decision by both European and African antislavery activists, it bolstered the political aspirations of British and North American industrial and financial bourgeoisie, who employed workers rather than owning slaves and therefore supported wage labor over slave labor. Politically, moreover, abolition hurt the aristocratic political rivals of the bourgeoisie, who tended to be slave-owners.

The gradual abolition of the Atlantic slave trade had an important impact on the large numbers of enslaved Africans, originally intended for the export trade, who slowly accumulated in various coastal regions of West Africa. With no destination across the ocean, these enslaved Africans became available for labor within the coastal African societies and contributed to the rise of "legitimate" products useful for European factories. Among the most important of these products were oil crops (especially palm oil and peanut oil), which could be used as industrial lubricants. Africans also produced other raw materials such as gum arabic, cotton, and indigo for the cloth industry as well as important crops for European bourgeois consumers including coffee, tobacco, and tea.

How were these vital industrial products produced, transported, and processed? In many cases, Africans themselves were involved as entrepreneurs. European merchants in Africa, many of whom were trying to retool from active slave trading, promoted the establishment of model farms and even plantations. They competed with Africans and people of mixed African and European heritage (and even Afro-Malay or Afro-Indian heritage) to dominate the market in palm oil and other resources.[10] In the 1820s, French merchant houses began to build plantations around the Senegal River using local laborers to grow crops like groundnuts for the European market. However, a coalition of local traders, many of whom were Euro-African, and other inhabitants opposed these plantations—not because they were against groundnut cultivation but because they were competing to grow groundnuts themselves (on small-holdings).[11] In other parts of Africa, too, local groups and individuals—many of whom were merchants, free peasants, and officials serving African states—competed with Europeans to provide raw materials, lubricants, and nutrients to the factory system.[12] At the same time, other Africans started businesses that distributed the products of the factories deep within the continent. Of course, many Africans also served as laborers; many were not paid wages but instead were share-croppers, renters, or even enslaved laborers.

*Modernization and Industrialization in Africa*

Many of the merchants involved with the trade of raw materials and manufactured products were also in favor of industrializing their own regions along the lines of Britain. Sometimes called "modernizers," these coalitions of traders, professionals, religious and state leaders, and merchants often consciously pursued such strategies as building new infrastructure, introducing novel practices and ideas, and even changing the social fabric of their societies in order to compete in the global industrializing economy. They spoke and wrote about these ideas in newspapers like *The Africa Times*, which was read widely in Sierra Leone, Liberia, the Gold Coast, and the coastal areas of what is today Nigeria. In 1869, one such professional, Doctor James Africanus Horton, even wrote a book promoting the idea of forming constitutional states along the West African coast akin to Britain and the small polities of Germany.[13] Although these modernizers engaged with the ideas of the British bourgeoisie, it would be simplistic to think of them as prowestern. Many of them endorsed the idea of developing economies and states similar to those of Europeans, but they also integrated local ideas of how state and society should function. In addition, they complained frequently about the pricing practices of European merchants and the policies of British and other officials in their regions, opposed building big plantations, and objected to the involvement of European corporations in the transport of crops from the interior. In other words, although they wanted to participate in and profit from the industrial revolution, they were not necessarily "westernizers."

In West, South, and East Africa many of the modernizers of the nineteenth century were members of Christian churches, while others were members of local religions. Still others were Muslims. One leading Muslim modernizer was Muhammad Ali, who effectively ruled Egypt from 1805 to 1849. Ali's rise to power was partly a result of the upheaval in Egypt following France's 1978 invasion. Ali was one of the leaders of a force sent by the Ottoman emperor to fight the French and retain Egypt for the empire. Instead, he seized power himself with the support of prominent local officials and religious leaders.

Over the course of Muhammad Ali's reign, he set out to modernize Egypt—in part, so that it could not again be easily invaded by modern armies like that of the French. He began with quite a lot of support, because many Egyptians were shocked by the ease with which the French had defeated their own garrison and impressed by their industrial goods. Ali began the modernization campaign by transforming landownership and agricultural production to allow for large plantations of cotton and other cash crops, as well as by building infrastructure such as canals, railways, and telegraph lines. He also sponsored the rise of nationalist modernizing thinkers such as Shaykh Rafia'a al-Tahtawi—who pushed for critical engagement of the relationship between Egyptian and Islamic identity and industrialization[14]—and built a modern army to defend Egyptian independence. However, modernization did not benefit everyone: the new plantations relied on hard work from rural dwellers who, like their contemporaries in Britain, had often lost their land. Moreover, just as Britain's industrial revolution may have relied in part on Africans enslaved to work in the Americas, Egypt's relied to some degree on Sudanese who were enslaved to work on Egyptian cotton farms.

*Settlers and "Big Men": Social and Political Change in Nineteenth-Century Africa*

On the other end of the African continent as well, rural Africans' experiences mirrored those of rural Britons during the period of the first industrial revolution, if somewhat later. Unlike any other part of Africa except Algeria, the southern tip of Africa experienced a large influx of European settlers early in the nineteenth century. Here, the transfer of ownership from local people into the hands of a small number of European farmers and herders followed the contours of European settlement in the territory. During the seventeenth century Dutch-speaking indentured servants of the Dutch East India Company and, later, independent farmers (known as "boers") carved out farms in what is now Cape Town as well as across the rocky terrain of the cape flats into the district of Stellenbosch. Gradually, these farmers spread out, building a wine industry, cattle ranches, and other types of farms. Among these laborers were enslaved or otherwise unfree Asians and Africans, who did much of the work.

In the mid-eighteenth century, European settlement of southern Africa began spreading eastward into the eastern Cape area. Here Europeans encountered large numbers of isiXhosa-speaking Africans known as amaXhosa, who initially resisted their advances. Following the British seizure of the Cape Colony in the early nineteenth century, reinforcements arrived—British soldiers initially and then, in 1820, large numbers of British subjects. Many of these "1820 settlers" were left over from the industrial revolution—mostly poor townspeople considered to be surplus population in

Britain and lured to South Africa by promises of land and help from the colonial government. Lacking the knowledge to farm the land they were given, they initially retreated into towns from where they traded with the amaXhosa. However, as they acquired the capital and skills they needed, many of these settlers began to herd sheep whose wool they provided to the factories of northern England. Thus they began to spread out and acquire land. This expansion lasted throughout much of the nineteenth century, culminating in the fencing off of large areas of land in the 1880s.[15] In the process, as we will see below, many of the amaXhosa were forced to transition from landowning free farmers and herders to workers on the big enclosed sheep farms of the eastern Cape.

In most of Africa, however, few if any European settlers arrived during this period. Thus the majority of African societies remained self-governing, at least until the 1890s for most of the continent and in some areas into the early twentieth century. Even in many of these regions, however, the industrial revolution shaped the transformation of local societies to varying degrees throughout the eighteenth and nineteenth centuries. In East Africa, this period saw the development of long-distance trade connecting Africans of the interior with Swahili-speaking African and Omani Arab merchants of the coast, who in turn traded with Asian and European ocean-going merchants. Factory-produced goods penetrated deep into the interior of central Africa, and raw materials came to the coast along a number of major routes stretching from east to west. The groups living along these routes, such as the Yao-speakers of the Lake Malawi area, reorganized themselves to control the new commerce, sometimes developing large trade networks or bigger states in the process. In other cases, as in the Pangani Valley of modern Tanzania, communities located along the trade route pushed aside larger but more distant states, leading to a fragmentation of the local political situation. Meanwhile, in the late nineteenth century, the emergence of massive plantations on the east coast of Africa drove a demand for slaves from the continent's center that deeply affected social organization patterns in the interior. There is some evidence that not only states but also family organization fragmented under the pressure of slave raiding in this region. In some areas, for example, the lack of security made ritual visits to relatives very difficult, thereby weakening the ties that bound uncles to nieces and nephews.

In West Africa, struggles to control the palm oil trade likewise led to political factionalization. This was especially true in the delta of the Niger River, one of the most important palm oil—producing regions in the world. Here, the palm oil business promoted competition not only between European merchants and Africans (and among African states and societies) but also between local corporations or "houses." In this dynamic setting, smart businesspeople could rapidly build trading empires. One such individual was Jubo Jubogha, or "Jaja," of Opobo. Enslaved to a trading corporation or "house" in the state of Bonny as a youth, Jaja rose to prominence and eventually came to dominate the palm oil trade in the region. He overcame rival houses and even maneuvered British buyers along the African coast into dealing directly with importers in Britain.[16] In the 1870s, his business empire was one of the major forces in the global palm oil business. On a smaller scale, men and women in the French-controlled island towns of St. Louis and Gorée in Senegambia sought to control the trade in groundnut oil and other goods. Some of these merchants were women born of European fathers and African mothers. Known as "signares," they used their two-sided family connections to act as intermediaries between producers in the African interior and merchants from France and other European countries.

All of these changes had varying effects on the social systems of African societies. In some areas, new labor and financial arrangements broke up or altered extended-family relationships. For example, in many parts of nineteenth-century Africa, inheritance usually passed at least partly through the maternal branch of the family—meaning that men left their property (and, in some cases, their names) to their sisters' sons and daughters rather than to their own children. In this way, wealth was redistributed among members of the family rather than concentrated in the hands of individuals. However, Africans who traded with Europeans entered a very different system in which property was privately owned by individuals (usually men) and passed on from father to son. Some of these Africans also organized large business networks operating on a cash basis and adopted a system of passing these assets on to their sons, thus breaking matrilineal ties based on the communal ownership of land. This system spread from merchants to entrepreneurial cash-crop farmers; the latter, too, recognized the advantage of owning their land on an individual basis. In this way, the penetration of cash economies and the linked ideals of capitalism operated to break the power of the extended family.

In regions where large plantations or enclosed ranches were built, the power of the extended family was often broken down even further. This was particularly true in southern Africa. In the eastern Cape, some British magistrates purposefully tried to limit the power of "chiefs" and family heads by limiting the size of amaXhosa communities in areas that they controlled. On the plantations of coastal East Africa, slaves from the interior were torn from their families and placed under the control of taskmasters instead.

Ironically, while the industrial revolution, the abolition of the Atlantic slave trade, and the growth of "legitimate trade" were supposed to promote wage labor in Africa, as they had earlier in Britain, these processes in reality caused at least a short-term rise in economic forms of enslavement *within* Africa.[17] Enslaved Africans who would otherwise have been shipped off the continent instead pooled in coastal areas of southeast and western Africa, and some were redirected into producing and transporting palm oil and other goods. Many of these individuals remained enslaved, although probably most of the production and transportation of goods within Africa continued to be carried out by family labor and through extended networks of sharecroppers, renters, and other types of laborers. In addition, enslaved women and men may have been redirected into the households of wealthy African entrepreneurs and members of the bourgeoisie to serve as domestic laborers and, in some cases, concubines.

Although the rising class of bourgeois African merchants, professionals, and other leaders was in many cases related to important families in rural areas, in the nineteenth century it began to build or join existing urbanized communities in trading towns along rivers and at the African coasts.[18] These cities and the infrastructure that served them was not dedicated to processing goods, as in Britain but, rather, was largely limited to moving raw materials out of the continent and importing finished goods from British and European factories in return. This was true even in North Africa, where the cities of the Maghreb from Morocco to Libya developed a wide taste for European goods for the first time in history. Life experiences in Africa's cities during the period of the industrial revolution were diverse, of course, but they shared an influx of European influences. These included new aesthetics—such as an appetite for rectilinear buildings—as well as ideas, products, and, in some cases, migrants. As with other aspects of the industrial revolution, Africans strove to control this flow and turn it to their own benefit. While they were not always successful, their economic success in this period may have been partly responsible for Europeans' turn toward formal colonialism in the late nineteenth century as African merchants' success at controlling production and prices led their European counterparts to demand that their governments embark on the formal conquest of Africa in the 1880s and 1890s. Whether or not this is correct, certainly it is not right to talk about the industrial revolution or African history in this period without considering their relationships to each other.

## AFRICAN PERSPECTIVES ON THE INDUSTRIAL REVOLUTION

Although African experiences in the era of the first industrial revolution were diverse, two examples can help to illustrate the ways in which the industrialization of Britain and the shifting global economy affected many Africans' everyday lives and how Africans themselves thought about these changes. The first example utilizes oral histories collected by an African intellectual in the 1880s to tell the story of amaXhosa-speakers in the eastern Cape during the 1850s. The second makes use of court testimony to highlight living conditions among enslaved working youths in the eighteenth-century Gold Coast (the southern region of modern Ghana) and of newspaper articles to demonstrate the perspectives of the wealthier classes of the region.

### The AmaXhosa and the Great Cattle Killing

The experiences of the amaXhosa people of southern Africa represent perhaps the most advanced penetration in Africa of the rural land enclosure system developed in Britain during the first industrial revolution. From about the 1820s onward, the amaXhosa, like many British peasants before them, gradually lost control of vast tracts of land through a series of wars that transferred territory to British settlers or at least placed many amaXhosa under the rule of British "magistrates." In these "directly ruled" territories, as in Britain, large areas of the land itself were transformed from small family plots and communally owned pastoral grasslands into privately owned sheep ranches producing wool for British factories. Then, in the 1850s, a British governor named Sir George Grey undertook a radical social program that forced amaXhosa within the directly ruled territories into road-working gangs, broke up the power of amaXhosa chiefs by forcing them to live in small villages consisting of no more than twenty structures, and promoted Christian missions as schools to teach Africans to accept their lot as workers for British landowners. At the same time, European settlers mistakenly imported a disease that affected cattle—bovine pneumonia (also called lung-sickness). By 1855, this disease was killing amaXhosa cattle at the rate of five thousand head a month. Another disease affected the staple maize (corn) crop around the same time. Thus, by 1856, the amaXhosa were "economically . . . against the wall."[19] Many became workers on mission and settler farms, and the chiefs of the directly ruled territories began to accept salaries as government officials, thereby losing the last of their independence.

To the east of the directly ruled territories, large amaXhosa-speaking populations still remained technically independent, especially in the region known as Gcalekaland. However, even these populations were deeply affected by the changes described above. Crowded onto smaller and less fertile plots of land by an influx of refugees from the directly ruled territories, they, too, suffered from losses of cattle and crops. This was not only an economic issue but a deeply social one as well. For the amaXhosa, cattle served as social capital. Wealth in cattle meant social status—and for men, adulthood was partly proven by possession of cattle. Cattle were transferred from a man's family to a woman's in cases of marriage, and lawsuits (including those for adultery or sexual transgressions) were settled through payments of cattle. Without cattle, the whole social structure of society was in danger of breaking down.

It was during this crisis that a fifteen-year-old girl named Nongqawuse went down to her family's maize fields on the Gxarha River in Qolora, where her job was to chase away the birds. On this day, together with her cousin Nonkosi, she heard voices coming from the river. Two strangers introduced themselves as Sifubasibanzi ("wide-chest") and Napakade ("forever"). Only Nongqawuse seemed to be able to communicate with them. They told Nongqawuse to communicate to her uncle Mhlakaza that he must convey a message from the other world. The message was that the amaXhosa should kill their cattle and stop cultivating their crops, and that on a said day, if they did as they were told, the dead would arise.

The isiXhosa-speaking scholar William Gqoba collected oral histories of this event in the 1880s and translated the words of the two strangers as follows:[20]

> You are to tell the people that the whole community is to rise again from the dead. Then go on to say to them that all the cattle living now must be slaughtered, for they are reared with defiled hands, as the people handle witchcraft. Say to them there must be no ploughing of land, rather must the people dig deep pits (granaries), erect new huts, set up wide, strongly built cattlefolds, make milksacks, and weave doors from buka roots. The people must give up witchcraft on their own, not waiting until they are exposed by the witchdoctors. You are to tell them that these are the words of their chiefs—the words of Napakade and Sifubasibanzi.

This quote does not directly talk about "industrialization" or "land enclosures," of course. Rather, it focuses on "witchcraft." Yet it is possible to draw a connection between these concepts. For the amaXhosa, witchcraft was related to greed as well as to disease and other misfortunes. By using the term "witchcraft," then, Nongqawuse was expressing the belief that the loss of land and diseases afflicting the amaXhosa, their crops, and their cattle was the result of an impure practice, and that only by "cleansing" their practices, their herds, and their crops could the amaXhosa come to retake the land they had lost and restore their wealth and social system.

Mhlakaza immediately began to proselytize this message to his neighbors and to destroy his own crops and cattle. Although many amaXhosa were skeptical, the ruler of Gcalekaland, Sarhili, was converted into a believer in July 1856 and used his influence to convince many of his chiefly officeholders and advisors to do the same. Even many amaXhosa living under direct colonial rule joined in. What happened next is described by Gqoba:

THE ORDERS OF THE CHIEFS

On reaching their homes, the chiefs assembled their subjects and made known the news of the ancestors who were expected to return to life, fresh and strong, of the promised coming-to life-again of the cattle they were about to slaughter and of those that they had slaughtered long ago. Nongqause had said that anyone who, on slaughtering his ox, decided to dispose of its carcass by barter, should nevertheless engage its soul, in order that on its coming back to life it should be his property. And she had said that all those who did not slaughter their cattle would be carried by a fierce hurricane and thrown into the sea to drown and die. The community was split in two. One section believed that the resurrection of the people would come some day, but not that of the cattle. Thereupon, father fell out with son, brother with brother, chief with subjects, relative with relative. Two names emerged to distinguish the two groups. One group was named amaTamba (the Submissive), that is, Nongqause's converts. The other was called amaGogotua (the Unyielding), that is, those who were stubborn and would not kill their cattle. So some slaughtered their cattle, and others did not.

THE EIGHTH DAY

As the killing of the cattle went on, those who had slaughtered hurriedly for fear of being smelt out began to starve and had to live by stealing the livestock of others. Then everybody looked forward to the eighth day. It was the day on which the sun was expected to rise red, and to set again in the sky.

Then there would follow great darkness, during which the people would shut themselves in their huts. Then the dead would rise and return to their homes, and then the light of day would come again.

On that day the sun rose as usual. Some people had washed their eyes with sea-water at the mouth of the Buffalo. Some peered outside through little apertures in their huts, while those who had never believed went about their daily outdoor tasks. Nothing happened. The sun did not set, no dead person came back to life, and not one of the things that had been predicted came to pass.

Such then was the Nongqause catastrophe. The people died of hunger and disease in large numbers. Thus it was that whenever thereafter a person said an unbelievable thing, those who heard him said, "You are telling a Nongqause tale."

As Ggoba notes, the cattle killing and crop burning did not succeed in bringing back the wealth and ancestors of the amaXhosa. In fact, in its aftermath many were forced to become laborers for European farms and on mission stations, while others starved to death. Sir George Grey refused to help the starving, and in fact tried to limit missionaries and even British settlers from extending aid to amaXhosa unless they agreed to become laborers. As a result, the independence of the amaXhosa was essentially ended.

How should we understand these events? Although many scholars have put forth explanations, we will concentrate on the links between the industrial revolution and the cattle killing.[21] The main argument here is that it's possible to interpret this episode as an attempt by the amaXhosa to respond to the pressures of rapid social and economic change brought about by settler capitalism. To us, with our "modern," scientific, and secular worldview, it may seem to have been an "irrational" response, but to the amaXhosa, with their own understanding of the world, it was perfectly rational.

Historians have perceived several links between settler capitalism and industrialization, on the one hand, and the cattle killing episodes, on the other. First, the cattle killing was at least partly a result of the material losses of the amaXhosa in the decades leading up to the war. Years of crop failures and the onset of lung sickness contributed to this misery, as did the amaXhosa's gradual loss of land to settler-owned farms that provided wool for the factories of Britain.[22]

For the amaXhosa living under direct colonial rule, this misery was compounded by the changes devised by Sir George Grey, including the weakening of chiefs and the forced mobilization of amaXhosa as laborers.

In fact, Grey managed to turn the chaos to his own benefit and that of the European settlers of the region. For this reason, some amaXhosa believed then, as do some today, that Grey may have been behind the whole process; indeed, some suspect that he hid by the river and influenced Nongqawuse to "invent" the story of meeting two strangers. While this seems unlikely, it is certainly true that Grey wanted to transform the amaXhosa into a dependent class of "useful servants, consumers of our goods, contributors to our revenue."[23] This end was essentially achieved by the cattle-killing episode.

The impact of missionary Christianity also cannot be underestimated. While the Christian missionaries were certainly not entirely allied to the government, and even tried to help starving amaXhosa in the aftermath of the cattle killing and crop burning, their Christian ideas nevertheless may have been part of the prophecies of Nongqawuse. The idea of the rebirth of ancestors, for example, may have emerged from Christian ideas of "resurrection," although it was cast as an amaXhosa-style "prophecy." Indeed, historian Jeff Peires suggests that Nongqawuse's uncle Mhlakaza may have been a former convert and preacher named Wilhelm Goliath who "lapsed" from the Christian faith but nevertheless brought some of its apocalyptic ideas back with him to Gcalekaland.[24]

The amaXhosa also merged their understanding of local trends with news of global events. For example, they were aware of the British involvement in the Crimean war against Russia. Learning that in 1854 the Russians had killed a former British governor of the Cape, Sir George Cathcart, some amaXhosa came to believe that the Russians were resurrected amaXhosa. Similarly, the Indian Rebellion in 1857 led a few amaXhosa to believe that the Indian mutineers were their ancestors reborn.

But the cattle killing was also shaped by profound social and cultural factors. By the 1850s, the loss of cattle due to sickness as well as land alienation and official policy may well have destroyed much of the social infrastructure of amaXhosa society. Lacking access to cattle, young men in turn may have found it difficult to marry. As a result, some may have pursued illicit sexual relationships, including those deemed incestuous or nonconsensual. Normally, such relationships would have been punished through cattle fines.

Since there was a shortage of cattle, however, the amaXhosa authorities could not fine men for such transgressions against sexual morals. Moreover, in the occupied areas, such "traditional" regulations would have faced interference from colonial magistrates trying to impose their own power by holding hearings in formal colonial courts.

If sexual transgressions against unmarried (or, in some cases, married) women were becoming more common during this period, it is possible to interpret the cattle-killing and crop-burning episode through a gendered lens: perhaps Nongqawuse's prophecy was a protest by women (and particularly by "a woman") against the changing moral and social situation. Indeed, historian Helen Bradford has suggested that Nongqawuse herself may have been an incest survivor and that her prophecy may have been influenced by her personal experience.[25] Through this lens, the prophecy's focus on "cleansing" society as well as the demand that the men destroy their main wealth— their cattle—take on new meaning.

The cattle killing episode did not complete the transformation of amaXhosa livelihoods, but it was certainly a watershed moment. Over the next several generations, most of the amaXhosa would complete the transition to industrial workers and wage-paid farm workers, often in very poor conditions. Even as early as the 1850s, however, amaXhosa society was being fundamentally changed by the spread of British authority and the growth of settler-run farms feeding the voracious appetites of factories in Britain. The cattle killing incident illustrates one way in which the amaXhosa responded—namely, through a synthesis of a localized conception of prophecies and Christian ideas of resurrection that they hoped would help them to reclaim their land, wealth, and social order.

*Laborers and the Bourgeoisie on the Gold Coast*

The region known in the eighteenth and nineteenth centuries as the Gold Coast comprises most of the coast of what is today Ghana and the forested area toward the interior. This area has been involved in trans-regional trade since at least the sixteenth century, including the sale of gold and kola nuts across the Sahel and Savanna into North Africa and the Islamic world.[26] In the sixteenth and seventeenth centuries, the Gold Coast supplied gold to Portuguese and Dutch merchants in exchange for enslaved Africans brought by the Europeans from other regions of the continent. These slaves were then used locally in the gold mining industry. Only in the 1670s did the Gold Coast become a net exporter of enslaved Africans.

Trade in the region was dominated for varying periods by networks of merchants such as the "Akani," but by the late eighteenth century merchants associated with the state government of the growing Asante Confederation regulated much of the commerce between the coast and the interior. These traders were active in the Atlantic slave trade, transferring captives acquired by the Asante government in wars or as tribute to coastal trading positions. They then sold the captives to European merchants, with whom they had uneasy relationships of competition and collaboration. The abolition of the Atlantic slave trade gradually ended this arrangement, and in the ensuing commercial crisis Europeans as well as Africans scrambled to find a way to replace the slave trade. In 1778, a Danish entrepreneur named Dr. Paul Isert had tried to grow coffee near the town of Accra using enslaved laborers, and in the early nineteenth century other Europeans tried sugar, cotton, and tobacco.[27] However, the crop that actually took off in the area was palm oil, which had become important as an industrial lubricant.

In contrast to southern Africa, very few Europeans settled in the Gold Coast, or indeed anywhere else in West Africa, during the nineteenth century. Thus there was no system of settler capitalism here. Rather, most palm oil in the region was probably grown on small farms worked by extended families. There is evidence, however, of other types of landowning and labor arrangements. The most dramatic of these may have been the "huza" system of the Krobo people.[28] The Krobo lived in mountainous territory, and the huzas were a style of farm uniquely suited to their environment, as they consisted of long parallel rectangular strips reaching away from a road or stream up the low slopes of the mountains.

The Krobo in the seventeenth and early eighteenth centuries probably had a relatively decentralized political structure in which priests were important leaders. In the late eighteenth century, the Krobo were fortunate in that many of their neighbors had weakened each other in a series of wars, allowing them to occupy rich agricultural land just as palm oil was becoming a profitable crop. As a result, the Krobo came to dominate its production. The palm oil farmers quickly rose in importance within Krobo society; many could afford to send their children to the tuition-charging mission schools and, with the assistance of their formally educated children, were able to make commercial alliances with merchants in the big towns of the coast and trade routes.

As the Krobo expanded by occupying or purchasing land in neighboring areas, they tended to subdivide these newly acquired regions in the same way as they had in their mountainous home territory. Palm oil grown on these farms was then carried to large cosmopolitan towns, where traders spoke all of the languages of the region—Ewe, various Twi dialects, the Adangme language of the Krobo themselves, the Ga language of their close cousins in nearby Accra, and even languages from far away such as Hausa. Some towns even had large European populations.[29] The oil was carried to the big ports of the coast, such as Accra, and then shipped to factories in Britain.

As they spread into new areas, individual Krobo farmers tended to acquire multiple farms, sometimes located quite far apart. By the 1880s, many important farmers were extremely wealthy. Of course, they did not have enough family to work all of the farms, and it seems that at least some of their laborers were enslaved individuals.[30] For example, the Konor (king) of the Yilo Krobo state in 1851 produced palm oil on dozens of huzas worked by his "slaves and children" and processed it at a central farm under the control of his wives.[31] Evidence of the Konor's farming empire shows that women played a key role on the farms. In general, as wealthy men became involved in traveling among their farms and arranging export arrangements, their wives and other key women of their households took over such roles as growing food, making goods for local markets, and processing palm kernels to get at the oil.

However, not all women (or men) found positive opportunities in the new economy. Because the tropical rainforests harbored diseases that killed domesticated animals, almost all of the palm oil was carried to the coast by humans, who, in return, brought industrial goods such as cloth and firearms as well as locally produced fish and salt. Many of these carriers were full members of local communities and were paid wages for their work, but a heightened demand for carriers drove a renewed bout of enslavement that did not diminish during the nineteenth century. Despite the criminalization of slavery in the British-controlled regions of the coast in 1874, there is evidence that throughout the late nineteenth century large numbers of young men and women and even children were serving as enslaved "carriers" who transported palm oil into the international market and returned with salt and finished products to the interior of West Africa. Much of this evidence comes from court records of the period in the British-controlled trading cities of Accra and Cape Coast:

SCT [Supreme Court Testimony] 5/14/15 Queen v. Quatto Bras, a Fanti, 26 February 1875, Cape Coast Judicial Assessor's Court

Quatto Bras: "Before the war I was trading in Ashantee and when the war came I ran away. When I went back I was paid the two women and girl for the things I had sold. . . . I brought them to the coast to carry salt for me."

SCT 2/15/12 Queen v. Kwamin Mintah, 11 February 1896, Accra Supreme Court

Kofi Binprah: "Defendant came and asked for carriers. Six of us went for 10/ [ten shillings] each. Five went home after Accra but I stayed with the accused. When I could not go on he threatened to flog me. Accused refused to let me go and [sold] me to some Ashantee people."

This need for carriers also led to new justifications and means of seizing free people to work as slaves. For example, some profit seekers began to seize young people for the debts of their relatives or even their unrelated country-people, as indicated in this record:

SCT 2/4/6 Queen v. Cobina Byai, 3 March 1871, Accra Divisional Court

Dokoo: "One of my relatives owed money for rum. Defendant paid the debt. He came and asked me to pay. I could not, so he seized seven relatives. I said why so many people for such a small debt? He replied his expenses had amounted to 1500 heads [of cowries].

Of course, not all of the enslaved were put to work on farms or as carriers, as noted in this report from a colonial official:

> R. E. Firminger to Colonial Office, 30 April 1889, West Kensington
> "The Akims supply Kintampo with kola nuts, take away slaves, ivory and cattle. The slaves . . . if docile are kept to work Akim farms. Many of the women are taken as slave wives or concubines, while the children are brought up to work as domestic slaves."

What was life like for these unfree workers? Unfortunately, they left little written evidence behind, but some of what we have learned about their lives comes from sources like oral traditions and proverbs. However, there are a few records from this place and time in which enslaved workers *can* tell us about their lives. For example, after defeating Asante in an 1873–1874 war, the British began to impose antislavery ordinances in some places along the coast. The ordinances allowed a few enslaved workers, especially those in domestic settings working for farming families or the new bourgeoisie, to seek their freedom. As Inspector R. E. Firminger's report notes, many were children. Here is how some of them described their lives as unfree domestic workers.

> SCT 17/5/6, Queen v. Aceday Ancrah, 5 October 1887, Accra District Court
> Amina (girl of 10 or 12): "I . . . went with accused to her house. [She] sent me to get water and wood. . . . If I did not get some she beat [me]. I was always hungry."

> SCT 17/5/9 Queen v. Afelu 25 March 1890, Accra District Court
> Ramato: "Some time ago I came from Salagah [north of Asante] with my master. We stopped in Accra about two months and returned to Salagah. My master always told me 'my mother stayed with her master. I must be patient and stop with him.' When we came here I heard my mother was sick at Salagah. I asked my master to let me go and see but he refused. If I am not a slave why can't my master allow me to go and see my mother now she is sick? When we went down to Kwitta my master used to flog [beat] me always."

SCT 5/4/19 Queen v. Quamina Eddoo 10 Nov 1876, Cape Coast Judicial Assessor's Court

Abina: "[T]he defendant gave me two cloths and told me that he had given me in marriage to one of his house people, and I remonstrated with defendant. I asked him how it was ([since] I had been left by Yowawhah to live with him, and that he would return), that he had given me in marriage to one of his people. On this I thought that I had been sold and I ran away. At the time the defendant said he had given me in marriage to Tandoe. And the defendant said that if I did not consent to be married to Tandoe he would tie me up and flog me. I heard I had country people living at Cape Coast, and for what the defendant said I ran away and came to Cape Coast. I swept the house, I go for water and firewood and I cooked and when I cooked I ate some. I went to market to buy vegetables."

Each of these witnesses was a young woman or girl who claimed to have been illegally treated as a slave within territory claimed by Britain, where the morals of the industrial revolution had swept abolitionist policies into place. While the court records largely reflect questions asked by the judges to determine whether or not these young witnesses could be described as having the status of "slaves," many of them nevertheless managed to tell us about what it was like to lack control over their own daily lives.

Some of the people for whom they worked as carriers, farm workers, or domestic laborers were also writing about their plans for their country. Among the English-literate of the coastal towns, especially, development and industry were important issues. By the nineteenth century, these bourgeois professionals and merchants were keenly concerned with building an infrastructure to support their commercial endeavors. Many of them became firm Christians and imbibed a sense of morals and ideals developed by the British industrial and financial bourgeoisie of the time. These views came out in newspapers like *The African Times* (which was begun in 1860 by middle-class and upper-class Englishmen and Afro-British intellectuals to help "modernize" and "civilize" parts of Africa), *The Church Missionary Intelligencer*, *The Sierra Leone Journal*, and *The Anglo-Colonial*. These resources helped English-speaking Africans and Africans of the diaspora share ideas and news about the places in which they lived.[32] *The African Times* was especially widely read in Sierra Leone and along the Gold Coast, from which many readers sent letters that made up the bulk of the paper. These letters expressed their writers' hopes and ideas for the future and were sometimes also presented as editorials. An excerpt from one such editorial is reprinted below. It was probably written by Ferdinand Fitzgerald, a West African—born professional and merchant living in Britain who edited the paper.

### "Native Capitalists," *The African Times*, May 23, 1868 (unsigned)

In one point all countries are alike. For the development of their material resources, and consequently for their general progress, they have need of an element which does not exist per se, but must be created or imported. This element is wealth; and wealth is the realized surplus product of industry after the supply of the wants of those employed in it. . . . [In T]he British possessions on the West Coast of Africa . . . there is no chance of any Imperial expenditures on those public works which are absolutely indispensable to a rapid development of material resources; no immigrants are likely to come in bringing realized capital with them; and it will be only after a large expenditure of capital that lands, even in British West African possessions, will be considered to offer such a security as to induce the loan of British capital upon them. From this it follows that if West Africa is to progress, it must be chiefly, if not entirely, by means of her own resources. In other words, there must be a creation of native capitalists. And the time has arrived at which this creation ought to take place. But it never can take place while the realized surplus product of industry goes out of the country. That realized surplus, which, in the infancy of trade and resources, went almost inevitably into the hands of the British merchant and trader, and has thus been lost to the country, must now be kept at home, for it is on the keeping it at home in the hands of natives that a rapid progress in Africa absolutely depends. . . . The question is, how is this to be accomplished? It must be done partly by them and partly for them. They must exercise prudence, self-restraint and self-denial, as well as industry and intelligence; and they must be aided in England by zeal and faithfulness, and the most strict and scrupulous honesty in dealing with them. . . . When once a race of native capitalists is created in the West African settlements—capitalists who can afford to detach a portion of their wealth from their particular branch of trade for the construction of public works, other capital will come in to help them in the regeneration and advancement of their country, upon terms that will not kill while affecting to benefit.

This excerpt displays the ambivalence felt by many Africans of the period. Fitzgerald, like many of his contemporaries, believed in building an economy like that of industrial Britain. However, he was also convinced that British merchants were exploiting Africa. In calling for a class of African entrepreneurs, Fitzgerald was suggesting that Africans deepen their engagement in the industrial revolution but strive to keep the profits for themselves. He held up many of the bourgeois moral values promoted by the British middle class as admirable—self-restraint and hard work, especially—yet clearly doubted that British traders could be counted on to deal fairly with Africans. In this way, his editorial was indicative of a class that sought to control the commerce of the industrial revolution for their own benefit. In the Gold Coast, such feelings translated into political projects. The most famous of these is the Fante Confederation project of the early 1870s, in which African merchants, professionals, and lawyers declared an independent state with a European-style government and laws favorable to commerce and industry. Although this state did not come to fruition, the attempt to create it expressed the hopes and aspirations of the African bourgeoisie of the period.

Of course, not all Africans were as deeply affected by the industrial revolution as those described above. In much of Africa, the engagement with European-centered commerce was less pronounced, and life was much more extensively shaped by local factors. The spread of formal colonialism in the following few decades, however, would transform much of the rest of Africa and deepen its dependency on—and links to—the global, capitalist, industrialized economy. As in the Gold Coast and the eastern Cape, this would lead to social and cultural as well as economic and political transformations.

## QUESTIONS

1. What roles were played by Africans in the first industrial revolution?
2. In what ways did the first industrial revolution affect Africans' societies and lifestyles?

3. How did the enclosure of land and the influx of diseases in the eastern Cape region affect the amaXhosa? How did Nongqawuse's followers talk about these issues?

4. How did the industrial revolution affect labor and lifestyle in the late-nineteenth-century Gold Coast?

5. In what ways do the opinions of the African author of "Native Capitalists" reflect commonly held ideals of the British bourgeoisie during the first industrial revolution? How does he seem to criticize British merchants and traders?

## FURTHER READINGS

Inikori, Joseph E. *Africans and the Industrial Revolution in England: A Study in International Trade and Economic Development.* Cambridge: Cambridge University Press, 2002.

Lewis, Jack. "Materialism and Idealism in the Historiography of the Xhosa Cattle-Killing Movement 1856–7," *South African Historical Journal* 25 (1991): 244–268.

Peires, Jeff. "Suicide or Genocide? Xhosa Perceptions of the Nongqawuse Catastrophe." *Radical History Review* 46, no. 7 (1990): 46–57.

Reynolds, Edward. *Trade and Economic Change on the Gold Coast, 1807–1874.* New York: Longman, 1974.

Rodney, Walter. *How Europe Underdeveloped Africa.* Washington: Howard University Press, 1982. Originally published in 1972.

Searing, James F. *West African Slavery and Atlantic Commerce: The Senegal River Valley, 1700–1860.* Cambridge: Cambridge University Press, 1993.

Sundiata, Ibrahim. *From Slaving to Neoslavery: The Bight of Biafra and Fernando Po in the Era of Abolition, 1827–1930.* Madison: University of Wisconsin Press, 1996.

Sutton, Inez. "Labour in Commercial Agriculture in Ghana in the Late Nineteenth and Early Twentieth Centuries," *Journal of African History* 24 (1983): 461–483.

## NOTES

1. Robert B. Marks, *The Origins of the Modern World: A Global and Ecological Narrative from the Fifteenth to the Twenty-First Century,* 2nd ed. (Lanham, MD: Rowman and Littlefield, 2006).

2. Eric Hobsbawm, *The Age of Revolution: Europe 1789–1848* (London: Weidenfeld & Nicolson Ltd., 1962).

3. Two excellent analyses are Peer Vries, *Via Peking Back to Manchester: Britain, the*

*Industrial Revolution, and China* (Leiden: CNWS, 2003), and G. Riello and P. O'Brien, "Reconstructing the Industrial Revolution: Analyses, Perceptions and Conceptions of Britain's Precocious Transition to Europe's First Industrial Society," *Economic History* 84 (2004): 1–41.

4. Kenneth Pomeranz and Steven Topik, *The World That Trade Created: Society, Culture, and the World Economy* (London: M. E. Sharpe, 2006); Eric Williams, *Capitalism and Slavery* (London: Andre Deutsch, 1964).

5. Robin Blackburn, *The Making of New World Slavery: From the Baroque to the Modern 1492–1800* (New York: Verso, 1997).

6. David Landes, *The Unbound Prometheus: Technological Change and Industrial Development in Western Europe from 1750 to the Present* (Cambridge: Cambridge University Press, 1969).

7. Joseph E. Inikori, *Africans and the Industrial Revolution in England: A Study in International Trade and Economic Development* (Cambridge: Cambridge University Press, 2002), p. 481.

8. Inikori, *Africans and the Industrial Revolution in England*, p. 482.

9. Walter Rodney, *How Europe Underdeveloped Africa* (Washington: Howard University Press, 1982; originally published in 1972).

10. One useful book in this respect is Martin Lynn, *Commerce and Economic Change in West Africa: The Palm Oil Trade in the Nineteenth Century* (Cambridge: Cambridge University Press, 1997).

11. The evidence of this is mostly to be found in the National Archives of Senegal, files 2B4 and 2B5, and in the French overseas archives.

12. Christopher Chamberlin, "Bulk Exports, Trade Tiers, Regulation, and Development: An Economic Approach to the Study of West Africa's 'Legitimate Trade,'" *Journal of Economic History* 39 (1979): 419–438.

13. James Africanus Horton, *West African Countries and People* (Edinburgh: Edinburgh University Press, 1969; originally published in 1868).

14. Afaf Lufti al-Sayyid Marsot, *Egypt in the Reign of Muhammad Ali* (Cambridge: University of Cambridge Press, 1983).

15. Lance van Sittert, "Holding the Line: The Rural Enclosure Movement in the Cape Colony, c. 1865–1910," *Journal of African History* 43 (2002): 95–118.

16. Sylvanus Cookey, *King Jaja of the Niger Delta: His Life and Times, 1821–1891* (New York: NOK Publishers, 1974).

17. James Searing, *West African Slavery and Atlantic Commerce: The Senegal River Valley, 1700–1860* (Cambridge: Cambridge University Press, 1993), pp. 49–51.

18. Bill Freund, *The African City: A History* (Cambridge: Cambridge University Press, 2007), pp. 37–64.

19. Noel Mostert, *Frontiers; The Epic of South Africa's Creation and the Tragedy of the Xhosa People* (New York: Alfred A. Knopf, 1992), p. 1178.

20. William Gqoba, "The Cause of the Cattle-Killing at the Nongqause Period," translated by A. C. Jordan, in *Towards an African Literature: The Emergence of Literary Form in Xhosa* (Berkeley: University of California Press, 1973), pp. 111–112, 113–115.

21. The formative analysis is Jeff Peires, *The Dead Will Arise: Nongqawuse and the Great Xhosa Cattle-Killing Movement of 1856–7* (Johannesburg: Ravan, 1989). I use this analysis extensively in later sections of the chapter.

22. See Julian Cobbing, "Review of *The Dead Will Arise: Nongqawuse and the Great Xhosa Cattle-Killing Movement of 1856–7*," *Journal of Southern African Studies* 20, no. 2 (1994): 339–341.

23. Imperial Blue Book 1969 of 1855, George Grey, March 17, 1855, pp. 56–69; quoted in Peires, *The Dead Will Arise*, p. 57.

24. Peires, *The Dead Will Arise*, pp. 33–36.

25. Helen Bradford, "Women, Gender and Colonialism: Rethinking the History of the British Cape Colony and Its Frontier Zones, c. 1806–1870," *Journal of African History* 37 (1996): 351–370.

26. Paul E. Lovejoy, *Caravans of Kola: the Hausa Kola Trade 1700–1900* (London and Zaria: Oxford University Press, 1980).

27. M. A. Kwamena-Poh, *Government and Politics in the Akuapem State, 1730–1850* (London: Longman, 1973).

28. Louis E. Wilson, "The 'Bloodless Conquest' in Southeastern Ghana: The Huza and Territorial Expansion of the Krobo in the 19th Century," *International Journal of African Historical Studies* 23 (1990): 269–297.

29. Ibid., p. 290.

30. Brodie Cruickshank, *Eighteen Years on the Gold Coast of West Africa*, vol. 1 (London: Hurst and Blackett, 1853), pp. 244–245.

31. Basel Mission Society archives, D-1.4a, Dieterle, May 31, 1852, Akropong.

32. The newspapers were also read in Britain and the British Caribbean. See K.A.B. Jones-Quartey, *History, Politics, and the Early Press in Ghana: The Fictions and the Facts* (Philadelphia: Afram, 1975), pp. 117–118; Christopher Fyfe, *A History of Sierra Leone* (Oxford: Oxford University Press, 1962), pp. 335, 337.

# 3

# When Satiety and Avarice Marry, Hunger Is Born

## *African Voices of the Colonial Era, ca. 1896–1945*

### Tim Carmichael

## GLOBAL CONTEXT

On March 1, 1896, Ethiopian Emperor Menilek's trans-regional, multiethnic army mobilized near Adwa and—despite exhaustion and food shortages—crushed a major invasion by Italy, an industrializing European state attempting to boost its national prestige through colonial conquest. Ethiopia's triumph preserved the African country's political independence during the Age of Imperialism and enhanced its global image and reputation, already considerable owing to its millennium and a half of Christian heritage and numerous references in the Bible.[1] In the decades that followed, Ethiopia came to embody a living international symbol of African potential that belied the prevailing Western belief that lighter-skinned people were somehow superior in God's eyes.[2] The African nation-state subsequently inspired colonized Africans, and others around the continent and throughout the world, to oppose European racism and colonial rule, often employing Christian allusions and imagery as they did so. This "Ethiopianist" symbolism was notable since Europeans had previously used Christianity and Biblical arguments to justify the Atlantic Slave Trade and, more recently, had used their faith to legitimize their subjugation and exploitation of nonwhite "races" in colonized territories, even when conquered peoples of color were co-religionists.

Ethiopia remained an independent state until the 1930s, when Benito Mussolini's fascist Italy attacked and temporarily occupied Ethiopia, in clear violation of the Charter of the League of Nations (the precursor to the United Nations), of which both Italy and Ethiopia were members. Article 10 of the charter stated: "The Members of the League undertake to respect and preserve as against external aggression the territorial integrity and existing political independence of all Members of the League." Yet the other member-states stood by while Italy invaded Ethiopia.

Despite this brief occupation, Ethiopia never experienced the sort of long-term exploitative colonial rule that plagued the rest of Africa and other regions of the world. That fact, alongside Ethiopia's historic nature as a Christian outpost that long maintained peaceful trade relations with its Arab and Black Islamic neighbors, as well as Christian Europeans further afield, makes Ethiopia a particularly interesting region in which to explore African attitudes toward colonial domination at the hands of white-skinned Christians.[3]

## European Imperialism in Africa

Beginning in the late nineteenth century, the industrialization of European economies and the emergence of the "nation-state model" as a focus of political loyalty contributed to the domination of a minority population of European residents over the majority of Africa's peoples and political and economic structures. To justify this domination, Europeans portrayed Africans as sub-human and in need of enlightenment and assistance in their evolutionary development toward "humanness." European authors of the time described Africans as devoid of history, as having lived in isolation for millennia, and as lacking intelligence—all racist notions that are demonstrably false.

The roots of European colonialism—the establishment of formal European control over African political and economic structures—can be traced to the late-eighteenth-century industrial revolution (see Chapter 2). The industrial revolution transformed European societies, created new demands for both natural resources and markets for finished goods, and provided Europeans with the industrial technology that permitted them to impose their rule, relatively efficiently, on much of the rest of the world. A convenient way to understand the process is to look at European motivations, the means by which they fulfilled them, and the timing by which their motives and means meshed.[4]

The timing of the European conquest of much of Africa was no coincidence but, rather, can be directly traced to several factors within Africa. In 1867, in southern Africa, areas of which were already under European rule, diamonds were discovered near Kimberley, sparking a new onslaught of white immigration from around the world. Then, in 1869, at the other end of the continent, Khedive Ismail of Egypt opened the Suez Canal, a massive engineering achievement that produced numerous unforeseen consequences. First, to finance the project, Egypt took out huge loans from European (primarily French and British) creditors, thereby making the country and its future a matter of direct concern to these bankers. Second, when the canal opened, ships were able to travel from England to India (and farther into the Indian Ocean) by traversing the Mediterranean and Red Seas, rather than circumnavigating the African continent.

For London, the opening of the Suez Canal was monumental. In 1858, Great Britain had taken over India, which soon became the "jewel in the British Crown." From that date forward the political, economic, and military ties between the two territories assumed supreme importance to politicians, merchant banks, and military leaders in London. Moreover, India was an important stopping point for merchants traveling farther east in the Indian Ocean basin or to China. Through the opening of the Suez Canal, "the voyage from London to Bombay was shortened by fifty-one percent, to Calcutta by thirty-two percent, and to Singapore by twenty-nine percent."[5] This development expedited official and financial correspondence and greatly lessened expenses for the transport of trade goods as well as military personnel and equipment.

Owing to the importance of India (and of China) to British prestige and wealth, the Suez Canal quickly became a major concern for London, but also for politicians in Paris, since French money lenders had provided major financial support for the project. The deeply vested interests of both France and Britain in the same foreign territory, Egypt, foreshadowed later jealousy and intrigue elsewhere, as Europeans raised the stakes in their ongoing game of global political chess. Indeed, the following decade witnessed growing competition between white governments evaluating their positions in the global capitalist economy.

The 1870s were also significant in terms of the development toward European colonialism. The relatively new ideology of "nationalism"—the forming of emotional bonds between physical strangers who live within a relatively large territory imagined to be somehow unified, as opposed to Europe's historical sense of identity as a locally centered one based on loyalty to a lord or regional family or king—created not just new forms of individual and collective identity but also new rivalries. One field in which these rivalries played out was in the competition between European states for the acquisition of foreign territory.

Some nationalists and merchants of the time believed that the more colonies a nation possessed, the more powerful it would be; their logic averred that establishing control of anticapitalist, closed markets in overseas territories would enable merchants to (1) set as low as possible the prices that they would pay for natural resources and labor purchased abroad, and (2) set as high as possible the prices that they would charge for industrial-produced goods marketed abroad. In the process of controlling both ends of the equation, businesspeople would vastly increase their profits and their ability to contribute to government expenditures at home.

Pious Christians also promoted Europe's overseas expansion. They were inspired by religious fervor similar to the zeal that drove the medieval Crusades, and they were stirred up over the social upheavals that had ravaged European societies during the industrial revolution, including massive rural-to-urban migration, the extreme alcohol abuse that resulted from the discovery of distillation, and the stresses on fundamental social structures (such as families, friendship, and economic support networks) that resulted from these major societal changes. Moreover, some Christians were outraged by reports that the international slave trade from Africa had not been completely eliminated (see Chapter 1). Thus, missionaries and their supporters campaigned for European governments to live up to Christian ideals by providing military protection to evangelical endeavors in the so-called Dark Continent. This sense of a religious "mission" benefited from Charles Darwin's observation of natural phenomena in the Galapagos Islands, which led to his publications on issues such as evolution and survival of the fittest. Racist European philosophers, with little or no scientific training, applied these ideas to the topic of physical differences between humans, suggesting that variations in skin color and other physical features equated to differences between species.[6] They then used their racist thought, garbed in pseudo-science, to encourage other Europeans to believe that it was the moral duty of their Christian societies to uplift lesser-evolved (i.e., darker skinned) people and raise them to the level of full humanity.

This kind of thinking linked material progress with racial appearance—and when such a mindset was disseminated by politicians, capitalists, and the religious elite, it met a ready audience in the European general public, among whom literacy rates were rising, as was a taste for newspapers and exciting stories from around the world. Indeed, the growing impression that the number of colonies a nation possessed determined its level of prosperity and power was a significant contributor to European popular support, and even demand, for leaders to pursue and expand the conquest of foreign lands.

For decades, historians have debated the details of these issues, as well as the timing of specific incidents of conquest, treaty signing, claims to sovereignty, and so on. For our purposes, the myriad details are less important than the fact that many events and forces came to a head at relatively the same time.[7] Nationalists pushed their governments toward a colonial agenda so as to compete more favorably with rival nations; capitalists urged governments to provide military protection for their overseas enterprises and investments; clergy called for supporting missionary activities; and ordinary people, inspired by their prideful nationalist feelings, also hungered for colonial ventures. There was thus a variety of interests that politicians sought to convert into one coherent policy, and colonialism became an easy and convenient political issue to exploit.

Yet this will to colonize did not necessarily mean that Europeans could actually carry out their colonial ambitions. What made it possible in practice was industrial technology. Beginning with primitive steamboats in the early 1800s, nineteenth-century technologies that became essential to military conquest and colonial administration included quinine, which greatly reduced European fatalities from malaria; various new firearms, culminating in the development of the machine gun, an extremely efficient killing machine; steam power and flat-bottomed boats for long-distance and rapid river travel; submarine cables for near-instantaneous international communication; and railroads for travel, military deployments, and commerce.

As conquest and "pacification" of African territories became easier and more cost-effective, European interest in the continent increased, picking up pace throughout the 1870s and rising rapidly in the early 1880s. At first pioneered largely by explorers, merchants, and missionaries, European attention toward Africa took on economic dimensions that later impacted politics. One key example is Egypt, already mentioned above. In building the Suez canal, Khedive Ismail put his country deeply into debt to European creditors. And when Ahmad Urabi, a military officer, led a popular rebellion against his government, the French and British feared that his administration would cease loan payments and possibly cut off access to the canal. Therefore, in 1882, the British invaded and took over Egypt and control of the Suez Canal, a move that angered the French and exacerbated Anglo-French rivalry.

Elsewhere on the continent, adventurers and agents from European states were signing a flurry of treaties with African leaders, trying to establish exclusive trade relations and forge political alliances against their European rivals. The resulting competition rose in intensity until the German chancellor, Otto von Bismarck, called for a meeting to discuss the African continent calmly, so that tensions would not result in military clashes or war between white peoples. Meeting from late 1884 until early 1885, the Berlin Conference laid down the ground rules for establishing land claims in Africa that all European nations would respect. Prominent among them was the notion of "effective occupation," by which no nation could claim a territory without establishing some sort of administrative presence. This development was significant because it emphasized early on the importance of creating some sort of physical administration as a requirement to gain international acceptance of legal sovereignty. Otherwise, it was thought, conflicts would be more likely to erupt between multiple European powers claiming the same land in Africa.

## AFRICAN EXPERIENCES

Amidst the processes of imperialism that led to some Europeans' ability to impose their political and economic will on vast swathes of the world, some states were able to preserve their political freedom. For example, Thailand, Afghanistan, and Japan escaped Europe's formal colonial rule in Asia, as did Iran, Saudi Arabia, and northern Yemen in the Middle East. In Africa there were two territorial exceptions to European colonialism. The first of these was Liberia. Assisted by prejudiced whites who feared the influence that free blacks would have in American society, Liberia was established as an independent country by African Americans who saw little hope for their futures in the racist system of the United States and thus desired to return to the "motherland," where more opportunities would be available to educated and skilled people regardless of their skin color. On the other side of the continent, Ethiopia defended its independence militarily, crushing the Italians at Dogali (1887) and Adwa (1896) and securing international recognition of its independence through diplomatic treaty negotiations with the world's leading governments.

Although Liberia and Ethiopia are the exceptions to European colonial conquest in Africa, other Africans did not remain passive victims to invasion and intrigue; instead, they responded in a variety of ways to the threat of foreign military conquest or political subjugation. Moreover, because Africans did not accept racist European ideas of white superiority, they found inspiration in Ethiopia as a continental leader, citing both the many references to Ethiopia in the Christian Bible and the fact of Ethiopia's 1896 military defeat of a modern European army. The same reasons contributed to Ethiopia's symbolic importance in the early decades of the twentieth century among African-descent communities in the global diaspora, including the United States.[8]

In light of these facts and Ethiopia's unique position in African colonial history, it is worth investigating Ethiopians' late-nineteenth- and early-twentieth-century views of a system that they witnessed spreading across the African continent, particularly among neighboring countries. What did Ethiopians know about colonialism, and how did they acquire that knowledge? What did they think they could do about it? What did they try to do about it? As European rule encroached on Ethiopian territories from all directions, Ethiopians clearly saw colonialism as a threat, but some also perceived novel opportunities and sought to manipulate the changing circumstances to their own and their country's future advantage in an increasingly global world.

*Europeans Through Ethiopian Eyes in the Nineteenth Century*

For centuries, modern Europe's interest in Ethiopia had related to a post-Crusades legend about Prester (Priest) John, a Christian monarch in the East who, it was hoped, could be contacted and persuaded to join a Pan-Christian alliance to retake the Holy Lands for the faith, ideally crushing Islam in the process. Europe's professional scholarly interest in Ethiopia began in earnest in the mid-1600s, when the German Job Ludolf began publishing on Ethiopian languages, culture, and history. Still, even in the centuries that followed, firsthand knowledge of the country came only from a small number of missionaries and a handful of explorers, among whom the best known is the Scotsman James Bruce, who trekked to the Horn of Africa in 1769 in a search to locate the source of the Nile.

Contacts between Ethiopia and Europe intensified in the early 1800s, when Ethiopian political elites began exchanging letters with their European counterparts.[9] The Africans were largely interested in European technology and skills, such as weapons, machinery, carpentry, architecture, and art. But central to it all was an awareness of shared Christian faith, which Ethiopians specifically articulated in their manifestations of friendship and requests for political alliances. Christian Europeans were implored to intercede on Ethiopia's behalf in relations with Christians elsewhere—for example, in Alexandria, Egypt, the center of the Coptic Church that appointed patriarchs to lead Ethiopia's Orthodox Church; as well as in Jerusalem, where destitute Ethiopian pilgrims were frustrated that they did not receive greater assistance from the more affluent Armenian community, whose Christian beliefs were closely related to Ethiopian ones. These types of communications demonstrate that while Ethiopians recognized that Europe possessed certain industrial technologies that the ancient African nation did not, they certainly did not regard Europeans as superior in any way. Instead, they viewed white-skinned Europeans as fellow Christians, who should—if their religious convictions were sincere—unite with Ethiopia.

These early-nineteenth-century communications took place in the context of Ethiopian internal political divisions. For almost a century, various regional kings had vied for ultimate power in Ethiopia—the imperial throne—but none was able to achieve this objective. The destructive period of disunity ended in 1855, when a former frontier bandit defeated his rivals and was crowned as Emperor Tewodros. Subsequently, his attempts to advance political and fiscal reforms alienated conservatives and the church, and he faced an additional challenge in his desire to expel Egyptian forces from Ethiopia's Red Sea coast. Regarding Queen Victoria as a fellow Christian monarch, Tewodros requested assistance, but her failure to respond left him feeling rebuffed. Aggravated by the increasing problems within his realm and irritated by the lack of a response, Tewodros imprisoned the British consul and several Swiss and German missionaries.

When word of Tewodros's actions reached London, Her Majesty's Government sent another envoy to resolve the dispute, but Tewodros took him hostage as well. In response, in 1868, the outraged British organized a large invasion force consisting of close to fifteen thousand soldiers (plus their thirty thousand support staff), nineteen thousand horses and mules, seventeen hundred donkeys, almost six thousand camels, forty-four elephants, sixteen cannons, two mortars, sixteen rocket-launchers, and other examples of the latest weaponry. Named the "Napier Expedition" after its commanding officer Sir Charles James Napier, the force defeated the Ethiopian army, liberated the prisoners, and looted innumerable Ethiopian treasures.[10] Tewodros committed suicide toward the end of the battle. Popular Ethiopian nationalist sentiment portrays his action as a heroic defiance: he preferred to end his own life than allow himself to fall into the foreign enemy's hands. While there may be a degree of truth to this idea, it is more likely that he was overwhelmed by all his failures as emperor and this battle was merely the final straw. Thus the nationalist portrayal is at least partially reductionistic, relying on twentieth-century Ethiopian views of European colonialism to interpret events and actions in the precolonial era.

Having achieved the exceptionally costly military objective of freeing a small number of hostages, Sir Napier turned his forces around and started marching back to the coast. In the process he gifted a large amount of guns and ammunition to a certain Ethiopian governor, Kasa Mercha, who as a rival of Emperor Tewodros had facilitated the British march inland.[11] Kasa later employed that weaponry to subdue adversaries and capture the emperorship himself, whereupon he adopted the regnal name Yohannes.

Ethiopians had long been skilled warriors inspired by martial culture, but the Napier Expedition and Yohannes's use of the British weaponry given to him further emphasized the potentially enormous military power of industrial Europe. Various Ethiopian kings and governors therefore began stepping up their efforts to acquire as much modern weaponry as possible, to strengthen their own positions around the country and, ideally, to depose Emperor Yohannes and gain the throne for themselves. In the long run, the most successful of these lords was King Menilek, who governed the southern province of Shewa and proved to be a master at playing off rival European powers against each other. The Horn of Africa in general, and Ethiopia in particular, were of interest not only to the British but also to their French and Italian rivals. These Europeans were only too happy to strengthen regional kings and governors in an attempt to weaken the head of state, Emperor Yohannes. Ethiopians were of course aware of what was happening and sought to encourage or discourage it, according to circumstances and their own interests. Seeking to strengthen Ethiopia internally, Emperor Yohannes tried to shore up his relationships with his primary rival, Menilek. In a letter seeking reconciliation, he stated:

> The Italians are not a serious people; they are intriguers; and all this must be something which the English are doing to me. The Italians have not come

to these parts because they lack pasture and abundance in their own country, but they come here because of ambition, in order to aggrandize themselves, because they are many and not rich. But with the help of God, they shall leave again humiliated and disappointed and with their honour lost before all the world.[12] They are not a people who can frighten us. . . . If the two of us always remain united, we shall with the help of God overcome not only the weak Italians, but also the strong people of other nations. As Adam wanted to enjoy the forbidden fruit because of ambition to become greater than God, and instead found nothing but chastisement and dishonour, so it will happen to the Italians.[13]

Meanwhile, taking full advantage of competing European interests, Menilek had built up a considerable arsenal, making him the only serious candidate for the emperorship when Yohannes died fighting Mahdist Muslim forces in the west, soon after writing the above letter in 1889. Soon after, King Menelik of Shewa successfully became Emperor Menelik of all of Ethiopia. That Menilek had long been developing a plan to secure power and establish a national state—upon his own terms and with the support of European allies—is apparent in numerous sources. For example, more than a decade earlier, he had sent two letters to Queen Victoria of England. In the first, he sought to establish a relationship based upon shared Christian identity and mutual hostility toward Islam:

Two years ago the viceroy of Egypt took all the ports of the Red Sea from Massawa all the way to Berbera, and even Harer among the Isa, a Somali clan. He wants to possess them and exchange the crown of Ethiopia, which has a cross at the top, for one with a Turkish [Muslim] crescent. But even if our crown loses the cross we hope with the help of God never to become the Muslim's slave.[14]

A month later, after accusing the Egyptians of pretending to be opposed to the slave trade while actually participating actively in it, Menilek again stressed the shared Christian identity of both England and Ethiopia, as well as Ethiopia's historical claims to lands suddenly desired by foreign nations:

How can I be prevented from using the port which was ours from the time of my grandfather and great-grandfather, when I say that I shall buy all the weapons with my money, and that I shall give all the European workers that come to me twice the salary and place the country of the pagans under my control, and that I shall destroy all evil-doers?[15]

Clearly, Emperor Menilek, like other Ethiopian rulers before him, did not feel different from Europeans in terms of skin color or race. Rather, he felt that religion was the primary factor—in other words, that faith was the fulcrum around which different societies would forge unity or become divided. This argument, however, did not work well in late-nineteenth-century Christian Europe, since neither Protestant nor Catholic European Christians regarded Coptic or Orthodox Christianity as legitimate, any more than they regarded each other as legitimate. Still, the religious connection remained salient for Ethiopian leaders and thinkers seeking international alliances.

### Ethiopians and the "Scramble for Africa"

In the meantime, following Britain's occupation of Egypt in 1882, resistance in the Sudan (under Egyptian rule) led to the decision to evacuate British-Egyptian troops from that region. Rather than mount another expensive invasion to help relieve the Sudan garrisons, the British envisioned that their isolated encampments could be more cost-effectively withdrawn with the assistance of troops from the neighboring nation of Ethiopia. A British naval officer was thus dispatched to parlay with Emperor Yohannes, who demanded that, in exchange for cooperation, the Red Sea port of Massawa, then under Egyptian control, would be restored to Ethiopia. The British officer refused, but agreed to allow the "free transit" of goods (including weapons) to and from Ethiopia under British supervision. Naïvely assuming that white Christians would honor their promises, Ethiopian forces helped to evacuate besieged British troops from the Sudan.

Although Britain and Egypt did abandon Massawa less than a year later, they did not turn it over to Ethiopia. Instead, in order to obstruct possible

French expansion, London encouraged Italy to occupy the port. The Italians moved in and immediately blocked the arms trade to Yohannes. Soon they also expanded their control over areas surrounding Massawa, and then gradually began creeping inland. A few years later, the emperor's commander in the area, Ras Alula Engeda, confronted this provocation, and at the Battle of Dogali in January 1887 his troops killed about five hundred Italians, with only eighty or so wounded Europeans managing to escape with their lives. The defeat shocked Italy and helped to bring a more hawkish government to power in Rome. Two years after that, Emperor Yohannes moved his army to fight against Sudanese Muslim warriors in the west, thereby helping the British, but also inadvertently providing the shamed and angry Italians with an opportunity to build up their occupation of the region around Massawa in the east.

As part of their campaign of weakening Yohannes in the north, the Italians had earlier intimated that they were open to talks with his southern rival, King Menilek. After Yohannes died fighting the Sudanese in 1889, Menilek initiated those talks, a diplomatic exercise conducted in the town of Wichale. The ensuing treaty of amity and commerce was finalized in May 1889; however, a discrepancy in the translation created tensions between the two signatories. The Italian version of Article 17 *required* Ethiopia to use Rome as its intermediary in all foreign relations, but the Amharic version stated only that Ethiopia could request Rome's services if it wanted to do so. Italian forces moved inland, occupying new districts and announcing to the world that "on the basis of Article 17, Rome claimed a protectorate over Ethiopia in conformity of Article 34 of the General Act of the Congress of Berlin of 26 February 1885."[16] At first unaware of this development, Menilek continued his efforts to secure domestic power and was crowned emperor later that year.

By the end of 1889, when Menilek ascended to Ethiopia's imperial throne, the colonial situation in the Horn was as follows: the British had varying degrees of presence in Egypt, northern Somalia, Kenya, and Uganda (as well as continued aspirations in the Sudan), as did the Italians in Eritrea and southern Somalia and the French in Djibouti. Ethiopia—the outlier—remained unconquered, an independent African monarchy whose ruling elite had adhered to Christianity for more than a thousand years.

The newly crowned Emperor Menilek understood perfectly well that he faced a variety of external threats, so he moved to expand his territory and entrench his internal power. For unknown reasons, following the Wichale crisis he did not try to expel the Italians from Eritrea. He did, however, embark on a course of more aggressive international diplomacy, aided in particular by France, which channeled large amounts of armaments to Ethiopia as tensions with Italy rose. In April 1891 the emperor wrote to European powers, defining his country's boundaries and denying the Italian right to declare a protectorate. His letter contained these stern statements:

> Since the kingdom of Ethiopia is an independent kingdom, We felt, when We heard this rumour [that Ethiopia had become an Italian protectorate], that it was something which degraded Ourselves and our kingdom, and have made known the error to you. And as We Ourselves [have done], We hope that the Italian government has not failed to make known to you the translation error.[17]
>
> [Moreover] We have no intention of being an indifferent spectator while far distant powers make their appearance with the intention of carving out their respective empires in Africa, Ethiopia having been for fourteen centuries an island of Christianity in a sea of pagans. As the Almighty has protected Ethiopia to this day, We are confident that He will protect and benefit her in the future. We have no doubt that he will not let her be divided under the subjugation of other governments.[18]

French assistance to Ethiopia was, of course, based on self-interest. Beyond the money to be made smuggling war materiel, officials in Paris were still angry about the British occupation of Egypt in 1882 and London's later encouragement of the Italians in Eritrea. In 1895, the French demanded that the British respect their earlier promise to depart Egypt once stability was restored, a condition the French believed had been fulfilled. A member of the French Chamber of Deputies threatened that if the British did not withdraw, then French forces in western and central Africa would march across the continent to take control of the Upper Nile, giving them dominion over the waters that to this day are the lifeblood of Egypt. A side benefit would be that the French could monopolize trade across the Sahara, from Senegal in the west to the Horn in the east—and also block the idea of a "Cape to Cairo" (i.e., South Africa to Egypt) swathe of Africa united by British rule and railroads. London, motivated by its own interests in Egypt, soon responded that the entire Nile watershed was British territory and any threat to it would be tantamount to an act of war. The stakes rose rapidly and British and French forces from various bases around the continent scrambled to establish their effective presence in Sudan and thereby shore up their nation's political position. Ultimately, British and French forces met at the remote Sudanese outpost of Fashoda, and after a tense exchange the French backed down so as to avoid war between the two European nations.[19]

The whole experience, however, strengthened British resolve to try to keep the French as weak as possible in Northeast Africa, where the sole French territory was the tiny colony of Djibouti, of economic interest only as one of the Red Sea harbors for Ethiopia's imports and exports. Yet the British were unwilling to allocate the resources necessary to extend their own colonial presence there. So what to do? Italy had been a late-comer to the game of colonialism and remained not only hungry for more territory but also eager to avenge the humiliation of Dogali and frustration over the Treaty of Wichale dispute. The British had earlier encouraged Rome to move into the Horn as a British proxy—upholding anti-French, pro-British interests and costing British taxpayers nothing. The hawkish administration in Rome thus encountered no complaint from London when it decided to invade Ethiopia, aiming to unite its colonies in Eritrea and southern Somalia.

Mobilizing forces from all parts of his empire, Emperor Menilek marched north to confront this latest Italian challenge. Following services at an early-morning Orthodox Christian Mass, on March 1, 1896, his more than 100,000-strong army attacked and wiped out the Italian army of 14,500 soldiers. Within a matter of hours, "Italy lost 70 percent of its forces, an incredible disaster for a modern army."[20] Explaining this lopsided victory is not difficult. The Ethiopians were battle-hardened warriors and better armed than their opponents; they had overwhelming numerical superiority and were fighting on their own land, protecting their own country and people. Moreover, the Italians were "blinded by racism and cultural arrogance"[21] and, as a result, woefully misjudged the military skills of Ethiopia's commanding officers.

However, at the time of these events westerners were incapable of or disinterested in admitting reality. Instead, to explain how a supposedly primitive African army could so decisively defeat a European power, Europeans embarked on a systematic reevaluation of history, proposing in the process that Ethiopians are not Africans but really quasi Caucasians! This convoluted way of thinking posited that centuries of "inter-breeding" between Caucasian immigrants and black locals had produced a people who looked African but had Caucasian blood flowing in their veins, and that their white-person blood explained Ethiopian civilization and military prowess.[22] While Europeans expended energy and resources to construct such awkward and absurd ideological explanations to justify their racist prejudices and military incompetence, Ethiopians viewed Adwa and their success very differently.

The best example of the Ethiopian perspective is one that has developed into an iconic theme in Ethiopian art circles: paintings depicting the clash of Ethiopian and Italian forces at Adwa (see Image 3.1). Tracing back many decades, this genre exhibits numerous variations, but most Adwa paintings contain some common elements, including written words to identify individual leaders, groups (e.g., clergy, riflemen), or events (e.g., Italians fleeing the battlefield). Prominent among the commonalities is the presence of St. George, a patron saint riding a white horse in the heavens and overseeing the Ethiopian defense while encircled by a flag of Ethiopia's national colors.[23] In most Adwa paintings, leaders of both sides are depicted, with Emperor Menilek (usually shaded beneath an umbrella and wearing his crown) and Empress Taytu (who helped to inspire the troops and is often depicted with a weapon in her hands) on the left; on the right there are various Italian officers, sometimes named and sometimes not. Underscoring the pious Orthodox elucidation of the Italian army's demise, the Ethiopian side also includes priests carrying a *tabot*, which is a replica of the Ark of the Covenant (or the Ten Commandments)—thereby suggesting evidence of Ethiopian Christians as God's chosen people. The Ethiopian appeal to God for aid against unjust attack is additionally visible in the *käbäro* drums, used in the Orthodox liturgy.

Image 3.1: Painting of the Battle of Adwa

Both sides fly their national flags and are heavily armed, though the depiction of weaponry varies from artist to artist; in the painting reproduced here, the machine guns accurately reflect how well-armed the Ethiopian forces were, though the number of cannons inaccurately suggests a stronger Italian force. Often present in Adwa paintings are Red Cross tents, denoting the provision of medical care for the wounded.[24] Artists seeking to render a particularly patriotic interpretation place such tents only on the Italian side, apparently because the white invaders, as the weaker combatants, had a greater need for internationally funded medical assistance. Finally, another common feature—a borrowing from historical traditions of Ethiopian church painting, which distinguishes stylistically between the forces of good and evil—is the depiction of the enemy (or demonic forces) from a side profile, with only one eye visible, and Ethiopians (or good Christians) from a full-face view, with both eyes showing. Whereas during this era of colonialism it was common in Europe to depict Africans as less than human, or as primitive and barbaric, Adwa paintings make no effort to dehumanize the Italians. Rather, their focus is on their own people, glorifying Ethiopia, the emperor and empress, the clergy, Ethiopian warriors, and their combined efforts that resulted in an internationally historic victory.

Following the Battle of Adwa, European diplomats flocked to Ethiopia to sign treaties of friendship with the government. The order in which they did so is still reflected today in the numbers displayed on diplomatic license plates; for example, diplomatic plates marked with the number 4 are for American officials, since the United States was the fourth nation to recognize Ethiopian sovereignty. Those marked 1 to 3 are for the Italians, French, and British, respectively. The legal protections that this international recognition provided to Ethiopia facilitated Menilek's efforts to advance modernizing reforms, a strategy designed to reduce future threats from European colonial powers. Resisted by the country's conservative political and religious elite, the reforms that Menilek managed to push through included the 1907 creation of a Council of Ministers, including Ministers of the Interior; Foreign Affairs; Finance; War; Agriculture; Commerce and Customs; Public Works; Palace, Post, Telegraph, and Telephones; Religion and Education; Justice; and Health. These appointees were entrusted with responsibilities relevant to their defined duties. The formation of the Council meant that for the first time in Ethiopian history an emperor had devolved and delineated national administrative responsibilities in a formalized and clear way. This approach mirrored European political structures, thereby (hopefully) undermining the ability of the Italians or anyone else to claim that Ethiopia was a primitive country and needed to be subjected to colonialism. Perhaps more significant is that Menilek's novel 1907 proclamation forever changed the political playing field in Ethiopia and opened up possibilities for new types of thinkers to achieve political success. The most important of these was Ras Tafari Mekonnen, the future Emperor Haile Sellassie I.

*Haile Sellassie, Benito Mussolini,*
*and the 1935–1936 Fascist Conquest of Ethiopia*

Tafari's father, Ras Mekonnen Walda-Mikael, was a leading military commander and provincial governor, who was also related to Emperor Menilek and served as Ethiopia's foremost ethnographic expert on Europeans and

European cultures. He died in 1906, leaving his fourteen-year-old son Tafari orphaned. Tafari then moved to the capital city, Addis Ababa, and entered Emperor Menilek's imperial court, where despite his youth he proved to be an astute student of statecraft. With a potential claim to the future imperial throne, yet lacking living parents to politick on his behalf, Tafari had to play his cards carefully. Menilek had named his grandson Iyasu as his successor, but Iyasu's tolerance of a nondominant religion (Islam), his penchant for sleeping with other men's wives, and his other youthful indiscretions alienated many persons of influence, including prominent nobles, Orthodox clergy, and foreign diplomats.

Manipulating Ethiopian and European fears of Islam during World War I, as well as the Orthodox Church's concern about Iyasu's apparent pro-Muslim leanings, Tafari managed in 1916 to secure his appointment as Crown Prince. His success was admirable, since it reflected a skillful ability to maneuver between the competing interests of conservative Ethiopians in both political and religious circles, as well as Europeans in the diplomatic community—three politically influential social groups that did not always see eye to eye.

Tafari clearly realized that European colonialism continued to pose a threat to Ethiopia, even after his country's spectacular victory at Adwa. He also understood that Ethiopia's economy was not sufficiently developed to create a military industry that would enable the country to defend itself against outside aggression again. Therefore, in opposition to Ethiopian conservatives and to racist Europeans, he placed his trust in international law and successfully promoted Ethiopia's admission to the League of Nations in 1923, a membership that he hoped would guarantee international protection against possible invasion (see the League's Article 10, quoted above).

Building on the 1907 Council of Ministers' proclamation and discussions with foreign officials, Tafari's portrayal of the "justness" and "modernity" of his style of administration was an effective stratagem for earning the support of European diplomats and proved to be helpful when the League considered Ethiopia's application. The great personal efforts Tafari made at the time attest to his belief that League membership would mitigate against future foreign attempts to intervene in his country's affairs. His faith in the power of the law was proven again in 1931, when as emperor of the country he drew on European models to promulgate the country's first written constitution, a strong assertion of the intended primacy of law in future Ethiopian governance. Envisioning the law as something to be respected by all civilized nations, the emperor declared: "Everyone knows that laws bring to men the greatest benefits, and that everyone's honor and well-being depend upon the wisdom of the laws, whereas depravity, shame, iniquity and denial of justice result from the non-existence or insufficiency of laws."[25]

Yet across the Mediterranean, during the 1920s, Italians remained shamed by the legacy of Adwa, were angry at being treated as second-class Europeans by the power brokers who negotiated an end to World War I, and were suffering under a weakened postwar economy. They thus had good reason to yearn for hope—which they discerned in the bombastically conservative rhetoric of Benito Mussolini, a fascist ideologue intent on restoring Italian national honor. Part of his violently conservative plan for the future was to restore the glory of the Roman Empire, something that could be accomplished only by expanding the reach of Italian colonialism. He believed that conquering Ethiopia would serve that purpose, unite Italy's colonies in Eritrea and Somalia, and, in the process, give Italy control over the Horn of Africa's most fertile region. He also provided economically poor Italians with fantasies of the agriculturally prosperous lands they would "settle" in Ethiopia. Perhaps most significantly, the invasion would serve to avenge the humiliations of Dogali and Adwa. Indeed, both at home and abroad, for Italian patriots it would be an all-win situation.

In the face of this threat, Ras Tafari and his allies within Ethiopia believed, perhaps naïvely, that the international community would honor international law as enshrined in the covenant of the League of Nations, and thus Ethiopia could concentrate on developing itself outside of a colonial framework. Accordingly, the Ethiopian government channeled its resources toward internal development, in areas such as education, health, medicine, transportation, communications, and industry—the sorts of fields that European colonial policies had traditionally cited to justify their exploitation of nonwhite peoples (and that Western nations still espouse today as essential to improvement of global living standards). However, if Ethiopia's aims were well-intentioned, they were not universally respected, despite the fact that the political leadership in Addis Ababa viewed them as grounded in and protected by international law.

In late 1925, London and Rome agreed between themselves that the British, owing to their interests in the Nile waters, should have primary rights to build a dam at Lake Tana (in northwest Ethiopia), the source of the Blue Nile; and that the Italians should have the right to build a railroad across Ethiopia to link Italy's colonies in Eritrea and southern Somalia. Encouraged by France, Ethiopia complained to the League of Nations that this Anglo-Italian agreement was an infringement upon Ethiopia's sovereign rights as an independent country and as a member of the League of Nations. As a result of this legal challenge, London and Rome backed down and Tafari's and other Ethiopians' confidence in League protection increased. As Tafari continued to modernize his country, Ethiopia and Italy signed a twenty-year Treaty of Friendship and Arbitration in 1928. Ethiopia was seeking a promise of friendship and a commitment that future disputes would be resolved by the League. Italy was seeking a means by which it could more effectively penetrate Ethiopia.

In late 1930 Crown Prince Tafari was elevated to the imperial throne, a *de jure* commemoration of the long-existing *de facto* political reality, and he adopted the name of Emperor Haile Sellassie (meaning "Power of the Trinity"). The celebrations were elaborate, including the purchase of Imperial Germany's state coach for transporting the royal couple around town, numerous projects to beautify Addis Ababa, and efforts to create the infrastructure necessary to cater to a large number of foreign attendees. The latter included the Duke of Gloucester, the Prince of Savoy, colonial governors, and a large number of journalists who sent home articles and newsreel images of the events. The journalistic coverage of the elaborate pageantry was transmitted around the globe and left a lasting impression on many viewers, including several elderly Americans, most now dead, with whom this chapter's author has spoken over the years.[26]

Nonetheless, post–World War I discontent in Europe and the ravages of the Great Depression stoked the popularity of two ultra-nationalist, ultra-conservative demagogues: Adolf Hitler in Germany and Benito Mussolini in Italy. Although both were fascists, Mussolini despised Hitler and there were not yet enough shared interests to encourage a long-term formal alliance. Germany left the League of Nations in 1933, making League strictures irrelevant in its case, and the rest of economically depressed Europe watched with anxiety as fascism took firmer root in Mussolini's Italy.

By 1934 at the latest, Mussolini was intent on restoring a Roman Empire and had decided to conquer Ethiopia. In recent years his forces in southern Somalia had been expanding beyond their borders to occupy waterholes in eastern Ethiopia, which became a matter of concern to Addis Ababa. In December 1934, the members of a joint British-Ethiopian border demarcation team arrived at Walwal, well within Ethiopian territory. There they found Italian troops entrenched, and in an ensuing battle the Ethiopians suffered heavy losses. Mussolini nevertheless had the issue he needed to move forward, and demanded a public apology and punitive damages from Ethiopia. Bolstered by earlier success at the League of Nations as well as by Ethiopia's legally justifiable position, Haile Sellassie refused to bow to Mussolini's threat and took the dispute to Geneva. Unfortunately for him and the rest of Ethiopia, the global context had changed: Europe did not want to push Mussolini closer to Hitler, for as a team they posed a far greater threat than they did individually. The League powers thus prevaricated until they came up with a solution that was really a nonsolution—prohibiting arms sales to both countries, "a measure that hurt only Ethiopia"[27]—and in the end it encouraged Mussolini to invade Ethiopia in 1935.

With their country betrayed by the international community and facing yet another military invasion by Italy, Ethiopians rallied around the flag and many probably imagined that they would once again wipe out any Italian forces foolish enough to attack. The emperor encouraged them with such words as "The opinion of the world has been revolted by this aggression against us. God be with us all."[28] Yet he was surely less sanguine than his followers, since he knew that in the previous three decades Italy had industrialized its military and Ethiopia had not.

The Italians were so much better armed that from the beginning it was really no contest, but that fact was not accepted by Ethiopian warriors, who were anxious to fight for their country. An aspect of Ethiopian fervor—

Image 3.2: *Fukkära*

heated by memories of Adwa—may be seen in Image 3.2, which provides one example of the tradition of *fukkära*. Often translated as "war-boasting," this term refers to a warrior working himself into a frenzy, shaking his spear or other weapon, and shouting out everything he would do to vanquish the enemy when engaged in battle. Foot soldiers would run before their leaders, while cavalry would maneuver their mounts to demonstrate their horseman-ship. In delivering a *fukkära*, a battle-hungry man would typically praise him-self and his peers, their past military actions and exploits, and their inevitable future accomplishments. To build greater morale, certain members of the community would be named as respected and loved individuals whose lives and activities warranted protection and preservation, and past historical events would be cited as evidence of the success that would result for Ethiopia if everyone else would properly join. Listeners would shout out their approval to encourage the *fukkära* and other "boasts" that followed. [29]

The powerful emotionalism inherent in *fukkära* performances served to build morale and motivate individuals, who set specific goals for themselves such as to rip out the gullets of every enemy they encountered. As the Italians prepared to invade yet again, this time with tanks and airplanes and other industrial weaponry, Ethiopian foot soldiers and mounted cavalry rallied around their emperor and tens of thousands of them performed *fukkära* on a large marching field in the capital city (not far from where the national university is housed today). After the public performances, about a quarter-million Ethiopians marched north to defend their country from the Italian invasion on that front. Their patriotism and their *fukkära* is reminiscent of a short poem from the time of Adwa, forty years earlier:

> What a fool he is, the person from a European country [Italy];
>> How, having made the instrument of his death [modern weapons], can he give it away?
>> With the Wetterley [a type of rifle] which he brought, with the bullets which he brought,
>> [Our emperor] roasted and cracked the overseas barley [Italy].[30]

Yet such confidence could not overcome the disparity in military technology—over the previous decade Ethiopia had, after all, employed its resources in building up its social and economic infrastructures rather than its military strength—and from the beginning of the military conflict Italy's victory was almost a foregone conclusion. Moreover, Italian forces ignored international law and employed poison gas, which had been prohibited by civilized nations after World War I. Haile Sellassie personally witnessed such Italian war crimes when he marched north to rally his troops. From one bloody scene, he wrote to a French missionary, his childhood tutor and longtime friend. This communication evidences the continued Ethiopian focus on a shared Christian faith with Europeans, even though the latter continued to emphasize race over religion:

> To Father Jarosseau, from Haile Sellassie, Conquering Lion of the Tribe of Judah, Elect of God, Emperor of Ethiopia.
>> How have you been of late? Thanks be to God's beneficence, We are well. We have come to Desse to visit Our troops in the north and to carry out Our responsibilities. We [got] the letter that Pope Pius sent you expressing his sadness that blood is being spilled between two Christian nations, and

We were very happy that he wants to know Our thoughts [on the matter]. One day ago, on 6 December [1935] . . . the Italians not only spilled Christian blood pointlessly. Also, in violation of the law, what they did to our troops encamped outside of Desse was accomplished not by the might of their soldiery, but rather by the strength of mechanized vehicles. Moreover, they dropped explosive and incendiary bombs on the civilian population of the town. Because they gave no prior warning, many women and children perished. In addition to this, because they are devoid of humanity, they dropped forty bombs on the hospital, which was full of wounded, and on the military doctor's field hospital, even though they were clearly marked with Red Cross symbols that are visible from a distance. The two patients' wards were burned up, as was the one surgical unit, and an American woman nurse in the hospital was wounded severely. Can the people who do such things actually be regarded as one of the world's Christian governments?[31]

With no hope of military victory, Haile Sellassie chose to flee the country and carry on his battle diplomatically, in Europe. A couple months later he appeared before the General Assembly of the League of Nations to protest Italy's unprovoked and unlawful invasion of Ethiopia. He addressed the delegates:

I, Haile Selassie [Sellassie] I, Emperor of Ethiopia, am here today to claim that justice which is due to my people, and the assistance promised to it eight months ago, when fifty nations asserted that aggression had been committed in violation of international treaties.

There is no precedent for a Head of State himself speaking in this assembly. But there is also no precedent for a people being victim of such injustice and being at present threatened by abandonment to its aggressor.

He continued:

It is to defend a people struggling for its age-old independence that the head of the Ethiopian Empire has come to Geneva to fulfill this supreme duty, after having himself fought at the head of his armies.

I pray to Almighty God that He may spare nations the terrible sufferings that have just been inflicted on my people, and of which the chiefs who accompany me here have been the horrified witnesses.

It is my duty to inform the Governments assembled in Geneva, responsible as they are for the lives of millions of men, women and children, of the deadly peril which threatens them, by describing to them the fate which has been suffered by Ethiopia. It is not only upon warriors that the Italian Government has made war. It has above all attacked populations far removed from hostilities, in order to terrorize and exterminate them.[32]

In its entirety, the speech was moving and garnered international public sympathy. But the handful of powerful countries who controlled the League of Nations were more concerned with preventing an alliance between Hitler and Mussolini than with providing justice to a fellow member-state, and they prevailed in their effort to avoid having the League do anything meaningful, such as uphold its legal covenant. The many League members who supported the League's principles and desired to support Ethiopia were silenced.

Italy's subsequent occupation of Ethiopia lasted five years, during which the *Tequr Anbessa*—the Black Lion movement—maintained communications with Haile Sellassie, who was in exile in London and kept up a steady guerilla resistance to the Italian occupation. Ethiopia was thus never fully pacified by Rome. When World War II broke out, the British government, which had earlier refused to support the emperor, came to the conclusion that as a fellow enemy of Italy he might be useful. London thus changed course by 180 degrees and decided to aid Ethiopia's Black Lions in ejecting the fascist Italians from the Horn and restoring Haile Sellassie to his throne in 1941. Upon his reentry, the monarch was treated to a celebratory *fukkära* by *Dejjazmach* Belay Zelleqa, one of the resistance leaders:

I, the son of Zelleqa, am the standard [flag] bearer of Ethiopia,
  [I am] he who vanquishes Italy,
  He who avenges Ethiopia.[33]

Nonetheless, some of the British officers who participated in the liberation of occupied Ethiopia were colonialists from other parts of Africa—

white soldiers and administrators who still looked down on Africans as if they were children. In light of Ethiopia's long history, its religious traditions, its pride in Adwa, its modernizing efforts, its admission to the League of Nations, and the fact that many Ethiopians were multilingual and had studied in Europe and the United States, and were sometimes far better educated than their European counterparts, Ethiopians did not appreciate such treatment, which was paternalistic at best and racist at worst. Ethiopians' resentment was further based on the fact that by that time many of them had a sophisticated understanding of colonialism and how it operated as a system.

## AN AFRICAN PERSPECTIVE ON EUROPEAN COLONIALISM

A notable example is Haddis Alemayehu, who became one of the country's best known twentieth-century authors. Educated in the Orthodox Church, then by Swedish missionaries, and then at a modern high school in Addis Ababa, he taught for a few years and then participated in the Black Lion resistance. Captured by the Italians, he was sent to a prison camp in Italy. After the war he served in various government ministries, as Ethiopian consul in Jerusalem, and he spent a number of years in Washington, DC, where he took international law classes at American University.[34] In the mid-1950s he published a small book whose ungrammatical title means something like "Foundation of Stories" or "Once Upon a Time." The following tale, rendered into English for the first time here, is an allegory on colonialism and appeared in that volume. It was based on a long-standing trope in Ethiopian oral literature—specifically, one that uses cats and mice to reflect power disparities and the advantage of cleverness over physical strength, in true David and Goliath fashion. Apparently aimed at Ethiopian children, and those reading the story to them, this story reflects the 1950s view of a highly educated, noncolonized African on the topic of European imperialism and colonialism. Owing to his traditional education, his military service, his internment as a prisoner of war, his Orthodox and Protestant Christian backgrounds, and his international experiences, Haddis Alemayehu's classic cat-and-mouse story would seem to be of broad interest as an African statement about European colonialism.[35]

*"When Satiety Marries Avarice, Hunger Is Born"*

Once upon a time there were two independent kingdoms . . . the cats and the mice. Separated by a spacious ocean, they lived in complete ignorance of each other. . . . Eventually the cat kingdom, advanced in terms of population density, civilization, and power . . . faced a scarcity of resources for feeding its people and factories. Therefore, to prevent the vanishing of the cat civilization and the perishing of the cat race from famine, a strategy was . . . formulated whereby emissaries would be sent across the sea to explore the world . . . and acquaint themselves with the inhabitants. . . . A huge ship was constructed and . . . diplomats were selected from both the females and males famous for their beauty and political acuity. Having loaded various types of gifts, they set sail for the mice kingdom.

After traveling for many days and nights . . . the emissaries safely disembarked. The mice people were immediately panic-stricken. . . . The elders and old women began to chant, "*Egzi'o* [Oh Lord]!"[36] The brave youth girded themselves with their weapons . . . boasting that they would spill blood for their country's freedom and king's honor. [37]

The cat emissaries thought they were doomed when they saw . . . the mouse army . . . approaching while shouting loudly and proclaiming its martial prowess in a frightening manner. Seized by fear, the cats fled back to their ship, whence they waved white flags . . . and endeavored . . . to explain [that] they were peaceful visitors. . . . Calm prevailed . . . and the cats hesitantly descended from the ship. They greeted the mice military commanders with great courtesy and implored permission to appear before His Majesty the King. In the mouse palace . . . the guests approached, trembling, offered greetings and announced the purpose of their mission. They presented the finery and various gifts that they had brought and . . . the king and all of his princes marveled. . . .

When the mouse king and queen—as well as the mice aristocracy and ministers—appeared publicly, wearing the resplendent cat king gifts, the mice citizens filling the city square applauded and cheered happily, "May our mighty king live forever!" . . . When the ululations and applause subsided, the king spoke the following words: "Our[38] beloved people: having being sent by a king who is renowned like We are, these guests whom you see amongst us have come in search of friendship and close relations.[39] Therefore . . . We are declaring that it is the duty of every mouse . . . to make them content while they are here. . . ."

There was not a mouse in any house who was not discussing the visiting cats' great size, beauty, politeness, and civility. That night His Excellency the mouse king gave a dinner banquet . . . the likes of which had never before been seen. Feasting, the cat diplomats were amazed . . . that the mice could prepare such elaborate festivities in one day. . . .

The next day the cat diplomats appeared before the king and begged that he provide them with a guide and permit them to tour his realms. . . . The cat diplomats, along with their authorized and knowledgeable guides, studied the entire mice dominion. . . . When they returned to the capital . . . the mouse king asked, "Have you seen Our realms?"

The emissaries' leader replied, "Yes, your majesty. May God grant you a long life. The guides whom you assigned us took us everywhere and showed us everything. We have been really amazed by the expanse and prosperity of the king's territory . . . [and] one is at a loss for words to explain the generous welcome with which the fine mouse people accepted us. I am certain, King, that when we return to our country and relate this unforgettably friendly reception to the cat people, the extent of their joy will be endless. . . . Yet I beg that, after our having seen the vast lands and the peoples of the king, I be granted permission to present one idea based upon the research findings of the anthropologists who accompanied me."

"What are anthropologists?" asked the king.

"Anthropologists are scholars who know about the similarities and differences between races and can distinguish the reasons why one people evolved and another remained stunted."

Astonished, the king asked, "What a miracle! Are there scholars amongst you right now who possess such knowledge?"

"Your majesty, we have scholars with us who know far more than this."

"Your knowledge exceeds your beauty, and your beauty exceeds your knowledge," said the mouse king, glancing furtively at one of the cat ladies seated in front of him. . . . "Well then, what did these scholars discover in the course of their research?"

"They assured me that in ancient times the mouse and cat peoples were the same species. . . . The cats developed like this because they followed a strategy that improved their way of life and brought about a new civilization. Since the mice people did not do so, they remained in the same form as they were when they were created long ago."

"And is there a cure for our condition?" asked the king.

"I give you my word of honor, your majesty, that without a doubt, if our two peoples cooperate and help each other, then in a short time the mouse people will reach the physical and mental levels achieved by the cat people . . . but, it *is* necessary to sign one treaty," explained the cat diplomat.

The king exclaimed, "Goodness! If it is possible for mice to become cats, I would sign a million treaties, let alone one!" . . . Diplomats from the two sides parleyed and signed a treaty. First, so that in a short time the mice people's minds and bodies would be uplifted like those of the cats, the cat government agreed to send . . . specialists throughout . . . the mouse kingdom to open schools and . . . clinics. . . . Second, while cat experts would . . . perform operations in the mice kingdom . . . the bodies of all dead mice [would be sent] to the cat country so that learned cats could conveniently research, in a laboratory, the reasons why mice remained undeveloped. . . . When the treaty was signed, the leader of the cat diplomats delivered the following speech: "As you can see, the cat government and people do not derive any advantage from this accord. It is only the mice people who . . . can be considered the . . . beneficiaries. . . ."

Not long after the cat messengers returned home, many cat teachers, doctors, technical and other specialists flooded into the mouse territory. Schools, hospitals, and other offices were opened. . . . So that the major laboratory could research the causes of mice remaining less mentally and physically developed than cats, the mouse government began gathering corpses and transporting them to the cat country.

In the first year, not many corpses were loaded. In the second year, however, thanks to the vigorous medical services provided by the cat doctors the number increased tenfold. . . . In this way, the number began to multiply tenfold in each successive year.

The young mice attending . . . schools began learning about the geography of the cat kingdom, the history of the great cat people, the purity of the cat race, and about the major battles and victories achieved by the illustrious cat monarchs who arose throughout time.

The years came and went . . . but the mice still saw no sign of changing toward cat-ness. Moreover, since the education offered by the cat scholars created . . . feelings of intellectual and mental deficiency . . . the new generations experienced even more regret and frustration than the older generations had. . . . The reasons for this, from the mice point of view, were that (1) contrary to the treaty, the cat government had not been able to make mice into cats; (2) rather than teaching cat acumen to the mice, the education provided by cat scholars was fostering disagreements and differences; (3) rather than making mice into cats, the medicine dispensed by cat doctors produced completely detrimental effects; and (4) rather than explaining and publicizing the causes of mouse stunted-ness, the research laboratory established in the cat kingdom continually swallowed the mice corpses sent there and then issued no findings. . . .

As for the cats, they plotted . . . so that they could slaughter and eat fresh meat whenever they wanted, rather than having to wait until mice died. Consequently, the cat government brought forward a new treaty proposal expressing the gracious cat government's [wish] . . . that all school-age mice children should go to the cat country to be educated, and the young mice men and maidens should go there also, to undergo operations that would transform them into cats, after which they would come home. . . . In the end, everyone agreed to the treaty. . . . Therefore, each year many hundreds of thousands of mice persons began flooding into the cat country. . . .

After many years one mouse youth finally succeeded in stowing away on a transport ship and returning to his country. The entire mouse kingdom was filled with panic and terror when he passed on the news that all those who traveled abroad for purposes of education or medical care were actually butchered as cat food. Then and there, all the cats who had come to live in and civilize the mouse realms were massacred. When this news was heard in the cat country, all of the cat people were absolutely enraged. Yet one clique, the military commanders and aristocracy, was extremely happy because the slaughtering of their compatriots provided them with an excellent pretext for overrunning, plundering, and [formally] governing the mouse country. They began preparing to invade.

As for the mice people, they selected scholars and elders to advise on ... a resistance.... During the council meeting, the cats' treachery made some valiant mice's blood boil[;] ... however, a few wise mice elders explained that ... the time had passed when they could have triumphed over the cats by engaging in face-to-face combat. For example, one elder said, "My dear brothers, the time when we could have inflicted a battlefield defeat upon the cats is gone. The war's history may have been different if we had clashed head-on long ago.... Now, however, the cats know our country better than we do ourselves. Therefore, we should prosecute our war according to a strategy...."

Another mouse elder asked him, "What sort of strategy is there against an all-knowing enemy?"

"Don't worry, it's not just that they know us—we know them, too. Therefore ... they cannot dominate us to the same extent that they did before ..." commented the wise mouse elder.

"Okay then, tell us the strategy by which we will make war against them," said the mouse elders who had gathered for the council meeting. Squinting his eyes, the clever mouse pondered for a bit.... "Each mouse should dig a hole and make a fortification and remain there with his family members. But the hole must not be large enough for a cat to insert its head.... Second, it will be necessary for everyone to resist approaching any of the cats, even if they try to beguile and lure us out.... Third, we need to inform every mouse that, beginning today, we and the cats are mortal enemies, and this vendetta cannot be abolished even by blood. If we do all these things, where will it be possible for the cats to get us?" ...

Accepting the elders' advice, the mice people dug holes, constructed fortifications, and took shelter. Later, when the [members of the] cat army came ... each mouse peeked out of his house and began to chuckle at them. The cats tried to coax the mice out ... managing only to get ... lacerated lips and noses. Eventually, annoyed and out of patience, they returned home.

From that time onward a blood feud has existed between cats and mice. The cats maintain that the number of mouse corpses that they were given did not fulfill the amount that had been agreed upon by the treaties. Therefore, nowadays cats still revel in hunting down and eating the few vagabond mice who come out of their holes . . . and the mice still refuse to acknowledge the legitimacy of the cat claims. With neither side giving in . . . the feud continues.

As mentioned above, this story emerged from an established tradition in Ethiopian literature, that of using cats and mice to reflect extreme disparities in power. Such differentials might include the relationships between two warring countries, two unevenly matched sports teams, or a bully and his weaker victim, or any imaginable dichotomy in between. This verbal imagery long ago expanded into other genres, such as the visual arts, an example of which concludes this chapter (see Image 3.3). Painted around 1935, on the verge of fascist Italy's colonial invasion, it depicts a wedding between two factions that are militaristic, albeit with different strengths.[40] It shows that even while getting ready to cement their friendship with the cats through the institution of political marriage, the mice were wise enough to look beyond the cats' preparation of a lavish feast and anticipate perfidy; thus, while playing along with the cats, the mice simultaneously busied themselves constructing protective defenses. Significantly, the religious imagery is markedly more visible among the mice, a clear statement about which side the artist believed was favored by God.

Keep in mind the year in which this painting was created, and compare its message(s) with those of other source materials provided above: nineteenth-century letters, the painting of the Battle of Adwa, the remarks made by Emperor Haile Sellassie to his French missionary friend and the world, and Haddis Alemayehu's tale "When Satiety Marries Avarice, Hunger Is Born."

### QUESTIONS

1. Today Africa is home to more than fifty countries. How might Ethiopian attitudes toward European colonialism be expected to differ from those of other African peoples? Why?

2. What were the primary themes of Ethiopian-European contacts, connections, and communications throughout history? How and why did they

Image 3.3: Painting of the Wedding Between a Cat and a Mouse

come to change over the course of the 1800s? Here, consider developments within both Ethiopia and Europe.

3. What were some Ethiopian policies and actions designed to protect the African empire's national sovereignty against industrial European conquest in the late 1800s? How might they have related to the conclusions you formed in answering the previous question? Were they action or reaction?

4. How did various elements of Ethiopian culture inflect the ways in which Ethiopians expressed attitudes toward European imperialism?

5. In studying history, can literary works such as Haddis Alemayehu's story, translated above, be deemed useful? Why or why not?

### FURTHER READINGS

Henze, Paul. *Layers of Time: A History of Ethiopia.* London: Hurst and Co., 2000.

Holcomb, Bonnie K., and Sisai Ibssa. *The Invention of Ethiopia: The Making of a Dependent Colonial State in Northeast Africa.* Trenton, NJ: Red Sea Press, 1990.

Levine, Donald N. *Wax and Gold: Tradition and Innovation in Ethiopian Culture.* Chicago: University of Chicago Press, 1965.

Marcus, Harold. *A History of Ethiopia*. Berkeley: University of California Press, 1994.

Rubenson, Sven. "Adwa 1896: The Resounding Protest," in R. Rotberg and Ali Mazrui, eds., *Protest and Power in Black Africa*. New York: Oxford University Press, 1970.

Sbacchi, Alberto. *Legacy of Bitterness: Ethiopia and Fascist Italy, 1935–1941*. Lawrenceville, NJ: Red Sea Press, 1997.

Tibebu, Teshale. *The Making of Modern Ethiopia, 1896–1974*. Lawrenceville, NJ: Red Sea Press, 1995.

Zewde, Bahru. *A History of Modern Ethiopia, 1855–1974*. London: James Currey, 1991.

## NOTES

1. See, for example, Psalm 68:31: "Ethiopia shall soon stretch out her hands unto God," and Nahum 3:9: "Ethiopia and Egypt were her strength, and it was infinite."

2. Edith R. Sanders, "The Hamitic Hypothesis: Its Origin and Functions in Time Perspective," *Journal of African History* 10, no. 4 (1969): 521–532; Philip S. Zachernuk, "Of Origins and Colonial Order: Southern Nigerian Historians and the 'Hamitic Hypothesis' c. 1870–1970," *Journal of African History* 35 (1994): 427–442.

3. It is worth noting that Ethiopian views on colonialism are divided, often along ethnic and class lines; many Ethiopians view their own country as a colonial power since in the process of building the modern state and staving off European colonialism, the central government conquered and subdued dozens of previously peripheral ethnic groups. Although debates about internal and external colonialism are fascinating, they are not pertinent to the topic of this book and thus will not be discussed in the present chapter, which focuses on the attitudes of Ethiopia's political and cultural elite toward white European colonialism.

4. Daniel Headrick, *The Tools of Empire: Technology and European Imperialism in the Nineteenth Century* (New York: Oxford University Press, 1981).

5. Ibid., p. 155.

6. A classic example is Arthur de Gobineau, *The Inequality of Human Races*, trans. Adrian Collins (Los Angeles: Noontide Press, 1966).

7. Robert Collins, *Historical Problems of Imperial Africa* (Princeton: Markus Wiener Publishers, 2007); A. Adu Boahen, *African Perspectives on Colonialism* (Baltimore: Johns Hopkins University Press, 1997).

8. Fikru Negash Gebrekidan, *Bond Without Blood: A History of Ethiopian and New World Black Relations, 1896–1991* (Trenton, NJ: Africa World Press, 2005).

9. On the issues discussed in this paragraph, see David L. Appleyard et al., trans., *Letters From Ethiopian Rulers (Early and Mid-Nineteenth Century)* (New York: Oxford University Press, 1985).

10. British looting included taking children, the best known of whom was Warqenah Eshate, who grew up to become a medical doctor and diplomat. See Peter P. Garretson,

*A Victorian Gentleman and Ethiopian Nationalist: The Life and Times of Hakim Wärqenäh, Dr. Charles Martin* (Oxford: James Currey, 2012).

11. On the Napier Expedition, see Percy Arnold, *Prelude to Magdala: Emperor Theodore of Ethiopia and British Diplomacy* (London: Bellew Publishing, 1992), and Volker Matthies, *The Siege of Magdala: The British Empire Against the Emperor of Ethiopia* (Princeton: Markus Wiener, 2011).

12. This letter was written after Ethiopia's defeat of Italian forces at the Battle of Dogali, which is discussed later in the chapter.

13. Emperor Yohannes to King Menilek, exact date uncertain but during 1889, quoted in Sven Rubenson, *The Survival of Ethiopian Independence* (Addis Ababa: Kuraz Publishing Agency, 1991), p. 380.

14. Menilek to Victoria, November 9, 1878, quoted in Sven Rubenson et al., eds., *Internal Rivalries and Foreign Threats, 1869–1879* (Addis Ababa: Addis Ababa University Press, 2000), p. 288.

15. Menilek to Victoria, December 6, 1878, quoted in Rubenson et al., *Internal Rivalries*, p. 300.

16. Harold G. Marcus, *A History of Ethiopia* (Berkeley: University of California Press, 1994), pp. 89–90.

17. Quoted in Sven Rubenson, *The Survival of Ethiopian Independence*, Kuraz Publishing Agency: (Addis Ababa: 1991), p. 380. The capitalized "We" signifies the Royal first-person plural, used instead of "I" by Ethiopian emperors. This orthographical distinction is replicated in all translations provided in the present chapter, even if doing so differs from the quoted versions.

18. Quoted in Zewde Gabre-Selassie, "Continuity and Discontinuity in Menilek's Foreign Policy," in Paulos Milkias et al., eds., *The Battle of Adwa: Reflections on Ethiopia's Historic Victory Against European Colonialism* (New York: Algora Publishing, 2005), p. 110. Other books provide variations on the translated wording, but the general message is the same.

19. David Levering Lewis, *The Race to Fashoda: European Colonialism and African Resistance in the Scramble for Africa* (New York: Weidenfeld and Nicolson, 1987).

20. Marcus, *A History of Ethiopia*, p. 99.

21. Ibid., p. 97.

22. Harold G. Marcus, "The Black Men Who Turned White: European Attitudes Towards Ethiopians, 1850–1950," *Archiv Orientální* 39 (1971): 155–166.

23. A relic of the saint was carried by Ethiopians in the battle. Today, St. George is honored in many ways, including as the name of one of the country's leading beers and as the namesake of a popular football (soccer) team.

24. When the Red Cross first went to Ethiopia, confusion was encountered on many occasions because, historically, houses of prostitution advertised their business by hang-

ing a red cross out front. Red Cross volunteers thus faced requests for services they had not come to offer!

25. "Address Delivered by His Majesty Emperor Haile Selassie I, in the Presence of the Princes and Dignitaries, the Bishops and Heads of the Clergy, Etc., On the Occasion of the Signing of the Ethiopian Empire's Constitution, on the 9th Hamlie of the Year of Grace 1923 (July 16, 1931)," in William M. Steen, ed., *The Ethiopian Constitution* (Washington, DC: Ethiopian Research Council, 1936).

26. On a different issue, many Rastafarians link the emergence of their faith system and way of life in the diaspora to the former Ras Tafari's elevation to the emperorship as Haile Sellassie I.

27. Marcus, *A History of Ethiopia*, p. 141.

28. Haile Sellassie I, "Mobilization Proclamation," October 3, 1935, in *Selected Speeches of His Imperial Majesty Haile Selassie First, 1918 to 1967* (Addis Ababa: Imperial Ethiopian Ministry of Information, 1967), p. 304.

29. Getie Gelaye, "Fukkära," in Siegbert Uhlig, ed., *Encyclopaedia Aethiopia*, vol. 2 (D—Ha) (Wiesbaden: Harrassowitz Verlag, 2005), pp. 584–585.

30. E. Cerulli, "Canti popolari amarici," *Rendiconti della Reale Accademia dei Lincei* 25 (1916): 569. The comment about the Europeans supplying weapons to Ethiopia is a reference to the fact that Italy actually supplied a huge amount of armaments to Menilek over the years, seeking to undermine Emperor Yohannes by aiding his rival Menilek (as noted earlier in the chapter), but still thought that defeating him would be easy.

31. Ras Tafari to Abba Endreyas, 27 Hedar 1928 [December 7, 1935]. Document 28.01.194b, housed at the National Archives of Ethiopia, in Addis Ababa, translated by Tim Carmichael and Mekonnen Tegegn.

32. Haile Sellassie I, "Appeal to the League of Nations," June 30, 1936, in *Selected Speeches of His Imperial Majesty Haile Selassie First, 1918 to 1967*, Imperial Ethiopian Ministry of Information: (Addis Ababa, 1967), pp. 304–305.

33. Getie Gelaye, "Fukkära," p. 585. My translation is based on but revises Getie's, which goes: "The son of Zälläqä, the flag. He who defeats Italy, He who avenges Ethiopia."

34. See Reidulf K. Molvaer, *Black Lions: The Creative Lives of Modern Ethiopia's Literary Giants and Pioneers* (Lawrenceville, NJ: Red Sea Press, 1997), pp. 133–154.

35. Haddis Alemayehu (translated by Tim Carmichael), "Tegab Sessetenn Yagäbba Endähon Rähabenn Yewälledal," in *Tärät Tärät YäMäsärät* (Addis Ababa: Berhanenna Sälam Publishers, 1948 [1955–1956]), pp. 31–43. For reasons of English-language style and flow, this version is abridged and should not be considered a complete representation of the original, but omissions are clearly indicated by ellipses. The story pairs with a famous Kenyan tale related in the classic work by Jomo Kenyatta, *Facing Mount*

*Kenya: The Tribal Life of the Gikuyu* (New York: Vintage Books, n.d.), pp. 47–51. Another story about animals and colonialism is James Aggrey's "The Parable of the Eagle," reproduced in Leon E. Clark, ed., *Through African Eyes: Cultures in Change* (New York: Praeger, 1970), pp. 12–15.

36. *Egzi'o* is an Ethiopian expression cried out by devout Christians to invoke God's mercy during a disaster.

37. See the earlier section on *fukkära*.

38. This pronoun is a version of the royal "we," by which a king refers to himself in the first-person plural rather than singular (i.e., "We" rather than "I," or "Our" rather than "my"). See also Note 17 above.

39. Or: "affection and kinship."

40. Here, both cats and mice wear earrings, which in Ethiopian culture men were historically permitted to wear only after demonstrating martial valor, such as by killing a man, a lion, or an elephant.

# 4

## Isaac Fadoyebo at the Battle of Nyron

*African Voices of the First and Second World Wars, ca. 1914–1945*

### Saheed Aderinto

### GLOBAL CONTEXT

Both World War I (1914–1918) and World War II (1939–1945) had far-reaching social, political, and economic impacts around the world. These wars not only led to the deaths of millions of people and the destruction of infrastructure and social institutions around, but also reconfigured world politics as new polities such as the United States and the Soviet Union became world superpowers while others such as Germany suffered serious political setbacks. Africa's involvement in both conflicts was inevitable because the major European belligerents—Britain, France, Germany, Italy, Belgium, and Portugal—all had colonies in Africa. The African continent was therefore an integral component of the global economic and political system both in 1914 and 1939. The purpose of this chapter is to explore the experiences of Africans as soldiers and civilians in these two wars and to see the wars through their eyes. A particular focus will be on the British colony of Nigeria and the experiences of Nigerians abroad.

The effects of the two world wars were felt in virtually all regions of Africa, from Cairo (Egypt) and Johannesburg (South Africa), to Bathurst (now Banjul, the Gambia) and Mogadishu (Somalia). Both wars had dramatic costs, human and otherwise. Not only did African colonies supply material resources used by the major powers for prosecuting the wars, they also provided soldiers whose heroic performances have been documented by authors ranging from European war generals to professional historians and even soldiers themselves.[1] The continent lost about 150,000 of the more than 1 million soldiers and carriers mobilized for World War I (WWI).[2] And African casualties in World War II (WWII) were even greater, not only because it lasted longer but also because it broke out after colonialism had taken firm root in Africa. Indeed, various regions in Africa were theaters of conflict during both wars. During WWI battles took place in Togoland, the Cameroon, German East Africa and German Southwest Africa, and Egypt served as a staging ground for the British effort against the Ottoman Empire. Both North Africa and Ethiopia saw fighting during WWII. During WWII, African battlefields were as important as Europe's or Asia's because the outcome of war on the African continent was capable of determining the victory. Moreover, the enormous costs of prosecuting the war led the colonial powers to intensify their exploitation of Africans as producers of raw materials directly needed for the wars. This meant drafting Africans as laborers and building more mines and agricultural plantations across the continent. Finally, during both conflicts, to help finance the war effort, new taxation regimes emerged throughout the continent as inflation—a direct consequence of the shortage of both essential goods (such as food) and services—took firm root. In short, Africans could afford fewer goods and had to pay higher taxes to the imperial powers as a result of the war.

## AFRICAN EXPERIENCES

In this section we will examine African experiences during the two world wars, focusing on Nigerians enlisted in the colonial army, Nigerian nationalists, and market women. This will allow us to better comprehend the impact of the wars on both soldiers and nonsoldiers and the contributions of the war generations to nationalism, decolonization, and gendered politics.

All Africans—regardless of class, region, ethnicity, and race—were involved to one degree or another in the win-the-war efforts of the belligerents. Their experiences of the wars were shaped predominantly by the politics of individual colonial powers and the extent of their involvement in the wars.

This section is divided into three parts. In the first, we examine how Nigerians viewed and responded to recruitment into the colonial army. The next section explores how the wars transformed Nigerian nationalism, and the position of leading nationalists on these major events in world history. In the third section, we consider the impact of the wars on African market women, who protested wartime policies that affected their livelihood and social status. Although we will focus mainly on the experiences of Africans from the British colony of Nigeria, the issues discussed here are applicable to the entire continent. It is useful to note that Nigeria was not only the most populous country in Africa but also Britain's most prosperous colony, second only to India.

### Recruitment of Nigerians

While only about 50,000 Nigerians were recruited by the British during WWI, about 140,000 were enlisted for WWII. Britain had maintained a colonial army in Nigeria for decades before the outbreak of WWI in 1914. Indeed, the history of the colonial army—known as the West African Frontier Force (WAFF) and, later, the Royal West African Frontier Force (RWAFF)—is as old as the history of British incursion into Nigerian geographic area. As was the case elsewhere in Africa, colonial military units in Nigeria were predominantly African in their composition. These colonial troops were utilized in battles during the so-called Scramble for Africa in the 1880s. They were also used for maintaining law and order, and as the last security and defense option when regular police proved inadequate in clamping down on revolts and insurgencies that threatened imperialism. Most of the pioneering troops of the WAFF in the late nineteenth and early twentieth centuries were runaway slaves who joined the army in order to secure redemption.[3] Others joined because they felt that the army bestowed respect and honor, glorified masculinity, and ensured better remuneration.[4]

The outbreak of the two world wars changed the nature and pattern of enlistment in the colonial army, as well as the soldiers' roles and functions. While some Nigerians continued to voluntarily enlist in the army for the respect it conferred, others were driven to fight for the British because the army's wages and remuneration were relatively higher than those of many other casual jobs during the war. However, the British realized very early on that voluntary recruitment was incapable of producing the manpower needed to defend the British Empire. Hence during both WWI and WWII, the British demanded that chiefs and community leaders in Africa fill recruitment quotas in accordance with the size of the communities they led as well as the power they wielded among their people. Many chiefs cooperated willingly with the recruitment quotas. Alaafin (King) Ladigbolu of Oyo (in southwestern Nigeria) told the British at the outset of WWI that he would enlist 30,000 men and that the British should "not treat this as an idle boast. I say it from my heart and mean it."[5] During WWII, the chiefs of Sokoto province closely monitored the recruitment of soldiers, allowing even family members to fight in the war. These recruitment quotas were a disguised form of forced labor since most people would have preferred to stay in their villages and towns rather than fight a war that originated outside their immediate communities. In reality, then, some of the "recruits" were seized by force while others were simply told that the British officer wanted to see them and not briefed about the purpose of the invitation until they arrived at the training camps. Nwose, a recruit from eastern Nigeria, gave a firsthand account of how he was "volunteered" by the chiefs at the outset of WWI:

> We came back one night from our yam farm, the chief called us and handed us over to government messenger. I did not know where we were going to, but the chief and the messenger said that the white man had sent for us and so we must go. After three days we reached the white man's compound. Plenty of others had arrived from other villages far away. The white man wrote our names in a book, tied a brass number ticket round our neck and gave each man a blanket and food. Then he told us that we were going to the great war [as World War I was called]. . . . We left and marched far into the

bush. The government police led the way, and allowed no man to stay behind.[6]

But it is misleading to assume that the chiefs willingly volunteered their kinsmen and community members to fight in the wars. Rather, most of them acted under pressure and from fear of the political consequences of disobeying imperial directives. In Nigeria, as elsewhere in Africa, colonial administrators had the power to remove local chiefs at will for not following imperial orders such as the demand for recruits. Many chiefs felt that they had to comply with the recruitment policy in order to remain politically relevant. Yet not all of the chiefs complied with the recruitment order. Chiefs in places like Zungeru and along the Cross River refused to send their men to war and some northern emirs sent disabled men, referred to by British military officers as "a herd of cripples."[7]

How did everyday Nigerians react to conscription? Some fled their immediate community and sought haven in places where forceful conscription by chiefs was not enforced. Others ran into the remote forest far beyond the reach of both African and colonial authorities. Still others "bribed" the traditional rulers in order to be exempted from war duties. During WWI, especially, some Igbo chiefs were reported to have benefited from the gifts received from those unwilling to go to the war front. Desertion from the army was rampant as well, especially among carriers like Nwose who did not know they were going to the war front and fled during training or even from the battleground itself. And some Muslims deserted the army because they believed that fighting in East Africa would entail killing fellow Muslims from the Middle East. Private Obudu Kano's explanation of his desertion from the British army in 1917 captures this reasoning:

> I volunteered to go to East Africa but I did not understand what it meant. When I arrived at Obolo, Sergeant Tanko Jura, who was in charge of my section, said to me "I hear we go to war and we got to fight the Turk in Stamboul [Istanbul]: and he advised me not to go." Another soldier, Private Garuba Hadeija[,] reported that he heard "Some soldiers say that they were going to fight at Stamboul,["] so when them making away, I joined them.[8]

Another reason desertion occurred so frequently was that African recruits faced terrible conditions and had little chance to better their conditions or even have their complaints heard. Indeed, colonial armies were one of the strongholds of racism in Africa. Lack of Western education and the entrenchment of colonial racial prejudice, coupled with the military culture's doctrine of total obedience, prevented African soldiers from seeking redress even when made to march barefoot (except on the battlefield). In addition, the highest post an African could aspire to was battalion sergeant-major. Africans were never appointed as commissioned officers and were paid far less their enlisted white counterparts. They were also required to stand at attention to British soldiers, regardless of rank, and to salute white civilians.

Yet battlefield experience was precisely what transformed African soldiers' perceptions of white masters' racial supremacy and demystified the prevailing notion of their invincibility. African soldiers saw their highly respected white soldiers and officers falling, getting killed, and breaking down in the face of violence. According to G. O. Olusanya, a Nigerian World War II historian, "The Nigerian soldiers found out that they were subject to the same emotions, the same fears and hopes as white soldiers, a fact which convinced them that all human beings, irrespective of their colour, were basically the same when subjected to the same conditions."[9] "The myth of racial superiority"—according to Mokwugo Okoye, who fought in WWII—"received less sanction" after the war.[10]

## Nationalism and the Newspaper Press

The two world wars also had a significant impact on nationalists and journalists in Nigeria. The relationship between nationalism and the newspaper press is as old as the history of colonial incursion in the region.[11] Both emerged from the same elite, literate class. This class, in turn, had emerged during the mid-nineteenth century as a result of the introduction of Christianity to southern Nigeria by European missionaries. Trained largely to serve as clerks supporting the colonial state, the members of this small but highly influential elite soon began to use their knowledge of Western literacy to campaign against the economic, political, and social exploitation of Nigerians.[12] In fact, they launched the first wave of cultural nationalism in Nigeria during the late nineteenth and early twentieth centuries. The primary aim of this generation of "cultural nationalists" was not independence from Britain but, rather, a colonial society free of racial prejudice and based on respect for African culture. Their methods of mobilization included public protest and petitioning administrators both in Nigeria and Britain, but it was the newspaper press that would prove the most powerful instrument of nationalist agitation. The early nationalist newspapers, which emerged in the 1880s, included the *Times of Nigeria*, the *Nigeria Pioneer*, the *Lagos Weekly Record*, the *Nigerian Chronicle*, and the *Lagos Standard*. Reaching a wide readership and serving as watchdogs of the colonial masters, these newspapers frequently criticized colonial policies and actions deemed unacceptable. They were able to do this because of their independence from both the colonial administration and European financial interests. Indeed, the newspaper press, throughout a century of British presence in Nigeria, was the only modern economic venture completely monopolized by Nigerians. It therefore formed the central institution for the development of Nigerian nationalism—the call for an independent state for the Nigerian people.

The outbreak of WWI tested the ideological framework of the Nigerian nationalist struggle in that it required taking sides with either the exploitative colonial master—Britain—or Britain's European enemies, the Germans. Although Britain was politically unpopular in Nigeria, as in most of its colonies, the nationalists believed that the collapse of the British Empire and the possibility of a resulting German annexation would spell doom for Nigerians. This conviction was partly based on Nigerians' observation of the repressive German regime in nearby German Togoland and German Cameroons. The old saying that "a known devil is better than an unknown angel" best describes the nationalists' perception of that regional tragedy.

It is important to note that anti-German sentiments cannot wholly explain why nationalists supported the British during WWI. According to Akinjide Osuntokun, a Nigerian historian of World War I, some nationalist newspapers actually supported the British and reduced their criticism of the colonial administration during the war in order to avoid censorship. The administration had threatened to censor antigovernment publications during the war for fear that they would reduce public support for the British.[13] Meanwhile, the new elite split up as progovernment individuals and groups (otherwise called "collaborators") gained popularity with the British officers—a trend that sowed discontent among the mainstream nationalist groups.

No sooner had the war started than the nationalists began to use their newspapers to support it and mobilize people for the war effort. The following editorial in *The Nigerian Pioneer*, dated December 11, 1914, demonstrates the moral and African-cultural tone that characterized these newspapers' appeal to Nigerians to support Britain:

> The splendid spirit of patriotism aroused in the breast of all who count as citizens of the Empire by the present awful war, we trust and hope will continue for all time. It has kindled in the minds of everyone unity of purpose and sense of duty. . . . It is this which animates all to give their best, be it of blood or money for the sake of the Empire. The African is taught from early childhood the duty we owe one to the other. In times of joy and gladness, he rejoices with those with whom he is brought into intimate contact. In times of sorrow and sadness he shares in the grief of his neighbours. In times of distress and want he is taught to contribute towards the relief of those affected.[14]

The nationalist call for Nigerians to join the colonial army—which had been unpopular for its repressiveness as an arm of imperialism—was a major reversal. Ironically, the nationalists did not depict the recruitment quota as a form of forced labor despite the fact that they had campaigned vigorously against all forms of involuntary conscription in the prewar era. In fact, the nationalists injected new phrases such as "imperial patriotism" into the quest to raise money and other forms of support for the British. In particular, they organized concerts to raise money for war efforts and published the names of and financial contributions made by chiefs as well as district and provincial officers. Although the coastal city of Lagos was the main hub of the newspaper industry, the circulation of nationalist newspapers reached the interior of Nigeria and became the best and most readily accessible information on war news.

British victory in World War I led to the interwar years, which in turn ushered in new social and political developments that consolidated the hold of colonialism in Nigeria and across the African continent. Compared to prewar years, this period saw a higher number of administrators, an increase in European economic investment, and a deeper colonial infrastructure. Meanwhile, the cultural nationalism of the late nineteenth and early twentieth centuries was gradually supplanted by political nationalism, which demanded self-rule or independence. The number of educated elites and the level of nationalist agitation increased during the interwar years as the newspaper industry, which continued to be firmly dominated by Nigerians, blossomed in response to an unprecedented increase in the number of educated elites and the urbanization of the Nigerian population.[15] This expansion of literacy and newspaper readership increased Nigerians' awareness of their place in world politics, the ills of foreign domination, and the importance of self-determination. At the same time, a number of constitutional changes during the interwar years (e.g., the Clifford Constitution of 1922) gave Nigerians more voice in the administration of the colony and provided an effective platform for seeking redress.[16] The *Lagos Daily News*, the *Daily Service*, and the *West African Pilot*, three newspapers founded during the interwar years, radicalized political nationalism by criticizing virtually all colonial policies of the time.

Whereas World War I merely tested the loyalty of Nigerians to the British Empire, World War II tested the security of the British Empire itself, inspiring the drive toward independence. When WWII broke out most Nigerians, including leading nationalists, once again sided with the British. The news of Adolf Hitler's atrocities against the Jews and his fledging pronouncement of a German world empire prompted Nigerians to support the Allies and their professed mission of defending the humanity against an impending Nazi imperialism. On September 6, 1939, three days after Britain and France declared war against Germany, Honourable Alakija, a member of the Nigerian Youth Movement and Nigerian Legislative Council, convened a meeting chaired by Oba (King) Falolu of Lagos and attended by about ten thousand Nigerians.[17] The attendees publicly pledged their support for the British and resolved to mobilize human and material resources for the "mother" country of England. They equated the Allies' victory with freedom for all humanity. This sentiment is reflected in the following statement issued by Herbert Macaulay, a leading nationalist: "Victory for Democracy and the freedom of Mankind depends on our contributions, our determination, and our Loyalty."[18]

Anti-Nazi sentiments permeated nearly the entire fabric of Nigerian society, from schools and government establishments to sacred places like the church. While schoolchildren were being taught anti-Axis songs with lyrics like "Hitler that is throwing the world into confusion, push him with a shovel into the grave,"[19] priests were publicly preaching their anti-Nazi opinions to their congregations.[20] As in WWI, newspapers became the most effective tool for mobilizing support for Britain. Indeed, they can be viewed as the principal ideological weapon supporting the prosecution of the war not only in Nigeria but in the entirety of British West Africa. During the interwar period the newspapers had critiqued the truthfulness of news emanating from Britain, but once the war began, they uncritically published virtually all news released by the War Office in London. Generally, the newspapers' pro-Allied wartime efforts can be divided into three interrelated categories: supporting conscription, disseminating battlefield news, and encouraging civilians to contribute to the Win-the-War Fund. Let us take a critical look at each of these wartime newspaper activities.

In 1939 the British set up a quota scheme (as they had done in WWI), but this scheme met with only inconsistent success. As WWII progressed, the British adopted a new recruitment strategy of marketing the army to individuals as a professional career that equipped soldiers with entrepreneurial skills they could use for personal development after demobilization. This campaign aimed at changing Nigerians' beliefs that soldiers were solely trained to carry weapons and kill. Specifically, the British hoped to attract educated Nigerians by emphasizing the technical and professional jobs available in the army (see Image 4.1). In addition, recruits were assured that they would be voluntarily released at the end of the war. A 1943 recruitment advertisement with the headline "Young Men! Army Pays You to Learn a

Trade" went on to say "Young men with ambition, who have finished school studies, are paid by the Army to learn a trade."[21] The nationalists quickly seized upon the importance of this new policy in human and technological development of the colonial state they intended to inherit from the British. There was rarely a week in which the major Lagos newspaper did not urge Nigerians to join the army. The following *Daily Service* editorial dated November 23, 1942, illuminates this new pattern of thinking:

> We call the attention of Nigerian youths to the notice in today's issue explaining schemes which offer excellent opportunities for technical training in the Army in the hope that the fullest advantage will be taken of them. The rates of pay in the army have increased, bringing them to a level which we believe compare favorably with the rates of paid for similar trade in civil occupation. But quite apart from any question of personal advantage, this war against Hitler is essentially one of machines and one in which the technician has to play an important part. Unlike other wars in the past, the struggle against Hitler and his associates is of tanks, lorries, aeroplanes, guns of all kinds, armoured cars and a thousand and one other things which require the technician's skill not only to manufacture but to repair. In Nigeria, the training afforded by the Army will serve a double purpose. Already there are attempts at industrialisation of the country. This process we believe will be capable of much development after the war in the reconstruction period that lies ahead. Then the skilled workers in different trades will be a matter of great national need.

In addition to aiding in the recruitment of soldiers, the nationalist newspapers served as the most accessible information channel for battlefield news. They were certainly biased in their coverage of the war, as they reported only the Allies' battlefield successes and frequently mocked Hitler. Educated readers who cared about the success of the Allies and, by extension, the future of British imperial rule in Nigeria were entertained by front-page headlines such as "Over 200 Enemies Ships Have Been Sunk in the Mediterranean Since Allied Landing in Africa," "Germans Abandon Men and Materials in Their Flight from Egypt," "Senior German General Is

S. Q. M. S. Asuquo has a most excellent Army record, enlisting as a Clerk on the 13.12.40 he has risen in the short space of 3 years to the rank of Staff Quartermaster Sergeant. He is welfare officer for his Unit and spends a considerable part of his spare time forwarding books and newspapers to his African friends on Active Service, —A Nigerian who is doing his part in more ways than one.

# He will have a trade when
# Victory is won

Men are wanted for the following vacancies.

|  | Qualification |
|---|---|
| Clerks | Middle II and over |
| Nursing Orderlies (*i.e., Military Nurse*) | Middle II |
| Literate recruits for Signals and Artillery | Middle II if possible, but lower standard can be accepted |
| Drivers | Must be able to speak simple English |
| Carpenters | |
| Blacksmiths | |
| Bricklayers | |
| Painters | |
| Mechanics | |
| Fitters | |

also apprentices for all trades.

Applicants will be interviewed at the Commissioner of the Colony's Office, every Monday at 8 a.m.

Please apply in person and not by letter Bring your Certificate with you.

SPECIAL :

Experienced Stewards to be personal servants wanted

# JOIN *the* ARMY

Image 4.1: Army recruitment advertisement

Killed During Action,""Bad Day for Hitler,""40,000 Axis Prisoners Have Been Taken in Egypt,"" Crew of One British Tank Capture Italian Colonel and 600 Other Senior Officers," and "The Nazis Still On the Run." News of African soldiers' gallantry on the battlefield was regularly celebrated,[22] and the reserves were regularly treated to diversions such as parades and dances that, in turn, served as a means of raising funds for the war.[23] Another editorial—under the heading "Hitler Gets the Jitters"—summarized the impact of an Allied victory by stating: "The Germans and their friends appear to have been caught completely unawares this time and it does not seem as if they have been given much time in which to reorganize to meet the latest surprise."[24] Photos of captured German soldiers, Allied generals, war ships, and fighter jets were scattered across the front pages of the newspapers. One photo of US and Japanese fighter jets had this caption: "U.S. Carrier Avoids Bombers: An American aircraft carrier veers sharply in the South Pacific during an attack by Japanese planes. The bombs missed and the planes were driven off."[25]

It is important to note that the stories of battlefield success were meant to serve the joint purpose of encouraging the public to continue to contribute to British war efforts and helping to boost sales and profits for the newspapers' owners. When Sokoto province donated £8,783 (thereby increasing its total war contribution to £27,000),[26] the governor of Nigeria not only publicly acknowledged the donation but remarked that the money would be used for purchasing a bomber and painted a verbal picture of what the bomber would do: "[A]nd soon a Mosquito bomber bearing the name SOKOTO will be busy stinging the enemy with its tons of bombs." He also stated that the bomber "could bring the war home to the enemy."[27] A week later, another newspaper story confirmed the efficacy of the "Mosquito Bomber" in bringing the war to a logical conclusion: "It can outmanoeuvre most of Germany's best fighters. It has a range which brings practically the whole of Germany within its reach."[28] Sokoto province soon acquired national fame as the "protector of the empire," and other provinces and districts intensified war contributions in order to gain publicity and popularity among the colonial officers.[29] Children were included in the drive to secure maximum financial support for the British. The author of a *West African*

*Pilot* editorial, after praising Nigerian children for broadcasting letters of condolence to their British counterparts, remarked: "Broadcasting letters to boys and girls of Britain and admiring their courage will not do much. We want more than mere words of mouth."[30] The editorial expected school-children to contribute their "pocket" money to Win-the-War Fund.

Yet while the newspapers generally supported the British war efforts, they also criticized certain aspects of military culture deemed unacceptable. As noted earlier, the colonial army was one of the strongholds of racism in Nigeria, and there were few official channels by which soldiers could complain of their treatment and better their conditions. Thus the newspaper became the mouthpiece of soldiers who feared retribution if they challenged authority. Three areas of discrimination in particular attracted the attention of nationalist newspapers: (1) the racist barrier to commissioning African soldiers as officers, (2) pay and remuneration, and (3) corporal punishment. Several Nigerian newspapers criticized the British for not appointing Africans as commissioned officers, claiming that they deliberately put in place stringent requirements that African soldiers could not meet. After listing the seven requirements for appointment for commissioned officers,[31] the *Daily Service* editorial of June 19, 1943, remarked that ambitious soldiers "know that on paper all these things sound excellent, but they know also that in practice, few Africans will ever have a chance to rise to the post of commissioned officers."[32] The editors of the newspaper believed that Africans deserve to be appointed to significant positions of military authority because of their enormous contributions to the two world wars. They accused the British of creating a double standard and questioned the promise that the end of the war would usher in a democratic regime: "We have been told so often that this is a war for democracy while so many things happen to create doubt about such profession that we think it is a good thing for those in authority not only to state on paper but show by their conduct and practice that they are animated by democratic principles in the general ordering of present day society."[33] Nigerians did not receive commissions until three years after World War II, when Lieutenant L.V Ugboma became the country's first military officer.[34]

The newspapers also criticized the prejudicial British practice of paying

African soldiers less than their British counterparts as contradictory to the spirit of wartime solidarity. The *West African Pilot* was bold on this point: "Those who enlist expect good salary just as their white brothers earn. To the people death knows no colour and, as such, rates of pay should be adjusted in that spirit."[35] On corporal punishment, the *Daily Service* noted that public flogging of men was not a feature of civil life in Nigeria and should not be an appropriate manner of punishing soldiers who risked their lives for the freedom the humanity. Moreover, the newspaper editors believed that, if necessary, corporal punishment should also be extended to the white soldiers: "Both White and Black in the army are arranged in battle against a common enemy [Hitler]. Both cherish a common hope and a common desire. Both risk their lives for a better and brighter world, why for goodness sake should one by discriminated against?"[36]

In sum, while not formally calling for decolonization during the war, the free Nigerian press cautiously began to publish complaints about the treatment of African soldiers (complaints that would become more generally aired as the war ended), contributing to the eventual nationalist sentiment that would force the British to leave the country and lead to an independent Nigeria.

*Market Women*

Market women occupied an indispensable position in the political economy of colonial rule as producers, distributors, and marketers of essential commodities—especially food products. Women's monopoly of the domestic market economy is rooted in centuries of traditions, which empowered them as significant agents of authority and spirituality.[37] In the precolonial agrarian economy of much of Nigeria, while men cleared the farm and planted at the beginning of each rainy season, the roles of women and girls included harvesting the crops. They retained some for household use and sold the surplus in markets that met both daily and periodically. Through this role, women became the principal long- and short-distance traders in the country. Market women also played a key role in the transmission of culture and language across the region, thereby fostering intergroup relations.

The advent of colonialism—which functioned as a male-centered insti-tution—robbed women of the significant political and economic power they had wielded in precolonial times. On the other hand, it boosted domestic markets with imported goods from Europe and the Americas, thus adding new items of trade sold by women. Nevertheless, market women were among the key opponents of colonialism and played a role in nationalist or-ganizations. In fact, scholars have shown that the Nigerian National Dem-ocratic Party, the first mass-based political party in Nigeria, owed its success to market women.[38]

The cardinal position occupied by market women in the domestic econ-omy meant that they would be adversely affected during periods of crisis such as the world wars.[39] During WWII, food shortages emerged as a direct consequence of the mass recruitment of male farmers into the army, rural-urban migration, and the German naval blockade and submarine warfare. Such shortages were also, however, caused in part by colonial policies. The decision of the government to export cassava starch, arguably the most im-portant staple food crop, created a vicious circle of poverty and hunger, even in the food-producing communities of Nigeria.[40] Food shortages and infla-tion led to a price control system, a government interventionist policy of fix-ing prices of both imported and locally produced foodstuffs.[41] The Pullen Price Control System (named after Captain Pullen, the Controller of Price) fixed prices below the market value, defying the law of supply that had tra-ditionally determined the prices of commodities. Large trading firms such as John Holt and United Africa Company, which operated on behalf of the government and could trade in large volumes, replaced women as major dis-tributors and markets of consumer goods. The government resold these products to the public in sales centers (also known as Pullen Markets) around the country.[42] The scheme failed, impoverishing Nigerians and cre-ating a "black" or "underground" market for essential consumer goods.[43] Women composed protest songs to register their grievances against the new order. This excerpt provides an example: "I bought okro; I bought onion; I bought one penny worth of salt; but was inadequate for my soup; I would send a curse to the white men in Akure."[44]

The Pullen marketing system not only put the economic survival of women on the line, it also criminalized their commercial activities. Women caught buying or selling goods above fixed prices or quantities were prosecuted for an offense called "profiteering" (see Table 1.1). Sentences and the names of convicts were regularly published in the newspapers to serve as deterrent to other traders.[45] The newspapers responded to these government prosecutions by publicizing the prosecution of women and protesting the "un-African-ness" of sending women to jail.[46] They also criticized the police for punishing the traders and shielding large trading companies like John Holt for committing "profiteering" offenses themselves.[47] As a December 1, 1942, editorial in the *Daily Service* put it: "To sentence a women to one, two, or three months imprisonment for selling a tin of milk a penny over the price when the very firm from which she bought might be allowed . . . to raise its price the following day above the price at which the women sold seems to us rather hard lines, whether or not the law is no respecter of persons."[48]

The women themselves were not lax in registering their grievances against the new order. They held protest meetings with administrations to demonstrate their displeasure of wartime policies. In fact, the activities of market women's associations such as the Nigerian Traders Association and Lagos Market Women's Association gained frontline newspaper coverage.[49] Another protest song of the period accused the British of invading a space traditionally preserved for women:

Strange things are happening in Lagos;
   Europeans now sell pepper;
   Europeans now sell palm-oil;
   Europeans now sell yam;
   Though they cannot find their way to Idogo [a food-crop-producing community];
   And yet Falolu [the King of Lagos] is still in his palace and alive;
   Europeans were not wont to sell melon seeds.[50]

Alimotu Pelewura was the leader of Lagos market women for more than a half-century, until her death in 1952.[51] In a January 1945 meeting with

TABLE 4.1: Sample of "Profiteering" Offenses and Sentences

| Name | Offense | Sentence |
|---|---|---|
| Rabiatu Adekunle | selling beef above controlled price | fined twenty shillings |
| Moriamo Adunni | selling one bottle of groundnut oil for seven pennies instead of controlled price of six and a half pennies | fined ten shillings |
| Rabiatu Balogun | selling five bottles of groundnut oil for two shillings, eleven pennies instead of controlled price of two shillings, eight and a half pennies | fined thirty shillings |
| Abusatu Ashabi | selling native-produced rice above controlled price | fined seven shillings, six pennies |
| Murano Okubolade | selling beef above controlled price | fined three pounds or one month in prison |
| Lalatu Lawani | selling one packet of pirate cigarettes for eight and half pennies instead of controlled price of seven and a half pennies | fined six pounds or one month in prison |
| Moriyamo Moses | selling one packet of pirate cigarettes for eight pennies instead of controlled price of seven and a half pennies | fined five pounds, ten shillings or twenty-one days in prison |
| Adesola Ayo | selling one packet of pirate cigarettes for eight pennies instead of controlled price of seven and a half pennies | fined five pounds, ten shillings or twenty-one days in prison |
| Yaheya Adegun | selling 32 pounds of marrows for sixteen shillings instead of controlled price of ten shillings, eight pennies and 680 pounds of potatoes for eleven pounds | fined ten pounds |
| Nusiratu Alake | selling one Oloruka pan of farina coarse [a food product made from cassava] for four pennies instead of controlled price of three and a half pennies | fined seventeen shillings, six pennies |

Source: Collated from *Daily Service*, January 2, 1943.

Captain Pullen and the Oba (King) Falolu of Lagos, Pelewura threatened to direct women to close down all trading activities if the government did not honor their demands, which included a halt to imprisonment of women. The following day, the government offered to pay her a monthly allowance of £7.10 and to recognize her as the official leader of market women if she stopped mobilizing women against wartime emergency policies. She declined this offer and not only continued to mobilize women in the rural areas of Ijebu Ode and Sagamu but also worked with them to ensure that foodstuffs were not taken to Lagos unless the women's demands were met.[52] When the government frustrated her efforts to sell gari (a cassava product) to women by shipping it directly from the province, she held a press conference in which she issued a demand to the authorities to "[l]et them allow her men to buy gari directly from Okitipupa and she would arrange distribution in Lagos. . . . The food control authorities could have all the Ijebu producing districts for their own scheme but for God's sake they should allow gari from Okitipupa to come to Lagos."[53]

In addition to the failed price control system, another issue that brought women into direct confrontation with the government was the Income Tax Ordinance, which called for an income tax on women who made £50 or more annually.[54] Prior to the outbreak of WWII, market women had successfully resisted paying income taxes on cultural and economic grounds.[55] Culturally, the women in most African societies did not pay direct income taxes; hence both the market women and the male nationalists viewed the Income Tax Ordinance as a Western implantation. An attempt to tax the women of Ogoja and Owerri provinces had led to the Women's War in 1929, a major event in Africa's history of colonialism, nationalism, and gender. Economically, WWII was an especially inappropriate period in which to tax women. Thus on December 16, 1940, a group of market women led by Madam Rabiatu Alaso Oke marched to the office of the Commissioner of the Colony of Lagos to register their grievances and proceeded to issue a formal petition that was thumb-printed by more than two hundred women.[56] On December 17 and 18, several protest meetings attended by about seven thousand people forced the government to officially raise the minimum income on which taxes had to be paid—namely, from £50 to £200.

This represented a victory for the women, since very few earned such an income in 1945. The excerpt below is reprinted from the petition submitted to the government following a well-attended meeting of Lagos market women on September 13, 1943:

At a women's meeting held on Monday the 13th [i]n the schoolroom of St. Paul's Church Breadfruit Street, under the auspices of the Lagos Women's League;[,] it was unanimously decided that the following statement should be placed before His Excellency the Acting Governor, so that the women's side of this matter of profiteering in food stuffs should be heard.

1) That this meeting view with great apprehension the effects of the legal action against profiteering in foodstuffs and craves His Excellency the Governors kind intervention in the matter.

2) That this meeting holds that generally speaking there is no profiteering in foodstuff, for the dealer get their supplies from various places at various prices to which must be added transport charges and they sell with a small margin of profit to themselves.

3) That there had always been fluctuation of foodstuffs according to the season of the year, so prices cannot remain the same for any length of time.

4) That in many areas where farm lands have been acquired for the purposes of the Military, thousands and thousands of Palm trees have been destroyed, acres and acres of cassava and other crops fields have [been] ruined and consequently there must be scarcity of these commodities.

5) That thousands of farm laborers have had to leave their work to take up arms for the protections of the Empire, this has caused shortages of labour in connection with farm produces.

6) That these reasons and other have been the cause of the increase in the prices of foodstuffs and yet the Controller of Prices fixes prices as on pre-war days.

7) That these meeting strongly protest against the system adopted by the Controller of Prices and consider it as a very unfair one. He fixes prices of local commodities at pre-war rates and all imported goods he allows to be sold at prices in some cases four and five times more than before the war. The effect of such action is impoverishing the people. Let them [market women]

be allowed to buy and sell their commodities freely without restriction as was done during the Great War and the distress and confusion prevalent now will quickly disappear.[57]

## A NIGERIAN PERSPECTIVE ON WORLD WAR II

Any discussion of the two world wars without a critical acknowledgment of Nigerian participation and contributions would be grossly inadequate. Besides fighting on the side of their colonial masters, Nigerians donated money and labor toward prosecuting the wars, which originated outside the continent. And, more generally, Africa hosted some of the theaters of wars and bore the hardship accentuated by wartime policies. The stories about African experiences of the wars can best be told from the perspectives of the women and men who actually participated in them and were affected by wartime policies. What follows is one such story.[58]

### THE BATTLE OF NYRON

In the course of our journey down [the] Kaladan River in Burma in pursuit of the fleeing Japanese troops towards Rangoon some time in March 1944, we anchored at Nyron village one evening to pass the night after paddling our bamboo rafts for several hours. When we woke up the following morning and started running around to get ourselves prepared for the onward movement it never crossed our minds that the journey would come to an abrupt and disastrous end that very morning. As we washed our faces and brushed our teeth we did not realise that we were the target of an armed attack and that the Japanese troops had already cocked their guns waiting for the Commander's "open fire" order. We could not have known that we were seeing ourselves as a group for the last time and that in the next few minutes some of us would be lying dead or wounded while the lucky ones would flee in disorder. It did not occur to us and we could not have imagined that the dissolution of the partnership would be over in a few moments. I was not lucky enough to escape unhurt; it was the day I walked right for the last time as I have since been maimed for the rest of my life. The batch was being led by the unit's commanding officer Major Murphy of the Royal Army Medical

Corps and next to him was Captain Brown also of the Royal Army Medical Corps. There was a host of both British and African non-commissioned officers in the group.

At about 7.30 a.m. gunshots rang [out] from the opposite bank unexpectedly and I and other members of my Unit, 29th Casualty Clearing Station, ran for cover. The Japanese troops were on the offensive. A confused situation arose because we were badly positioned. The slanting nature of the river bank rendered ineffective our efforts to dodge the enemy bullets. In other words we could not do much to evade the gunshots in view of the fact that we were on the slope of a river. The heavy fire continued intermittently for more than one hour. A colleague of mine, Essien, and I took cover in the same place. Each time the Japanese stopped firing, I made a number of abortive attempts to get away from the area. I did not know in time that I had been wounded and I just kept on trying to move away. I was wondering as to what might have been responsible for my inability to lift myself off the ground and make a dash for shelter. As a young and healthy man I felt I possessed such a remarkable agility that I could run to safety in the event of an attack. Alas I was wrong in the estimation of my prowess. In addition to my not being able to crawl away I started to feel tired due perhaps to loss of blood. My right leg developed aches and pains. So was the left hand side of my abdomen immediately below my ribs. I made an attempt to peep at my right leg and the left hand side of my body and I saw a lot of blood. I then knew for sure that I had been hit by bullets on both parts of the body. I had a fractured femur very close to the knee and one bullet also pierced my stomach just below the ribs. Luckily, for me that bullet did not go deep enough to injure my intestine or any of the food canal organs. Of course, my battle dress had already been soaked with blood. It was also then that it occurred to me that I was in serious trouble and on the threshold of an agony that lasted for over nine months.

When I was trying to examine my body the movement might have attracted the attention of the Japanese soldiers who were still at alert position across the river and as a result several shots rang out again [striking] nearly all the grass around me. They all missed me miraculously. I really heard the sounds of bullets flying or whistling past my head almost uprooting the shrubs around the spot I laid my head. The situation was indescribable. The bullets would seem to be bouncing off my body particularly my head. I would have thought that I had developed supernatural powers were it not that two bullets had already been lodged in my body. It had only pleased God that the bullets should miss their target. In the meantime I noticed that Essien, who was lying quite close to me, was in pains but I did not see any blood stain in his battle dress. I heard him saying, "Take me O God! Take me O God!," all the time. After a short while, I observed that he was struggling for breath, gasping as doctors would say. He could no longer repeat "Take me O God." A few minutes later he stopped gasping and I then presumed that he was no more. I incurred the risk of being fired at once again by stretching my left hand in an attempt to reach his body but I was not successful. Feeling that the firing had ceased for good, I made another effort by crawling a little, just a little, towards his direction and touched his body. It was already cold and lifeless. I shivered.

At sunset Captain Brown, a Scot, emerged from nowhere and came straight to me and said: "Ebo my boy you are down o!" He had always been calling me "Ebo" because he felt my name "Fadoyebo" was too long for him to memorise. He therefore restricted himself to the last syllable or three letters. I complained of thirst, pains and tiredness. He went away and after a minute or two he reappeared with a flask containing tea and served me. What a brave soldier. It was apparent that all those who were lucky to escape death or being seriously wounded had run away except Captain Brown. I regarded the tea he gave me as the "Last Supper" because I thought I was going to die in the next few moments. I was already down with severe gunshot wounds, no medical attention and no hope of getting out of the predicament in which I found myself. Death was the next thing. After all a colleague of mine, Essien was lying dead by my side. It was Captain Brown who informed me that the commanding officer Major Murphy was badly wounded in the head and that he tried to apply some dressings. He asked me to sit up but I could not. He told me he would like to arrange for an improvised splint to support my fractured femur.

At that juncture the invading Japanese soldiers charged in with bayonets fixed to the nozzle of their rifles and took Captain Brown away from me. I heard him telling them: "I am Captain Brown, Medical Officer." I did not and still do not know what happened to him thereafter. I came to admire and respect the courage and gallantry he displayed. He was free to desert us like others but instead he kept going round to minister to the wants of those who were in dire need of assistance. He was not wounded, not even a [scratch] on his body and yet as a soldier and true to his profession, he stayed to succour comrades struck down by enemy bullets. Shortly afterwards, another set of Japanese troops came and asked me to get up. Of course they spoke in their language which I did not understand and later used their hands to convey to me what they were saying in Japanese language. I replied in English that it was not possible for me to get up. I could not even sit up. One of them, I still remember, pointed his rifle at me apparently thinking that the threat would make me attempt the impossible. In my view there was no need for him to harass me because I could not have waited for them to see me if I were fit enough to be on my legs. They spent roughly one hour ransacking the bamboo rafts with which we arrived at the scene and examining the pockets of those who were lying dead, perhaps for possible documents that might lead to information about the strength and strategy of the Allied forces. Before the arrival of the Japanese troops, some people in uniform, probably local militia men, came to the scene, looked around and went away without saying a word to me.

As I watched the Japanese soldiers searching our luggage I saw the huge frame of CSM [Company Sergeant Major] Duke lying still on the river bank with the tea mug clung to his hand. It was painful. When I saw the enemy troops coming to me a second time I thought they wanted to carry me away, mend my wounds and make me a prisoner of war. I was in terrible pains and anything that was likely to remove the agony or even lessen it would suit me, be it a prisoner of war camp or any other place. Nothing of that sort was forthcoming and for several days afterwards I had to bear the pain. Seeing the Japanese soldiers sailing away in their motor boats I felt that they were a set of callous people. On the other hand, it might be they had not the facilities for attending to ailments or that they went away to enable them [to] discuss my condition with their superior officers that would decide on what to do with me. I did not know in time that others like Sergeant David Kagbo, Sergeant Lamina and Moigboi Jagha were in a position similar to mine. Sergeant

Lamina and Moigboi Jagha later died of wounds while David Kagbo and I survived the ordeal through the inscrutable design of providence—a stroke of unbelievable luck. As soon as the Japanese went out of sight, the local inhabitants swarmed to the scene and looted our luggage. I saw them carrying away a number of things, some of them were even quarrelling with themselves perhaps as to who took what. The war had impoverished them a lot and I would not blame them for picking a few things that belonged to the dead or people who were severely incapacitated. Apart from clothing material and military equipment I could not think of any valuable property that could be looted as we had been warned not to carry along with us jewelry or other things of value.

Needless to say that I had little or no sleep throughout the night. The pains and thoughts of the uncertainty of what the morrow had in stock for me would not allow me to sleep. True to their promise my two friends brought food and water the following day at about 11 a.m. I ate a handful of rice and drank almost all the water. The rice was wrapped in leaves and the water was brought in a bamboo container—[a] hollow part of bamboo cane. As soon as my guests left I noticed that thick smoke was coming from the other side of the bush. I later discovered that it was [a] wild fire and thought the end had come because I could not move on my own away from the place if it happened to be engulfed by fire. The midday gentle breeze fanned the flame towards my direction and I was frightened. Although the area was made up of mostly little shrubs the kind people chose to drop me on a spot [having] some tall grass to prevent me from being easily detected. I started saying to myself that I would have preferred death through enemy bullets to being roasted alive. I closed my eyes and prayed to God requesting for His mercies and shortly after there was a mild cloud followed by an equally mild drizzle that reduced the intensity of the inferno and finally extinguished it. Incredible, unbelievable and yet it formed by those who took part in the final battle that the Japanese were fond of shouting "Africa Cha!" as they fled in disorderly retreat. I would not know the English translation of the Japanese word *cha*. Sweet revenge!

The British captain hired two "coolies" who arranged for an improvised stretcher with which I was carried. David Kagbo was, in my estimation, well enough to do the journey although he was still limping. At that point, one Tommy Sherman, another Sierra Leonean member of our unit, joined us from nowhere. I was seeing him for the first time since the day of the attack. He had no wound; he looked fresh and agile. The British captain who had only a Stengun and few rounds of ammunition informed us that he wanted to see whether he could smuggle us across the enemy occupied territory into safety. He was a combatant in full battle order and complete camouflage. In addition to his green battledress, he had his face and hands painted green. What we black soldiers needed was just the green dress as nature had already coloured our body. The white boys had the exposed parts of their body painted green to avoid being easily seen from a distance.

As we kept moving along the edge of a rice field my pains increased and I started screaming not too loudly any way. Jerky movement along an undulating rice field with a fractured femur that was not in any way supported could be extremely painful. After a few metres walk some friendly Indians came to inform us that a large number of Japanese troops were stationed along the direction we were heading for and as a result we decided to take another route. The British captain whose name I did not know was discouraged by that information and subsequently felt that it would not be safe for the group to take me along in that condition. In other words I was being branded a security risk because of my poor physical condition. Looking calm and completely disturbed, he checked his map and the magazine of his Stengun and came to the conclusion that even the ammunition he had would not be sufficient to defend all of us in the event of an attack. He was the only person armed. Others in the batch including my ailing self had not even a pen knife. He therefore, instructed that I should be taken back to the spot at which I was picked up and that David Kagbo should stay with me. Although David Kagbo's wound was not as bad as mine, the officer was in some doubt as to his ability to cross the enemy line safely along with others because there could be moments when one had to run fast or pass through difficult terrain. Probably the British captain also thought that I might die if I were left alone in that condition. Subsequent events proved that he took a sound decision. I certainly could not have survived if I were left alone. At that moment he had a number of problems to contend with: they included our ailing conditions and shortage of ammunition. One of the able-bodied soldiers in the group was not in complete camouflage, he wore a green jacket over a blue pair of shorts and held a white enamel bowl. There was nothing that could be done regarding the pair of pants as that was his only possession as far as clothing was concerned. The officer, however, ordered him to throw away the white dish and he did. A white material could easily be sighted from a fairly long distance.

David Kagbo and I were later informed that Tommy Sherman did not arrive and that nobody knew what happened to him. The probability was that he walked into a Japanese camp or ambush. Perhaps he is still living, who knows for sure? He certainly took a very expensive and wrong decision. David Kagbo and I were not surprised that he deviated from the views of an expert. He was a colleague we knew [only] too well; pleasant, efficient and agile but argumentative to the extreme. It was a pity that we only met briefly in company of the British captain and as such we had no time to exchange experiences. I would have loved to know how he managed to dodge the Japanese bullets. He was looking very well without a scratch on him. The only information he managed to pass on to us was that he tried to get the corpse of one of us, Moigboi Jagha[,] covered with dust a day before we came together under the "leadership" of the British captain. As David Kagbo and I were being led to our hideout I was looking at Tommy Sherman as he went the other direction holding a small parcel the contents of which I would not know. There was no doubt that he had lost all he had either to the ravages of the Japanese soldiers or the Indian looters. I never knew I was seeing him for the last time. Right from the outset the British captain appeared to be a brave and competent military officer. He certainly knew his job. In those days, all the infantry officers were invariably good geographers and they had to be in the interest of their profession.

## QUESTIONS

1. Discuss how Nigerians were recruited for World Wars I and II. How did they react to British recruitment policies?

2. How did the newspaper press support the British during the two world wars?

3. Examine the newspapers' condemnation of racism and prejudices in the colonial army. What kinds of experiences did they complain about?

4. Describe the experiences of market women during WWII. How did they mobilize against the draconian policies of the colonialists?

5. What does Isaac Fadoyebo's wartime memoir reveal about African soldier's battlefield experience?

## FURTHER READINGS

Chuku, Gloria, "'Crack Kernels, Crack Hitler'": Export Production Drive and Igbo Women During the Second World War," in Judith Byfield, LaRay Denzer, and Morrison Anthea, eds., *Gendering the African Diaspora: Women, Culture, and Historical Change in the Caribbean and Nigerian Hinterland* (Bloomington: Indiana University Press, 2010).

Fadoyebo, Isaac. *A Stroke of Unbelievable Luck: A Moving Account of the Experience of a Teen-age Soldier in the Battlefield During the Burma Campaign, 1944*. Madison: African Studies Program, University of Wisconsin Madison, 1999.

Killingray, David, and Richard Rathbone, eds. *Africa and the Second World War*. London: Macmillan, 1986.

Olusanya, G. O. *The Second World War and Politics in Nigeria, 1939–1953*. Lagos: University of Lagos Press, 1973.

Osuntokun, Akinjide. *Nigeria in the First World War*. London: Longman, 1979.

Page, Melvin. *Africa and the First World War*. New York: St. Martin's Press, 1987.

## NOTES

1. See, for example, David Killingray, "'If I Fight for Them, Maybe Then I Can Go Back to the Village'": African Soldiers in the Mediterranean and European Campaigns, 1939–45," in Paul Addison and Angus Calder, eds., *Time to Kill: The Soldier's Experience of War in the West* (London: Picador, 1996); Peter B. Clarke, *West Africans at War, 1914–1918; 1938–1945: Colonial Propaganda and Its Cultural Aftermath* (London: Ethnographica, 1986); James K. Matthews, "World War I and the Rise of African Nationalism: Nigerian Veterans as Catalysts of Change," *Journal of Modern African Studies* 20, no. 3 (1982): 493–502; and Meshack Owino, "'For Your Tomorrow, We Gave Our Today': A History of Kenya African Soldiers in the Second World War" (PhD dissertation, Rice University, 2004).

2. Michael Crowder, "The First World War and Its Consequences," in J.F.A. Ajayi,

ed., *General History of Africa, Vol. 7: Africa Under Colonial Domination* (Berkeley: University of California Press, 1985), p. 282.

3. Sam Ukpabi, *The Origins of the Nigerian Army: A History of the West African Frontier Force, 1897–1914* (Zaria: Gaskiya Corp., 1987).

4. Ibid., pp. 30–32.

5. Ibid., p. 97.

6. James K. Matthews, "Reluctant Allies: Nigerian Responses to Military Recruitment 1914–1918," in Melvin Page, ed., *Africa and the First World War* (New York: St. Martin's Press, 1987), p. 97.

7. Ibid., p. 100.

8. Ibid., p. 107.

9. G. O. Olusanya, "The Role of Ex-Servicemen in Nigerian Politics," *Journal of Modern African Studies* 6, no. 2 (1968): 225.

10. Mokwugo Okoye, *Storms on the Niger: A Story of Nigeria's Struggle* (Nigeria: Fourth Dimension, 1981).

11. See J. S. Coleman, *Nigeria: Background to Nationalism* (Berkeley: University of California Press, 1958).

12. J.F.A Ajayi, *Christian Missions in Nigeria, 1841–1891: The Making of a New Elite* (Evanston, IL: Northwestern University Press, 1965).

13. Akinjide Osuntokun, *Nigeria in the First World War* (London: Longman, 1979), p. 71.

14. "Nigeria's Contribution to the War Fund," *The Nigerian Pioneer*, December 11, 1914.

15. For details on the history of education in Nigeria, see Adewumi Fajana, *Education in Nigeria, 1842–1939: A Historical Analysis* (London: Longman, 1978), and Babatunde Fafunwa, *History of Education in Nigeria* (London: Allen & Unwin, 1974).

16. Tekena Tamuno, *Nigeria and Elective Representation, 1923–1947* (London: Longman, 1966).

17. G. O. Olusanya, *The Second World War and Politics in Nigeria, 1939–1953* (Lagos: University of Lagos Press, 1973), p. 43.

18. Michael Crowder, "The 1939–45 War and the West," in J.F.A. Ajayi and Michael Crowder, eds., *History of West Africa* (New York: Columbia University Press, 1974), p. 609.

19. Olusanya, *The Second World War*, p. 51.

20. Ibid., p. 51.

21. "Young Men, Army Pays You to Learn a Trade," *Daily Service*, December 16, 1942.

22. "Wounded Nigerian Soldier Afna Abadi Gives Account of March Through Arakan Jungle," *West African Pilot*, June 21, 1944.

23. See the following articles in the *Daily Service:* "African Soldier Wins Military Medal & Is Decorated at Special Parade," January 25, 1943; "To-night Victory Dance," April 16, 1943; "School Children Hold Dance Parade to Raise Money for Win-the-War Fund," November 10, 1942; "Entertainment for Our Boys in Khaki," November 10, 1942; and "Eight Army's Brilliant Victory," November 6, 1942.

24. "Hitler Gets the Jitters," *Daily Service*, November 12, 1942.

25. "U.S. Carrier Avoids Bombers," *Daily Service*, May 3, 1943.

26. "Sokoto and the War Efforts," *Daily Service*, March 1, 1943.

27. "Sokoto's £8,783 Will Help Buy Mosquito Bomber," *Daily Service*, April 30 1943.

28. "The Mosquito Bomber," *Daily Service*, May 8, 1943.

29. Samples of newspaper publicity of contribution include "The Oba of Benin's Fund Now £1,000," *Daily Service*, January 29, 1943; "Alake Tours Food Producing Centres and Urges for More Production," *Daily Service*, November 25, 1942; "Ijebu People Make Big Drive to Aid War Efforts," *Daily Service*, December 12, 1942; and "War Effort in the Provinces," *Daily Service*, November 16, 1942.

30. "British Children's Appeal," *West African Pilot*, April 28, 1941.

31. The conditions for commissioning Africans included the following: "(1) he [the soldier] must be a serving soldier (i.e., serving in the ranks), (2) that he must have a good educational standard, (3) that he must be recommended by his Commanding Officer, (4) that he must not be over 25 years of age, (5) that he must be recommended by three reputable persons who knew him before he joined the army, (6) that he be approved by a Board of three senior officers and (7) that he passes through an Officers Cadet Training Unit." See "Africans and Commissions in the Army," *Daily Service*, June 19, 1943.

32. Ibid.

33. Ibid.

34. Three others were commissioned during the following year: Lieutenant J. T. Aguiyi-Ironsi (who would later become Nigeria's first military Head of State and one of the victims of the July 1966 coup), Lieutenant Wellington Bassey, and Lieutenant Johnson Ademulegun. The number of commissioned Nigerian officers had increased to twelve by 1954. See C. N. Ubah, *Colonial Army and Society in Northern Nigeria* (Kaduna: Baraka Press, 1998), pp. 234–235.

35. "Recruiting for Nigeria Regiment," *West African Pilot*, August 1, 1941.

36. "Discrimination in the Army," *Daily Service*, January 13, 1945.

37. A good source of information on this topic is Bessie House-Midamba and Felix K. Ekechi, eds., *African Market Women and Economic Power: The Role of Women in African Economic Development* (Westport, CT: Greenwood Press, 2005).

38. Nina Emma Mba, *Nigerian Women Mobilized: Women's Political Activity in Southern Nigeria* (Berkeley and Los Angeles: University of California Press and Institute

of International Studies, 1982), pp. 199–202.

39. For more on women's economic activities during WWII, see Gloria Chuku, "'Crack Kernels, Crack Hitler': Export Production Drive and Igbo Women During the Second World War," in Judith Byfield, LaRay Denzer, and Morrison Anthea, eds., *Gendering the African Diaspora: Women, Culture, and Historical Change in the Caribbean and Nigerian Hinterland* (Bloomington: Indiana University Press, 2010).

40. See Toyin Falola, "Cassava Starch for Export in Nigeria During the Second World War," *African Economic History* 18 (1989): 73–89; Toyin Falola, "'Salt Is Gold': The Management of Salt Scarcity in Nigeria During World War II," *Canadian Journal of African History* 26, no. 3 (1992): 412–436.

41. Wale Oyemakinde, "The Pullen Marketing Scheme: A Trial in Food Price Control in Nigeria, 1941–1947," *Journal of the Historical Society of Nigeria* 6, no. 4 (June 1973): 413–423.

42. Ayodeji Olukoju, "'Buy British, Sell Foreign': External Trade Control Policies in Nigeria During World War II and Its Aftermath, 1939–1950," *International Journal of African Historical Studies* 35, nos. 2/3 (2002): 363–384.

43. See the following articles in the *Daily Service:* "Black Market" in Local Foodstuffs," January 6, 1943; "Capt. Pullen Admits the Controlled Price of Fowls Leaves No Margin for Profit," August 25, 1944; "The Law Is An Ass," August 29, 1944; "Plebiscite on Pullen Market," August 15, 1945; "Pull Out the Pullen Markets," August 13, 1945; and "The Pullen Market," July 9, 1945.

44. Akure is the administrative headquarters of Ondo Province of Western Nigeria. See Olusanya, *The Second World War,* p. 63.

45. See the following stories in the *Daily Service:* "Three Women Who Profiteered Are Fined 10/, 20/, and 30/ [10, 20, and 30 Shillings] Respectively," December 21, 1942; "Lady Caught at Pullen Rice Stall," January 22, 1944; "Woman Who Profiteered in Gari Is Sentenced to 2 Months," November 21, 1942; "Woman Who Profiteered in Pirate Cigarettes Is Fined £5.10," December 29, 1942.

46. "Imprisonment of Women for Profiteering," *Daily Service,* November 6, 1942.

47. "Letter to the Police," *Daily Service,* December 24, 1942.

48. "Penalties Inflicted for Profiteering," *Daily Service,* December 1, 1942.

49. See "1,000 Market Women and Petty Traders Attend Maiden Meeting of Nigerian Traders Association," *Daily Service,* January 15, 1943, and "Benin Market Women Present Petition to Authorities Against Embargo on Lorries Carrying Foodstuffs," *Daily Service,* November 18, 1942.

50. Olusanya, *The Second World War,* p. 64.

51. Cheryl Johnson, "Female Leadership During the Colonial Period: Madam Alimotu Pelewura and the Lagos Market Women," *Tarikh* 7, no. 1 (1980): 1–10.

52. Mba, *Nigerian Women Mobilized,* p. 228.

53. Ibid., p. 229.

54. "Lagos Women Make Protest Against Payment of Income Tax," *Nigerian Daily Times*, December 18, 1940.

55. National Archives Ibadan, Comcol 1, "Taxation of Women in Lagos," December 18, 1940.

56. Cheryl Johnson, "Grassroots Organizing: Women in Anti-Colonial Activity in Southwestern Nigeria," *African Studies Review* 25 (June–September 1982): 140–141.

57. National Archives Ibadan, Comcol 248/121, "Proceedings of a Meeting of Women Held in the Schoolroom of St. Paul's Church on Breadfruit Street on Monday September 13, 1943."

58. The following excerpt is taken from Isaac Fadoyebo's *A Stroke of Unbelievable Luck: A Moving Account of the Experience of a Teen-age Soldier in the Battlefield During the Burma Campaign, 1944* (Madison: African Studies Program, University of Wisconsin, 1999), pp. 6–13.

# 5

## Pathways to Decolonization

*African Voices of the Fight for Independence, ca. 1880–1994*

Peter Adebayo

### GLOBAL CONTEXT

The purpose of this chapter is to revisit the issue of decolonization—the process of nationalist struggle that caused the European empires to give up their African colonies—from the perspective of Africans. Decolonization, an important theme in African history, has been experienced in different ways in different places. A political process on the surface, but with economic, social, and cultural implications, decolonization has frequently involved violence. In extreme circumstances, wars of independence followed revolutions. More often, there was a dynamic cycle in which negotiations failed and minor disturbances ensued, resulting in suppression by the police and military forces, escalating into more violent revolts that led to further negotiations until independence was granted.[1] European and American authors have often referred to this process as a "transfer of power," whereas African scholars understand it as a long process of struggle, spanning many decades, that which can be roughly divided into the following phases: 1900–1920, 1920–1940, and 1940–1970. During these phases, Africans adopted various strategies of resistance—from rebellions, insurrections, and militancy to peaceful and constitutional means. Consequently, decolonization has come to be known by various names—"the fall of colonialism," "regaining independence and sovereignty by African states," the "liberation movements," "struggle for independence," "nationalists' struggle," and "the anticolonial period in Africa."[2] These terms are discussed where appropriate in the chapter.

### African Decolonization in Global Context

Arguably, the starting point for understanding decolonization on a global scale was World War I, which emphasized the principles of self-determination. During World War I, the European powers implied that their colonial territories would be granted self-determination and democracy after the war. This propaganda was used by European governments—especially Britain and France—to mobilize African soldiers to fight against German forces in British and French colonies. After the war, European powers failed to adhere to this promise and many African soldiers, whose intellectual outlook had expanded during the war, returned home to mobilize forces against colonialism in Africa. Some soldiers, who returned "politicized and radicalized" from the war, formed national associations critical of colonialism, such as the National Congress of British West Africa formed in 1920 by the nationalists in Ghana.[3] However, these were generally small groups oriented toward the needs of an emerging middle class of formally educated men. In the same period, radical parties such as al-Wafd al Misri in Egypt and the Destour Party in Tunusia were formed to agitate for independence.

Two decades later, during World War II (1939–1945), African soldiers in India and other Asian countries such as Burma widened the political horizon of the soldiers who similarly returned home to mobilize the masses for the liquidation of colonialism. Again, European powers used the propagandistic message that they were fighting for democracy and self-determination to mobilize support for the Allied forces in African and Asian colonies, along with promises and implications that the colonies would be granted self-rule after the war. The principle that all people have the right to self-determination was espoused by British Prime Minister Winston Churchill and US President Franklin D. Roosevelt in the third part of their eight-point agenda in the Atlantic Charter of August 14, 1941, and, again, in the United Nations Charter signed in 1945.

Newly formed local political parties that focused on attaining independence and enjoyed widespread grassroots support after World War II probably had the greatest impact in accelerating the decolonization process. This was true in Asia, the Caribbean, and also in Africa, where the period 1945–1950 witnessed the growth of the first organized and widespread political parties outside of Egypt. Founded in almost every corner of the continent, these parties differed dramatically from one another. What they had in common, however, was the ability to appeal to large groups of people and the objective of expelling the overseas empires and their colonial apparatus. This commonality bound together, for example, the Mouvement pour le Triomphe des Libertés Démocratiques (MTLD) in Algeria, the Ashiqq (Brothers) and Umma (Nation) Parties in the Sudan, the Rassemblement Démocratique Africain (RDA) throughout French West and Equatorial Africa, the Kenyan African Union (KAU) in Kenya, and the Mouvement pour L'Évolution Sociale de l' Afrique Noire (MESAN) in Central African Republic.

The emergence of the United States and the Union of Soviet Socialist Republics (USSR) as superpowers and their cold war dispute also contributed to the pace of decolonization. The two superpowers generally supported ending colonial rule and wooed emergent nations through economic aid, technical expertise, and military assistance; especially persuasive was the series of aid programs offered to African nationalist forces struggling for independence. US public opinion in support of nationalist movements helped to undermine the British and French will to rule in much of Africa. Angola, Mozambique, and Guinea-Bissau received military and financial aid from the Soviet Union while struggling to overthrow Portuguese colonial rule in the 1970s, and the United Nations promoted self-determination for colonized peoples by acting as a forum for peaceful resolution of independence struggles. The United Nations Charter explicitly supported the principle of international accountability in Articles 73 and 74, and UN practices aided the decolonization process in Africa.[4] These external factors, combined with the formation of grassroots political parties, marked a significant turning point in the history of Africa's decolonization.

*Precedents and Cross-Currents*

In order to understand Africa's decolonization process, we will find it helpful to look briefly at earlier and contemporaneous liberation movements in North America, Latin America, Europe, the Middle East, and Asia. Consider, for example, the struggle for American independence in the 1770s, which was due less to social tensions within the thirteen British North American colonies than to a rather sudden and unexpected effort by the British government to tighten its control over the colonies and to extract more revenue in the form of taxes.[5] The impact of America's revolutionary war of independence was felt in both France and Latin America. In France, thousands of soldiers who assisted American colonists returned home full of enthusiasm for awakening the consciousness of the masses, helping to spur the French Revolution of 1789. The echoes of both the American and the French revolutions reverberated loudly in the French Caribbean colony of Saint Domingue, later renamed Haiti.[6] There, slaves led by the astute former slave Toussaint Louverture, held a massive revolt beginning in 1791, eventually overcoming internal resistance, outmaneuvering foreign powers, and defeating French forces. Haiti's independence was declared on January 1, 1804. This revolution would later embolden nationalist activities in Africa.

In Spain's Latin American colonies, revolutions in the early nineteenth century were shaped by preceding events in North America, France, and Haiti as well as by their own distinctive societies and historical experiences. Native-born elites in the Spanish colonies (known as creoles) opposed the Spanish monarchy's efforts to exercise greater power over its colonies and to subject them to heavier taxes and tariffs. Creole intellectuals were familiar with the concepts of popular sovereignty, republican government, and personal liberty derived from the European philosophers and the Enlightenment. This revolutionary thought was facilitated by the upheavals in Europe that developed from Napoleon Bonaparte's invasion of Spain and Portugal. One major result was the decolonization of continental Latin America and parts of the Caribbean.

However, while twentieth-century African anticolonial leaders sometimes referred to the Enlightenment ideals offered by Latin American and US revolutionaries and certainly saw the Haitian Revolution as an inspiration, the example of Asian states that managed to liberate themselves in the twentieth century was of more immediate relevance. In Asia, the independence of India in 1947 was especially inspirational. This decolonization was characterized by the nonviolent Indian independence movement led by Mohandas Gandhi, which was later imitated by emergent African Leaders such as Kwame Nkrumah of Ghana and Chief Obafemi Awolowo of Nigeria. Other African anticolonial leaders were inspired by the armed resistance of Asian anticolonial forces such as the Viet Minh in Vietnam to resist colonialism with force.

Equally significant for African anticolonial leaders was their connection to black Americans and other Africans of the diaspora. By the 1920s, W.E.B. Du Bois and Marcus Garvey urged African Americans to fight against oppression and racial discrimination in the United States. Both of these intellectuals were also greatly concerned about the suffering of Africans under colonialism. Garvey, in particular, taught his fellow African Americans to be proud of their skin color and preached in favor of the large-scale return of African Americans to Africa and the freedom of Africa from colonialism. Garvey prophesied that Africa's redemption was "coming like a storm."[7] His brand of black nationalism had three components: unity, pride in African cultural heritage, and complete autonomy. Garvey believed that people of African descent could establish a great independent nation in their ancient homeland of Africa. Meanwhile, Du Bois tried to bring black leaders in the United States of America, the West Indies, and Africa together so that they could cooperate toward the liberation of black people everywhere. Under his influence, five Pan-African Congresses were held between 1919 and 1945.[8] At the 1945 Pan-African Congress, delegates declared that "[i]f the western world is still determined to rule mankind by force, then Africans, as a last resort, may have to appeal to force in the effort to achieve freedom, even if force destroys them and the world." A resolution from the conference called on "the colonial workers, farmers and intellectuals to unite and form societies to fight against imperialist exploitation and for independence using such methods as strikes, boycotts, positive actions and other non-violent strategies."[9]

Future African leaders—notably, Nnamdi Azikwe of Nigeria and Kwame Nkumah of Ghana, both of whom studied in America in the 1920s—were influenced by the black nationalism of both Garvey and Du Bois. Garvey's ideas, in particular, affected their outlook and helped bring global awareness to the movement. Young Africans studying abroad joined organizations such as the West African Students' Union (WASU), which was founded in London in 1925 by Ladipo Solanke, a Nigerian student. The WASU, through its social and political activities, attracted numerous West African students in Britain.

## The Attitudes of the Colonizers

The process of decolonization was also influenced by the policies and attitudes of each of the great global empires. For instance, Africans in the British colonies were allowed more freedom of expression and association than those in the Portuguese or Belgian colonies. Consequently, liberation struggles in the British colonies were generally peaceful and constitutional, whereas the Portuguese colonies fought protracted liberation wars. In colonies with many European settlers, a military fight was ultimately necessary for independence, even those in British hands (e.g., Kenya) or under French control (e.g., Algeria).

However, the struggles in British colonies were fundamentally different from those in the French colonies. In the 1950s, the British realized that the rebellious colonies were becoming a financial and geopolitical burden, largely due to the efforts of anticolonial protestors, whereas the French believed that they had to reassert their national prestige by maintaining control of their colonies. This difference in attitude was exacerbated by the disparity between the two empires' governing systems. In the British system the governor of each colony (advised by his legislative and executive councils) was in charge, with only general guidelines from London. By contrast, the French system endeavored to evolve a common "philosophy" of administration for all colonies, and colonial affairs were managed more directly from Paris.[10] Accordingly, the nationalist leaders of the British West African colonies concentrated their efforts on influencing their local colonial administrations whereas those of the French colonies focused more on influencing Paris directly. This may explain why French colonial Africa's experience of decolonization was so different from that of British colonial Africa. In short, France's decolonization was bloody and bitter whereas Britain's was relatively peaceful, if not painless.

The other colonial powers, Portugal and Belgium, pursued their own colonial policies. Portuguese leaders perceived their colonies (Angola, Mozambique, Guinea, and the Cape Verde islands Sao Tome and Principe) as appendages of the metropole, spending half of the country's annual budget to maintain military control of these colonies and using them as a means of securing employment for its citizens, who were encouraged to migrate to Africa to help solve Portugal's economic problems. Belgium, on the other hand, adopted a highly centralized policy for its colonial territories. The Congo was divided into five provinces; each had a governor and they were headed overall by a governor-general. The Belgian system of rule rested on a triple alliance of the state, the church, and big corporations. Local representation was considered to be unnecessary. The object of Belgian colonial policy was to create a prosperous black working class that would be content with prosperity instead of votes. The Belgian *Charter Coloniale* omitted freedom of association and freedom of the press as essential rights. Indeed, the Belgian colonial administration wished to remove the Congo from "politics" altogether and, toward this end, formed two related policies that aimed at removing the Congo from nationalist movements in the rest of Africa and at preventing the growth of a landed European class impatient with home control.

## AFRICAN EXPERIENCES

The continent-wide process of African decolonization can be roughly divided into three phases: 1900s–1920s, 1920s–1940s, and 1940s–1970s.

### First Phase (1900s–1920s): The Gradual Development of the Liberation Struggle

With the exception of Liberia and Ethiopia, the entirety of the African continent was colonized between the 1870s and 1910s. During this period,

Africans engaged in rural armed uprisings and other types of struggles against colonialism. They found it difficult to tolerate the restrictive and often inexplicable ways in which their lives were being reordered. The main objective of the anticolonial movement during this period was to either regain lost sovereignty by expelling the colonial administration or to press for reforms of the colonial system. Strategies included passive resistance as well as campaigns by secret associations, unions, political parties, and the new African-controlled Ethiopian and Pentecostal churches that had begun to emerge. Numerous rebellions also broke out, usually originating in rural areas rather than urban centers and often under the leadership of traditional rulers and priests. These rebellions were usually precipitated by measures introduced by the new colonial order such as taxation, alienation of land, compulsory cultivation of crops, colonial officials' tyrannical behavior, introduction of European culture in the form of Western education and Christianity, and condemnation of African culture and traditional ways of life. One rebellion in West Africa that focused on defending the old order was the Yaa Asantewaa war in 1900, which involved the Asante of Ghana. Other rebellions—such as the Egba revolt of 1903, the Gurunsi rebellion in 1915 in Upper Volta (now Burkina Faso), and the Hut Tax war in Sierra Leone in 1898—were largely uprisings against taxation and forced labor.[11] In the same period more than twenty-five organized rebellions occurred in the five central African colonies of Angola, Mozambique, Nyasaland (Malawi), Northern Rhodesia (Zambia), and the Congo as well as in southern Africa. An interesting aspect of these rebellions in the southern and central African regions was the involvement of cult priests and spirit mediums. The rebellion in Nyasaland in 1908, for example, was led by the Tonga priest Maluma, who urged "black people to rise and drive all the white people out of the country." Similarly, Mbona cult priests spearheaded the Massinga rebellion of 1884, and the priestess Maria Nkoie played a leading role in the rebellion in the Congo that lasted from 1916 to 1921.[12]

In East Africa, the largest uprising of this period was the Maji-Maji rebellion, which broke out in Tanganyika (now Tanzania) with the sole aim of driving out the Germans. Led by the traditional prophet Kinjikitiele, it covered an area of more than ten thousand square miles and involved more than twenty ethnic groups. The revolt started when the Germans levied new taxes in 1898 and forced locals to build roads and accomplish various other tasks for the government. Four years later, in 1902, the governor of Tanganyika ordered all of the villages of the colony to grow cotton as a cash crop; each was charged with producing a common plot of cotton. The African headmen of these villages were left in charge of overseeing production—a position that left them vulnerable to angry criticism from the population. This decision to force cotton growing on rural peasants, who had their own livings to make, was extremely unpopular across Tanzania and took a toll on their lives. Indeed, the social fabric of society was undergoing rapid change. The roles of men and women were altered to face the needs of the communities. Since men were forced away from their homes to work, women had to assume some of the traditional male roles; as a result, the resources of the village were strained and people were less able to remain self-sufficient. These outcomes created a great deal of animosity against the government. In 1905, a drought threatened the region. This, combined with opposition to the government's agricultural and labor policies, led to an open rebellion against the Germans that lasted from 1905 to 1907.

In places where colonial policies were particularly oppressive, such as the Belgian Congo, country-wide revolts frequently broke out. The biggest of these were the uprisings among the Azande (1892–1912), the Bakaya (1825–1906), the Kasango Nyembo (1907–1917), the Bashi (1900–1916), and the Babua and Budja (1903–1905). Similar revolts occurred in many other parts of Africa. Some of these revolts were carried out jointly by neighboring peoples who had little or nothing to do with each other before the advent of colonial rule. In eastern and central Africa, for instance, the Ndbele and Shona of Rhodesia (Zimbabwe), who had once been antagonistic toward each other, revolted together against the British in 1896–1897. And the Maji-Maji revolt against German rule in 1907 was the result of cooperation among many groups in southeastern Tanzania. Essentially rural movements, such revolts occurred at a time when the colonial powers were firmly establishing their control. In most cases they were easily suppressed by the colonial powers.

Religious insurrections were also common during the early years of colonial rule. In parts of Africa where Christianity had made a considerable impact, people sought liberation through such insurrections. In 1911 Charles Domingo founded an independent church in Malawi and used his pulpit to criticize colonialism. With rousing sermons he attacked Christian missions and Europeans, pointing out the contrast between their theories and their practices. One of his leaflets, published in 1911, employed the semi-pidgin English common during this period to express his disdain for European hypocrisy. Although such language may seem comical to us today, the sentiment was deadly serious:

> There is too much failure among all Europeans in Nyasaland. The combined bodies—missionaries, Government and Companies organizers of money—do form the same rule to look down upon the native with mockery eyes. It is sometimes startles us to see that the three combined are from Europe and along with them there is little Christiandom. . . . If we had power enough to communicate ourselves to Europe we would advise them not to call themselves Christiandon but Europeandom. Therefore the life of the combined bodies is altogether too cheaty, too thefty, too mockery. Instead of "give," they say take away. There is too much breakage of God's pure law as seen in James's Epistle, Chapter Five, verse four.[13]

In many African communities, separatist Christian churches arose under the leadership of native "messiahs" who declared that they had been sent to liberate the people. Their preachings sparked revolts against the colonial regime. Among many such uprisings, the two best-known ones were led in 1915 by John Chilembwe in Malawi (then Nyasaland) and in 1921 by Simon Kimbangu in the Belgian Congo. In some instances (e.g., Kimbanguism in the Congo), the political influences of these messianic movements persisted for many decades.[14]

### Second Phase (1920s—1940s): The Formation of Liberation Movements

The second phase in the struggle for independence, which commenced in the 1920s, was characterized by the influence of communism, the negritude movement, and the emergence of liberation movements. After the October

Revolution of 1917, the communists under V. I. Lenin came to power in Russia and the new Soviet Union government quickly began to operate internationally. In Africa, the Soviet government provided not only money but also training in political organization to African anticolonial leaders. Sierra Leonean Wallace Johnson and Jomo Kenyatta of Kenya had training in Moscow and were influenced by communist and socialist ideologies. So, too, were Kwame Nkrumah of Ghana, Amilcar Cabral of Guinea Bissau, and Agostinho Neto of Angola.

The emerging anticolonial movements in French West Africa were boosted during this era by the development of the consciousness of African identity known as the concept of negritude. Largely an intellectual and literary movement, negritude had its origins among Francophone Africa and Caribbean students living and studying in Paris in the 1930s. Here young scholars such as Leopold Senghor (who later became the first president of Senegal) and Leon Damas began to develop a philosophy of "blackness," which stressed the shared culture of all those of African descent.[15] Its inspiration was *Légitime Défense*, a literary journal started by French-speaking West Indians. This movement developed the idea of negritude, which became identified with the journal *Présence Africaine*. Its great theorists were the Martiniquan poets Étienne Léro and Aimé Césaire. Negritude reflected the special conditions of French-speaking Africans in the world of the French. Unlike the British and the Belgians, the French believed in a colonial policy of cultural assimilation, sometimes mockingly described as turning Africans into "black Frenchmen"—a policy that included only a small elite. Eventually, many in this group began to feel smothered by the alien clothes and ideas forced on them, and stripped away their French cultural wrappings in order to discover their own true black skins. This intellectual revolt against enforced assimilation and the "search for the roots of African origin" is the essence of negritude.

The anticolonial movements of this period generally did not move to end colonialism decisively but, rather, called for reform in particular policies. They adopted diverse strategies against colonialism but also continued to use religious movements (as they had done during the first phase) as a way of expressing colonial protests. Even in cases where particular protests appeared to have immediate objectives—such as revolts against taxation, demands for increased employment of Africans, and demands for the return of lands seized by settlers—their underlying motive was the rejection of foreign domination (as we shall see below). Thus, although the pace of progress varied from colony to colony, the many separate local battles of this period should be seen as part of the main struggle for independence.

In North Africa, however, a few radical political parties formed that agitated for full and rapid moves toward independence. These parties were led by charismatic personalities such as the Sudanese radical nationalist Ali Abd al-Latif, who campaigned for liberation from the "slavery of the colonial power" and organized demonstrations and riots in the major towns. In 1924 the Sudanese military staged an unsuccessful revolt against British colonialism, and in 1920 a radical nationalist organization called the Destour party was formed in Tunisia. However, these groups would have to wait many years before their goals were accomplished.

Egypt was the only real exception to the general trend; indeed, it was the only country in which major nationalist progress was made during the 1920s. Egypt enjoyed two advantages: first, British occupation of Egypt was balanced by the continued authority of the Egyptian king and, second, before the British occupation, the Egypt government had begun to educate a new class of leaders in European-style schools. By the beginning of the twentieth century, the country had produced many such leaders and its nationalist movement was therefore very strong. Consequently, in 1922, Britain was compelled to grant independence of a limited sort to Egypt.[16]

### Third Phase (1940s–1970s): The Independence Struggle

For most African countries, the late 1940s marked the beginning of the third and culminating stage of the liberation struggle. Anticolonial feelings that had developed in the previous decades became more intense during World War II.[17] Major nationalist leaders such as Kwame Nkrumah, Jomo Kenyatta, and Nnamdi Azikiwe were politicized by the Italian invasion of Ethiopia in 1935, for example. After independence was attained, the emperor of Ethiopia put his country at the forefront of the unity movements by inviting African nationalists to a meeting that led to the formation of the Organization of African Unity.

These three leaders—Nkrumah, Kenyatta, and Azikiwe—deserve special attention. Kwame Nkrumah (1909–1972) was born in the British Gold Coast Colony, which would later become Ghana. He was trained in both the United States and the United Kingdom, and then returned to take an active part in politics. During the colonial era of agitation for independence, Nkrumah broke away from the politically moderate United Gold Coast Convention (UGCC), which called for a gradual evolution of British policy toward decolonization, and in 1949 formed the Convention People's Party (CPP), whose motto was "Self-Government Now." The CPP's Positive Action campaign quickly gained the support of rural and working-class people. Soon, however, Nkrumah and other party leaders were imprisoned by British authorities for organizing boycotts, strikes, and other forms of civil disobedience. In 1951, however, the British allowed a general election. The recently released Nkrumah won, becoming the "Leader of the Government Business" and, later, prime minister. In 1954, the country became virtually self-governing. After further negotiations with Britain, on 6 March 1957 at 12 a.m. Nkrumah declared Ghana "free forever."

Jomo Kenyatta, also known as Kamau wa Ngengi (1894–1978), was born to the family of Ngengi wa Muigai and Wambui in the village of Gatundu in British East Africa (now Kenya). Kenyatta was a member of the Kikuyi people. He entered politics after taking an interest in the political activities of James Beauttah, the leader of the Kikuyu Central Association (KCA). Kenyatta joined the KCA in 1924 and rose up the ranks; he also studied in London and Moscow.[18] Soon after the rebellion against British rule began in 1951, Kenyatta was arrested and indicted with five others on the charges of "managing and being a member" of the Mau Mau—a blanket label applied by the British to a group of radical anticolonial movements including the armed Land Freedom Party. He remained in prison until 1959, after which he was detained in a prison camp in a remote part of Kenya. He was still there when, following an extended military campaign, the state of emergency was lifted on January 12, 1960. The rebels suffered heavy losses but were ultimately successful in forcing the British to the bargaining table. In 1961 and

1962, Kenyatta led the Kenya African National Union (KANU) in negotiations as well as in the subsequent election, winning 83 seats out of 124. On June 1, 1963, Kenyatta became prime minister of the autonomous Kenyan government.

Benjamin Nnamdi Azikiwe (1904–1996), usually referred to as Nnamdi Azikiwe and popularly known as "Zik," was one of the leading figures of modern Nigeria nationalism and the first president of Nigeria in 1960.[19] A journalist, Azikiwe co-founded the National Council of Nigeria and the Cameroons (NCNC) alongside Herbert Macaulay in 1944. He became the secretary-general of the National Council in 1946 and was elected to the Legislative Council of Nigeria the following year. He went on to serve in the provincial parliaments allowed by Britain after World War II. In 1951, he became the leader of the opposition to the government of Obafemi Awolowo in the Western Region's House of Assembly. In 1952 he moved to the Eastern Region and was elected to the position of chief minister, and in 1954 he became premier of Nigeria's Eastern Region. On November 16, 1960, he became the governor general and on the same day became the first Nigerian named to the Privy Council of the United Kingdom. Following the proclamation of a republic in Nigeria in 1963, he became the first president. At the same time, Abubakar Tafawa Balewa was chosen as Nigeria's first prime minister.

These men and others like them took leadership positions and led their countries to freedom, partly through their own skills and partly owing to the new global situation after 1945. They found fertile ground for their ideas in the post–World War II period. The war not only produced a politicized class of veterans and galvanized the masses, it also discredited the racist ideologies that were used to justify European rule. In addition, it left the colonial powers exhausted economically and infrastructurally. Ever more reliant on the economies of the colonies, the imperial powers had to give in to the pressures of nationalists across Africa. The new nationalist leaders were emboldened by support from the United States and the Soviet Union—especially the 1945 press statement from Soviet foreign minister V. M. Molotov, who said: "We must first of all see to it that the dependent territories are enabled as soon as possible to take the path of national independence."[20]

Soviet attacks on colonialism placed the Soviet Union at the head of the radical anticolonial Afro-Asian group of states at the United Nations, forcing the British and the French to grant concessions to the anticolonial forces in order not to alienate the Afro-Asian states. Together with the rise of the United Nations and the Pan-African Congress of 1945, these external influences helped to solidify the strength of nationalist movements in Africa.[21] However, the strongest factor in the vigorous upsurge of nationalism after World War II was the intensification of feelings of anger, frustration, and disappointment over the inadequate political, social, and economic measures introduced by the colonial powers. Partly in response to criticisms and demands of the African nations during and immediately after the war, and partly to promote their own economic recovery, the colonial powers introduced a number of social, economic, and political changes. However, these reforms were too weak and too oriented toward economic investment from Europe to be satisfactory to the nationalists.

Anticolonial sentiment during this period was advanced through a proliferating number of African political parties, which, with broad popular support, focused on attaining rapid independence for their respective countries (although these parties were not allowed in Portuguese and Belgian colonies until 1954 and 1956, respectively).[22] In contrast to the parties and associations of the 1920s and '30s, which were generally made up of elites and mainly agitated for reform of the colonial system, these independent parties were grassroots oriented and more focused on the objective of attaining independence.

These changes were more significant to the success of the decolonization process in Africa than was the global context. This point was emphasized by historian A. Adu Boahen, perhaps the most important African scholar of decolonization to date:

> It is to Africans themselves and not to the colonial powers, the United Nations or any other powers that the initiative for and the accomplishment of the overthrow of colonialism should be attributed. In other words, the colonial powers did not voluntarily, smoothly or ingeniously hand over sovereignty and independence to Africans and scuttle out. With the sole exception

of Belgium, all the others were kicked out of Africa, politically though unfortunately not yet economically or even culturally, after protracted struggles that were sometimes peaceful and constitutional but often violent and bloody.[23]

## AFRICAN PERSPECTIVES ON DECOLONIZATION

### Decolonization in British and French West Africa

Ghana, formerly the British Gold Coast Colony, was the first colony in sub-Saharan Africa to attain independence, and managed to do so with minimal violence. Kwame Nkrumah was the main architect of the independence movement here. Between 1947 and 1957 he instituted the Positive Action Campaign, expanding the United Gold Coast Convention (UGCC) to more than five hundred local offices throughout the colony, all of which were capable of mounting local protests. However, the UGCC leadership did not support his strategy of mounting growing numbers of mass protests. Thus Nkrumah left the UGCC to form his own progressive political party, the Convention People's Party. The more aggressive strategy of this party was reflected in its motto (which, as noted earlier, was "Self-Government Now"), and on July 10, 1953, Kwame Nkrumah called for constitutional reform that would bring independence to Ghana. The CPP also took on a "pan-Africanist" vision that called for union or alliance with nationalist movements in other colonies. Following is Nkrumah's view on this issue:

> For centuries, Europeans dominated the African continent. The white man arrogated to himself the right to rule and to be obeyed by the non-white; his mission, he claimed, was to "civilise" Africa. Under this cloak, the Europeans robbed the continent of vast riches and inflicted unimaginable suffering on the African people. All this makes a sad story, but now we must be prepared to bury the past with its unpleasant memories and look to the future. All we ask of the former colonial powers is their goodwill and cooperation to remedy past mistakes and injustices and to grant independence to the colonies in Africa. . . . It is clear that we must find an African solution

to our problems, and that this can only be found in African unity. Divided we are weak; united, Africa could become one of the greatest forces for good in the world. Although most Africans are poor, our continent is potentially extremely rich. Our mineral resources, which are being exploited with foreign capital only to enrich foreign investors, range from gold and diamonds to uranium and petroleum. Our forests contain some of the finest woods to be grown anywhere. Our cash crops include cocoa, coffee, rubber, tobacco and cotton. As for power, which is an important factor in any economic development, Africa contains over 40% of the potential water power of the world, as compared with about 10% in Europe and 13% in North America. Yet so far, less than 1% has been developed. This is one of the reasons why we have in Africa the paradox of poverty in the midst of plenty, and scarcity in the midst of abundance.

Never before have a people had within their grasp so great an opportunity for developing a continent endowed with so much wealth. Individually, the independent states of Africa, some of them potentially rich, others poor, can do little for their people. Together, by mutual help, they can achieve much. But the economic development of the continent must be planned and pursued as a whole. A loose confederation designed only for economic co-operation would not provide the necessary unity of purpose. Only a strong political union can bring about full and effective development of our natural resources for the benefit of our people.

The political situation in Africa today is heartening and at the same time disturbing. It is heartening to see so many new flags hoisted in place of the old; it is disturbing to see so many countries of varying sizes and at different levels of development, weak and, in some cases, almost helpless. If this terrible state of fragmentation is allowed to continue it may well be disastrous for us all. There are at present some 28 states in Africa, excluding the Union of South Africa, and those countries not yet free. No less than nine of these states have a population of less than three million. Can we seriously believe that the colonial powers meant these countries to be independent, viable states? The example of South America, which has as much wealth, if not more than North America, and yet remains weak and dependent on outside interests, is one which every African would do well to study. Critics of African unity often refer to the wide differences in culture, language and ideas in various parts of Africa. This is true, but the essential fact remains that we are all Africans, and have a common interest in the independence of Africa. The difficulties presented by questions of language, culture and different political systems are not insuperable. If the need for political union is agreed by us all, then the will to create it is born; and where there's a will there's a way.[24]

Ghana became independent under Nkrumah only four years later, on March 6, 1957. This event had the effect of a revolutionary tonic, propelling other African leaders and nationalist movements to struggle for the attainment of independence. Some of its impact was psychological, as reflected in the statement of the great intellectual Frantz Fanon, who wrote that "the independence of a new territory, the liberation of the new people are felt by the other oppressed countries as an invitation, an encouragement and a promise."[25] Ghana also quickly gave material and organizational aid to other African independence movements. In 1958, Nkrumah organized an important meeting that brought together leaders from twenty-eight states to share ideas and strategies. The All African Peoples' Conference (AAPC) commenced on December 5, 1958, and lasted for eight days. The majority of these countries were not independent and were thus represented by heads of anticolonial political parties, movements, and trade unions. The chairman of the conference, Tom Mboya, a dynamic young labor union official from Kenya, opened the meeting by saying that "the problem is not to know if we want independence, but how to get it."[26]

The process of decolonization in other Anglophone African colonies was in some cases similar to that in Ghana. For instance, Nigeria's independence was also achieved without violence. In fact, it might have occurred even earlier than Ghana's if not for the fact that the three main political parties—the Nigerian National Council of Nigeria and the Cameroons (NCNC) headed by Nnamidi Azikiwe, the Action Group (AC) headed by Chief Obafemi Awolowo, and the Northern People's Congress (NPC) headed by Sardaruna of Sokoto—found it difficult to work in solidarity with one another.[27]

In French-held West Africa, decolonization was much slower—owing in part to French policy and in part to the strategy implemented by French-speaking African leaders concerned by the lack of resources and educated personnel in French West Africa. With administrative services still largely manned by France, most nationalist leaders in French West Africa—who were heavily dependent on French aid—realized that immediate independence without France's good will would be economically and politically difficult despite all its emotional attractions.[28] Just one year after Ghanaian independence, however, Sékou Touré, the leader of mineral-rich Guinea Africa, broke with this belief by telling French Prime Minister General Charles de Gaulle: "We prefer liberty with poverty to slavery with wealth."

Touré was inspired partly by revolutionary struggles for independence in French North African colonies such as Algeria, where the members of the Armée Nationale de Libération (ANL) were fighting the French forces. Touré would lead his country, Guinea, to become the first independent former French colony in sub-Saharan Africa in 1959, followed closely by much of French West and Equatorial Africa in 1960.

*Violent Struggles for Independence in Settler Colonies*

West Africa generally had few European settlers, so the nationalists there had a somewhat easier pathway to independence. French Algeria, by contrast, presents a classic case of independence achieved against the wishes of European settlers and thus pursued through violence. Large numbers of French and other European immigrants had settled in the country as early as the nineteenth century, and they generally refused to countenance independence under African leadership. First formed in 1954, the Algerian Front de Libération Nationale (FLN) issued a series of demands based on immediate independence:

> MEANS OF STRUGGLE: Struggle by every means until our goal is attained. Exertion at home and abroad through political and direct action, with a view to making the Algerian problem a reality for the entire world. The struggle will be long, but the outcome is certain. To limit the bloodshed, we propose an honourable platform for discussion with the French authorities:
>
> 1. The opening of negotiations with the authorized spokesmen the Algerian people, on the basis of a recognition of Algerian sovereignty, one and indivisible.

2. The inception of an atmosphere of confidence brought about [by] freeing all those who are detained, by annulling all measures [without] exception, and by ending all legal action against the combatant forces.

3. The recognition of Algerian nationhood by an official declaration abrogating all edicts, decrees, and laws by virtue of which Algeria was "French soil."

In return for which:

1. French cultural and economic interests will be respected, as well as persons and families.

2. All French citizens desiring to remain in Algeria will be allowed to opt for their original nationality, in which case they will be considered as foreigners, or for Algerian nationality, in which case they will be considered as Algerians, equal both as to rights and as to duties.

3. The ties between France and Algeria will be the object of agreement between the two Powers on the basis of equality and mutual respect.[29]

The French government, supported by the settler population, felt that it had the strength to resist these demands. Accordingly, the FLN's leaders decided that military action was the only way to remove the French and pursued a war for independence. In addition to and simultaneous with armed rebellion, they pursued a strategy of international diplomacy. In 1957, the Algerian independence issue was brought before the UN, putting a great deal of pressure on France. Although these strategies failed to rapidly achieve their objectives, after eight years of intensive fighting the French were forced to grant independence to Algeria in July 1962.[30]

Armed struggle similarly occurred in the British colony of Kenya. Here, the inability of the reformist and anticolonial associations formed in the 1920s and '30s to negotiate with the European settlers led to the formation of a more active and powerful secret society called the Land and Freedom Party, also known as "the Mau Mau." The Mau Mau organized a massive rebellion that erupted throughout the country in 1952 and was suppressed only in 1960. The Land and Freedom Party members' struggle forced the British to grant independence to Kenya on December 12, 1963.[31]

The Portuguese colonies of Africa also contained significant numbers of settlers and were liberated only through prolonged armed struggle. Liberation wars against Portugal began in Angola 1961, but the fragmenting of the anticolonialists into several groups slowed the path to independence here and in Mozambique. Still, by the 1970s Portugal was fighting three separate wars in Africa. The cost in manpower and money was so high that the Portuguese people overthrew their government in a coup in 1974, and the new government recognized the right of its African subjects to self-governance.[32]

Two other settler colonies—British Rhodesia and South Africa—present striking situations in which nationalist struggles were directed against the settlers who took a harder line for continued colonial rule than the British government itself. In Southern Rhodesia (modern Zimbabwe), one of the major issues was land, inasmuch as the settlers had appropriated much of the arable territory of the country in the early twentieth century. Prior to 1965, African resistance in this colony was largely nonviolent and directed at public opinion in Britain, which was shifting toward support of independence. However, in 1965, when Britain appeared to be giving in to the anticolonial forces, the Rhodesian settler government of Ian Smith issued the Unilateral Declaration of Independence (UDI), which declared Southern Rhodesia free from British white-only rule. Soon after, the national liberation war turned into a guerrilla conflict waged by two associated groups, the Zimbabwe African National Union (ZANU) and the Zimbabwe African People's Union (ZAPU). The conflict lasted more than a decade. Coupled with international sanctions on the white minority regime as well as support for rebels from other African countries such as Nigeria, this conflict eventually brought the white minority regime to its knees. Zimbabwe became a multiracial democracy in 1980, with ZANU leader Robert Mugabe as the first prime minister.

In South Africa as well, nationalist struggle was directed against a white minority regime that was technically independent of Great Britain. Under this regime, the country's black African majority had no political rights whatsoever within the central state. Black South Africans' struggle was therefore directed against this internal opponent rather against a distant imperial authority. The African resistance against the white minority had initially been characterized by peaceful and moderate protests in the 1920s and '30s. These protests, which were organized by the African National Congress (ANC) and other African organizations, primarily targeted two laws—namely, the Representation of Natives Act, which took the right to vote from the few previously eligible black voters in South Africa, and the Native Trust Land Bill, which deprived black Africans of their right to buy land outside the African reserves.[33]

As in other territories, World War II stimulated African resistance in South Africa and led to the formation of the ANC Youth League by university graduates, students, and educated workers. The most prominent leaders of the Youth League were African university graduates such as Nelson Mandela and Oliver Tambo and educated workers such as Walter Sisulu and Anton Lembede. Using the motto "'Africa's Cause Must Triumph," these young men and women criticized the ANC's traditional moderate methods of peaceful protest. As white minority rule became ever more racist and discriminatory, especially with the passing of the segregationist apartheid laws in 1948, they advocated direct mass action.

In 1949, the ANC reacted to these apartheid policies by adopting a program of action that called for the use of boycotts, strikes, civil disobedience, and noncooperation. Massive demonstrations by Africans as well as the Indian and mixed-race Coloured community shook the country during 1950. These groups formed a joint Planning Council to coordinate their efforts. Two years later they launched the famous Defiance Campaign of 1952, through which they defied a number of apartheid laws. Riots broke out in many cities, and 8,500 volunteers were arrested and imprisoned for deliberate acts of civil disobedience.[34] These activities undoubtedly strengthened the popularity of the ANC among Africans, who were also encouraged by developments in other African countries where nationalist forces were gradually driving out colonialism. However, the question of whether or not to move to militant tactics caused a split in 1958 between the ANC and the militant Pan African Congress (PAC).[35] On March 21, 1960, an unarmed crowd protesting against being forced to carry pass cards was shot at in Sharpeville. Sixty-nine of the demonstrators were killed and 178 wounded. Both the ANC and the PAC denounced the Sharpeville massacre; the government followed up with police raids, leading to the arrest of many leaders of both the ANC and the PAC. Eventually, the government banned both parties as threats to the peace.

Following the ban, both organizations went underground. Under Nelson Mandela, the ANC formed a militant wing, Umkonto we Sizwe (Spear of the Nation), to train guerrillas for the eventual war against the white minority regime.[36] In 1962, Mandela and other leaders were arrested and convicted of sabotage. During his twenty-seven years of imprisonment, Mandela became a powerful symbol of resistance.

Throughout the 1970s, underground nationalists leaders turned to armed struggle, setting up training camps in friendly African states and authorizing selected acts of sabotage and assassination. Meanwhile, students and workers took matters into their own hands in spontaneous uprisings in 1976 and 1983–1985. Through their protests they won massive international support for their cause, including sanctions levied against the South African government by the United States and Europe. This was an important step, as most Arab, African, and Soviet-bloc states had already refused to cooperate with South Africa, leaving it with few friends outside of the West.

One of the few African leaders able to protest the state openly was Bishop Desmond Tutu (b. 1931), the first black Archbishop of Cape Town and the head of the Anglican Church in South Africa. In 1984, he was awarded the Nobel Peace Prize for his role in speaking out against apartheid. Shortly afterward, he spoke before the United Nations Security Council, attacking South Africa's racial policies. Tutu's speech was pessimistic about the future—a reflection of the times and the crisis faced by South Africans in 1985, at the height of the uprising:

> I speak out of a full heart, for I am about to speak about a land that I love deeply and passionately; a beautiful land of rolling hills and gurgling streams, of clear starlit skies, of singing birds, and gamboling lambs; a land God has richly endowed with the good things of the earth, a land rich in mineral deposits of nearly every kind; a land of vast open spaces, enough to accommodate all its inhabitants comfortably; a land capable of feeding itself and other lands on the beleaguered continent of Africa, a veritable breadbasket; a land that could contribute wonderfully to the material and spiritual development

and prosperity of all Africa and indeed of the whole world. It is endowed with enough to satisfy the material and spiritual needs of all its peoples. And so we would expect that such a land, veritably flowing with milk and honey, should be a land where peace and harmony and contentment reigned supreme.

Alas, the opposite is the case. For my beloved country is wracked by division, by alienation, by animosity, by separation, by injustice, by avoidable pain and suffering. It is a deeply fragmented society, ridden by fear and anxiety, covered by a pall of despondency and a sense of desperation, split up into hostile, warring factions. It is a highly volatile land, and its inhabitants sit on a powder-keg with a very short fuse indeed, ready to blow us all up into kingdom come. There is endemic unrest, like a festering sore that will not heal until not just the symptoms are treated but the root causes are removed.

South African society is deeply polarized. Nothing illustrates this more sharply than the events of the past week. While the black community was in the seventh heaven of delight because of the decision of that committee in Oslo, and while the world was congratulating the recipient of the Nobel Peace prize, the white government and most white South Africans, very sadly, were seeking to devalue that prize. An event that should have been the occasion of uninhibited joy and thanksgiving revealed a sadly divided society. Before I came to this country in early September to go on sabbatical, I visited one of the trouble-spots near Johannesburg. I went with members of the Executive Committee of the South African Council of Churches, which had met in emergency session after I had urged Mr. P. W. Botha to meet with church leaders to deal with a rapidly deteriorating situation. As a result of our peace initiative, we did get to meet with two cabinet ministers, demonstrating thereby our concern to carry out our call to be ministers of reconciliation and ambassadors of Christ.

In this black township, we met an old lady who told us that she was looking after her grandchildren and the children of neighbors while they were at work. On the day about which she was speaking, the police had been chasing black schoolchildren in that street, but the children had eluded the police, who then drove down the street past the old lady's house. Her wards were playing in front of the house, in the yard. She was sitting in the kitchen at the back, when her daughter burst in, calling agitatedly for her. She rushed out into the living room. A grandson had fallen just inside the door, dead. The police had shot him in the back. He was six years old. Recently a baby, a few weeks old, became the first white casualty of the current uprisings. Every death is one too many.

Those whom the black community has identified as collaborators with a system that oppresses them and denies them the most elementary human rights have met cruel death, which we deplore as much as any others. They have rejected these people operating within the system, whom they have seen as lackies and stooges, despite their titles of town councilors, and so on, under an apparently new dispensation extending the right of local government to the blacks. Over 100,000 black students are out of school, boycotting—as they did in 1976—what they and the black community perceive as an inferior education designed deliberately for inferiority. An already highly volatile situation has been ignited several times and, as a result, over 80 persons have died. There has been industrial unrest, with the first official strike by black miners taking place, not without its toll of fatalities among the blacks. . . .

The South African government is turning us into aliens in the land of our birth. It continues unabated with its vicious policy of forced population removals. It is threatening to remove the people of Kwa Ngema. It treats carelessly the women in the KTC squatter camp near Cape Town whose flimsy plastic coverings are destroyed every day by the authorities; and the heinous crime of those women is that they want to be with their husbands, with the fathers of their children. White South Africans are not demons; they are ordinary human beings, scared human beings, many of them; who would not be, if they were outnumbered five to one? Through this lofty body I wish to appeal to my white fellow South Africans to share in building a new society, for blacks are not intent on driving whites into the sea but on claiming only their rightful place in the sun in the land of their birth. We deplore all forms of violence, the violence of an oppressive and unjust society and the violence of those seeking to overthrow that society, for we believe that violence is not the answer to the crisis of our land. We dream of a new society that will be truly non-racial, truly democratic, in which people count because they are created in the image of God. We are committed to work for justice, for peace, and for reconciliation. We ask you, please help us; urge the South African authorities to go to the conference table with the representatives of all sections of our community. I appeal to this body to act. I appeal in the name of the ordinary, the little people of South Africa. I appeal in the name of the squatters in crossroads and in the KTC camp. I appeal on behalf of the father who has to live in a single-sex hostel as a migrant worker, separated from his family for 11 months of the year. I appeal on behalf of the students who have rejected this travesty of education made available only for blacks. I appeal on behalf of those who are banned arbitrarily, who are banished, who are detained without trial, those imprisoned because they have had a vision of this new South Africa. I appeal on behalf of those who have been exiled from their homes. I say we will be free, and we ask you: Help us: that this freedom comes for all of us in South Africa, black and white, but that it comes with the least possible violence, that it comes peacefully, that it comes soon.[37]

The combination of internal and external pressures eventually persuaded many white South African that discussion with African nationalist leaders was the only alternative to a massive, bloody, and futile struggle to preserve white privileges. The outcome was the abandonment of key apartheid policies, Nelson Mandela's release from prison, the legalization of the ANC, and a prolonged process of negotiation, culminating in the country's first national elections as a democratic state in 1994. To nearly everyone's surprise, the long nightmare of South African apartheid came to an end without a racial bloodbath.

## QUESTIONS

1. In what ways did decolonization and anticolonial struggles elsewhere in the world influence Africans' own struggles for independence?

2. How did the attitude of the United States and the former Soviet Union accelerate the process of decolonization in Africa?

3. Examine the role of the United Nations in hastening the role of decolonization process in Africa.

4. Why do you think nationalist movements developed faster in British West Africa than elsewhere on the continent?

5. Read the FLN Declaration of 1954. How would you describe its tone? What were the organization's leaders asking for?

6. Compare Desmond Tutu's and Kwame Nkrumah's speeches. In what ways are their messages similar? In what ways are they different? What do these differences suggest about the diversity of African perspectives on decolonization?

## FURTHER READINGS

Ajayi, A.J.F., and Michael Crowder, eds. *History of West Africa*, vol. 2. London, Longman, 1974.

Akintoye, S. A. *Emergent Africa: Topics in Twentieth Century African History*. London, Longman, 1976.

Boahen, A. Adu. "Africa: Colonialism and Independence." In Raph Uwechue, ed., *Africa Today*. London, Africa Books Ltd., 1991.

Fanon, Frantz, ed. *Toward the African Revolution: Political Essays*. New York: Gore, 1967.

Gifford, Posser, and W. M. Roger Louis. *The Transfer of Power in Africa Decolonization, 1940–1960*. New Haven: Yale University Press, 1982.

Hargreaves, J. D. *Decolonization in Africa*. London: Longman, 1988.

Harris, P. B. *Studies in African Politics*. London: Hutchinson University Library, 1970.

Karis, Thomas, and Gwendolen M. Carter, eds. *From Protest to Challenge: A Documentary History of African Politics in South Africa, 1882–1964*. Bloomington: Indiana University Press, 1997.

Mortimer, E. *France and Africa, 1944–60*. London: Faber and Faber, 1969.

Rubin, Leslie, and Brian Weinstein. *Introduction to African Politics: A Continental Approach*. New York: Praeger Publishers, 1977.

Whitaker, Paul. "The Revolutions of Portuguese Africa." *Journal of Modern African Studies* 8, no. 1 (1970): 15–35.

## NOTES

1. J. D. Hargreaves, *Decolonization in Africa* (London: Longman, 1988), p. 10.

2. For a discussion, see A. Adu Boahen, "Africa: Colonialism and Independence," in Raph Uwechue, ed., *Africa Today* (London: Africa Books Ltd., 1991), p. 169–188.

3. Ibid.

4. Olajide Aluko, "Politics of Decolonization in British West Africa," in J. F. Ade Ajayi and M. Crowder, eds., *The History of West Africa*, vol.11 (London: Longman, 1974), pp. 622–663.

5. Raymond Betts, *Decolonization* (London: Routledge, 1997), p. 98.

6. Peter Jennings and Todd Brewster, *In Search of America* (New York: Hyperion, 2002), p. xix.

7. A. E. Afigbo et al., *The Making of Modern Africa, Vol. 2: The Twentieth Century* (London: Longman, 1986), p. 145.

8. S. A. Akintoye, *Emergent African States: Topics in Twentieth Century African History* (London: Longman, 1976).

9. Boahen, "Africa: Colonialism and Independence."

10. P. B. Harris, "The Process of Decolonization in Africa," in P. B. Harris, ed., *Studies in African Politics* (London: Hutchinson University Library, 1970), pp. 9–35.

11. J. B. Webster et al., "Sierra Leone 1787–1914: Mother of British West Africa," in James B. Webster, A. Adu Boahen, and Michael Tidy, eds., *The Growth of African Civilization: The Revolutionary Years: West Africa Since 1800* (London: Longman, 1967), pp. 147–149.

12. R. Oliver and Gervase Mathew, eds., *History of East Africa*, vol. 1 (Oxford: Oxford University Press, 1964), p. 120.

13. Boahen, "Africa: Colonialism and Independence," p. 187.

14. Akintoye, *Emergent African States*, pp. 8–18.

15. Colin Legum, "Pan-Africanism and Nationalism," in Joseph C. Anene and Godfrey N. Brown, eds., *Africa in the Nineteenth and Twentieth Centuries* (Ibadan: Ibadan University Press, 1972), pp. 528–539.

16. E. A. Ayandele, "Nationalist Movements in North Africa and the Achievement of Independence in the Twentieth Century," in Joseph C. Anene and Godrey N. Brown, ed., *Africa in the Nineteenth and Twentieth Centuries* (Ibadan: Ibadan University Press, 1972), pp. 199–215.

17. Ali Mazuri, *Africa's International Relations* (London: Heinemann, 1977), p. 577.

18. Guy Arnold, *Kenyatta and the Politics of Kenya* (London: Dent, 1974), p. 84.

19. Agbafor Igwe and Nnamdi Azikiwe, *The Philosopher of Our Time* (Enugu, Nigeria: Fourth Dimension Publisher, 1992), p. 25. See also K. A. B. Jones-Quartey, *A Life of Azikiwe* (Baltimore: Penguin, 1965).

20. *New York Times*, May 8, 1945.

21. Ibid.

22. Boahen, "Africa: Colonialism and Independence."

23. Ibid.

24. Kwame Nkrumah, *I Speak of Freedom: A Statement of African Ideology* (London: Heinemann, 1961), pp. xi–xiv.

25. Frantz Fanon, "Decolonization and Independence," in Fanon, ed., *Towards the African Revolution* (New York: Gore, 1967), p. 105.

26. Leslie Rubin and Brian Weinstein, *Introduction to African Politics: A Continental Approach* (New York: Praeger Publishers, 1977).

27. Richard Skalar, *Political Parties in Nigeria: Power in an Emergent Nation* (Treonton: Africa World Press, 2004).

28. Michael Crowder, "French West Africa," in J.F.A. Ajayi and M. Crowder, eds., *History of West Africa*, vol. 2. London: Longman, 1974).

29. Proclamation of the Algerian National Front, November 1954.

30. Akintoye, *Emergent Africa*. In contrast to Tunisia and Morocco, the nationalist struggle in Algeria became violent because of the large number of French settlers involved.

31. Ajayi and Crowder, *History of West Africa*.

32. Olajide Aluko, *Essays in Nigerian Foreign Policy* (London: Allen and Unwin, 1981). See especially ch. 15, "The 'New' Nigerian Foreign Policy," pp. 231–248.

33. Proser Gifford and W. M. Roger Louis, *The Transfer of Power in Africa: Decolonization: 1940–1960* (New Haven: Yale University Press, 1982), pp. 417–444.

34. Ibid.

35. Peter Walshe, *The Rise of African Nationalism in South Africa: The African National Congress, 1912–1952* (Berkeley: University of California Press, 1971).

36. See Howard Brotz, *The Politics of South Africa: Democracy and Racial Diversity* (New York: Oxford University Press, 1977), and Albert Luthuli, *Let My People Go: An Autobiography* (New York: McGraw-Hill, 1962).

37. Bishop Desmond Tutu, "The Question of South Africa," *Africa Report* 30 (January—February 1985): 50–52. Originally a statement to the United Nations Security Council issued on October 23, 1984.

# 6

## Moroccan Feminism as Universal Feminism

### *African Voices of the Feminist Struggle, ca. 1930–2000*

### Osire Glacier

GLOBAL CONTEXT

The purpose of this chapter is to discuss feminism as an African, and particularly Moroccan, experience and ideology. Most people in the West believe that feminism is a strictly western ideology and that feminism in nonwestern societies is a western import, or at best only produced by an "indigenous" westernized elite. The dominant narratives of world history locate the origins of feminism in Europe and the United States in the nineteenth and twentieth centuries. These world historians are themselves guided by a dominant set of feminist histories. Most of these histories of feminism were produced by Euro-American countries before the new millennium.[1] They are part of a vast feminist literature that was produced in the second half of the nineteenth century and the beginning of the nineteenth century in the West, rather than in the rest of the world.[2] The prevalence of this western dominance in the feminist literature has led scholars such as Miriam Schnier to argue that feminism could only have emerged in the West and not, for example, from Muslim *harems*, including Moroccan ones.[3] Feminist scholars like Schnier thus link feminism to western modernity, whose manifestations are the industrial revolution, the expansion of capitalism that attracted women to the job market, and the enlightenment philosophy that underlies individual rights and social movements.[4] In other words, in their view feminism is intimately bound to western economic development and democratic progress.

In the last decade, however, this historiography has begun to show interest in nonwestern feminisms, as we shall see below. Indeed, women's resistance—of which feminism is one of many forms of ideas, discourses, ways of life, individual or collective actions, and social constructions of inequalities between the sexes—is not solely a feature of western societies. In fact, such resistance has always existed and continues to exist in all human societies, although it is often ignored by historians. As the feminist theorist Chandra Mohanty has pointed out, whereas the history of western feminism has been amply studied, the history of feminism in the rest of the world is still untold.[5] For this reason, the present chapter begins by narrating the history of Moroccan feminism, while analyzing some key concepts of dominant feminist historiography such as *feminism, modernity, democracy,* and *westernization.* Ultimately, such an analysis demonstrates that Moroccan feminism is an integral part of *universal feminism,* which is defined as a series of ideas, discourses, and actions conveyed by isolated individuals or collective groups, with the goals of denouncing social constructions of inequalities between the sexes and of remedying the situation by promoting women's rights. Discourse is a series of narratives that are produced in a specific social and historical context, with a particular in mind—here the aim is the improvement of women's condition. Thus discourse posits the existence of strategies that depend on a given social and historical context. In other words, universal feminism is part of the lived experiences and perspectives of women in many places and times, and often appears as a dialogue among women as a group formed around common issues and interests. This chapter gives a voice to a number of Moroccan feminists so that the reader can appreciate these feminist discourses.

## A Brief History of Western Feminism

If ones considers the history of feminism as it is usually narrated, the pioneering feminists were European women who contested their conditions as women as early as the fifteenth century.[6] This is how Christine de Pizan came to be recognized as the first woman to have written in defense of women.[7] Other European women came afterward, such as Modesta di Pozzo di Forzi, Marie le Jars de Gournay, and Mary Wollstonecraft.[8] However, most other historical accounts suggest that modern feminism was born much later, during the nineteenth century in Europe and the United States.[9] The latter histories argue that the advent of women's collective organizations in this period distinguish modern feminism from the incidents of women's resistance of earlier centuries, which were largely acts of individual resistance. These collective organizations led to a social movement whose objective was to modify the laws and mentalities that perpetuated inequalities between the sexes. Having identified the nineteenth-century collective organizations as the point of origin for modern feminism, these historical accounts then classify modern feminism into three waves of thought and activism.

The first wave of feminist activism began in the nineteenth century and continued into the beginning of the twentieth century in the United States, Britain, Germany, and France. During this period, feminist activists primarily sought to promote women's suffrage, or right to vote. (For this reason, they are often called "suffragettes.") However, they also denounced other inequalities, such as imbalances within marriage and women's lack of financial autonomy.[10] Emmeline Pankhurst in Britain, Charlotte Perkins and Elizabeth Cady Stanton in the United States, and Jeanne Deroin in France are among the leaders of this movement.

The first wave of feminism ended when these suffragettes finally attained their goal. This occurred largely through the modification of the American, British, German, and French constitutions, all of which granted women the right to vote in the beginning of the twentieth century.[11] However, in subsequent decades, women realized that gaining the right to vote did not eradicate discrimination against them. Accordingly, in the 1960s and '70s, the second phase of feminism was concerned with all forms of discrimination against women.[12] This period corresponds to the women's liberation movement. Thus, expressions such as "Women's Liberation," "The British Women's Liberation Movement," and "le Mouvement de libération des femmes" began appearing in the United States, Britain, and

France, respectively, during the 1960s and '70s. These second-wave feminists focused more on personal and social issues rather than on political rights. Important topics included reproductive rights and birth control, equal pay and treatment in the workplace, and the division of labor in the home. The slogans "One is not born a woman, but becomes one" and "The personal is political" describe the spirit of the movement.[13] In short, these feminists argued that the inequality experienced by women in their interactions in the private sphere were indications of unequal power structures in the political sphere. Simone de Beauvoir, Betty Friedan, Kate Millett, and Shulamith Firestone are among the great thinkers of this phase.[14]

The third wave of feminism, which began in the 1990s, reflected new challenges faced by feminists in this era. Feminists were not only facing a backlash during this phase but also needed to fill some gaps left behind by feminist activities during the second wave.[15] Thus third-wave feminism included many distinct but overlapping critiques of earlier feminist thought. For example, postcolonial feminism emerged in this period to address the omission of nonwestern women from first- and second-wave feminist discourse. Postcolonial feminists argued (and continue to argue) that the dominant feminist discourse reduces feminist issues to the experiences of middle- and upper-middle classes of Euro-American women.[16] Similarly, this feminism highlights the fragmentary representation of nonwestern women depicted by the dominant feminist discourse.[17] Indeed, Chandra Mohanty argues that western feminists' writings about women in the rest of the world were produced through the processes of western academia.[18] One of the consequences of this hegemony is that most feminists' writings continue to portray nonwestern women, including African women, as a single bloc of oppressed women.[19] These women are imagined to be ignorant, poor, passive, and victimized. In other words, they are seen as the opposite of western women, who—according to most feminist writers—are educated, modern, active, and combative.[20] The postcolonial feminists did make progress, however. As of now, a few years into the new millennium, the new dominant feminist historiography considers feminism to include "multiple feminisms"—a diversity of voices within the multiplicity of human societies.[21]

*Western Feminism and Women of the World*

The history of feminism as it is typically narrated raises several issues. First, we need to add the label "western" to this history since it describes the development of western feminism, but not that of feminism throughout the world. It therefore contributes to the erroneous belief that feminism is exclusively a western ideology. Thus, for instance, in an historical and comparative study of women's movements throughout the world, Janet Chafetz and Anthony Dworkin maintain that there is no independent women's movement in North Africa, including Morocco.[22] As we shall see below, this is not correct.

Second, this dominant history clearly links feminism to of the ideas, structures, and social organization associated with western modernity, including the industrial revolution, urbanization, economic development, and democratic individualism.[23] According to this narrative, nonwestern feminism emerged exclusively from Europe, during the western colonial expansions, and not from any local conditions or actions.[24]

Linking the emergence of nonwestern feminism to its encounter with the West in this way implies that African, Asian, and other societies do not have an endogenous feminism. Yet, nonwestern feminism has always existed. It is just more difficult for western scholars to perceive. In order for this feminism to be seen, and therefore to be narrated, feminism must be redefined in such a way as to reflect the society and historical era being analyzed. This requires a shift in methodology. Numerous societies, including Morocco, favored the oral tradition until only recently. Therefore, in addition to seeking evidence of feminist discourses in the writings left by women, we need to examine their ways of life throughout the centuries. But we must also recognize that the feminist expression of a given period depends upon the limits that oppressive bodies impose upon it. In fact, to avoid being silenced, feminist expression often assumes only the permissible forms that power structures grant to dissident voices. As evidence of the kinds of feminism that careful work in this process can reveal, the following sections narrate the history of Moroccan women's resistance to social constructions of inequalities between the sexes from ancient times to the present.

## AFRICAN EXPERIENCES

This chapter focuses specifically on Moroccan feminism, but it's important to say a few words about the broader African context as well. As scholars who study women in precolonial African history have demonstrated, the roles and status of women have varied greatly across the continent and at different times. Some historians have even suggested that certain African societies did not have a fixed category of "woman" and that those who did often recognized the ability of men and women to cross into each other's realms.[25] This is not to say that women didn't face particular restrictions or suffer from lower status in some areas and periods in precolonial Africa. Indeed, evidence suggests that they often fought to gain or maintain rights and privileges through women's social organizations, contests over control of religious rituals and mystical power, and political action.

Women's diversity and flexibility decreased rapidly, however, with the advent of colonialism. Nineteenth- and twentieth-century European colonizers tended to not recognize the rights that women held in African societies—partly owing to their own cultural predilections but also because they worked more closely with African men, and particularly powerful male Africans, than with women. As a result, women's rights were rapidly eroded across much of Africa during the colonial period.

Nevertheless, African women managed to contest this erosion even during the colonial period. Many of their activities were individually based, but mass, organized defenses of women's rights also took place. A case in point is the Nigerian "Women's War" of 1929, in which thousands of women rose up against the British colonial administration and their appointed male chiefs to protest taxes on women who owned stalls in markets. Some of their protests took the form of songs and dances outside of chief's residences. Indeed, such performances were historically a form of protest employed by women. (In this instance, they were somewhat effective in reversing the new tax.) Although songs and dances would not fall under the traditional definition of "feminism," they provide a good example of action taken by women to redress inequalities and issues that particularly hurt women.

Similarly, despite the patriarchal structures of traditional Moroccan society, women found ways to participate in the public sphere. Patriarchy can be defined as a form of social organization in which the man as father functions as the mediator of authority in the family and, by extension, in society. Inevitably, patriarchy is accompanied by discrimination against women, including their submission to men; a preference for male offspring; and the transmission of the father's surname to the children. In precolonial Morocco, women were confined to the private sphere, with queens and princess relegated to the *harems*, and Islamic law dictated interactions between women and men. Certainly, the law favored polygamy and unilateral male divorce. At the same time, Islamic law guaranteed the respectful treatment of women. Individual women may have succeeded in participating in the public sphere during this period, but it wasn't until the advent of colonialism that women began struggling collectively against patriarchal structures. Indeed, they participated in anticolonial struggles, including armed conflict, when central Morocco became a French protectorate and Northern and Southern Morocco became a Spanish protectorate in the early twentieth century. While struggling against colonialism, women sought to improve their conditions by founding organizations and schools for girls. However, independence failed to bring about the social reforms desired by women. In fact, although postcolonial Morocco experienced profound social changes, the women in this region continue to face discrimination such as unequal access to education, to the labor market, and to structures of power. Yet from the precolonial era to the present day, they have opposed such discrimination. In short, by broadening the definition of feminism to include a conscious understanding of how social inequalities between women and men come into being, as well as an understanding of the ways of life that oppose these constructions, we can readily conclude that feminism has been an integral part of the Moroccan social fabric since ancient times.

## Women in Moroccan Political History

Many of the women who managed to overcome masculine power structures went on to play an important role in Moroccan political history from ancient times to the colonial era. Some were queens; others were political leaders.

For instance, Tin Hinan was the Tuaregs' queen and ancestress during the fourth century;[26] to this day, women and men inhabiting the desert proudly claim to be her descendants. Similarly, al-Kahina was the Berbers' queen. Her power extended from Tripoli to Tangiers in the seventh century,[27] and she was the only woman who fought the Arab Umayyad Empire's armies. Other women were *de facto* queens; as such, they ruled through either their husbands or their sons. One example is Zaynab al-Nafzawiyya, who, while serving as political adviser to her husband Yussef Ben Tachfine, was the *de facto* queen in the eleventh century; in this capacity she participated in the governance of one of the largest empires in the Maghreb, extending from Senegal to Andalusia and from the Atlantic to Algiers.[28] Another example is Khnata Bent Bakkar, who as political adviser to her husband, the sultan Moulay Ismaïl, and later to her son, was the *de facto* ruler of Morocco in the seventeenth century.[29] Thanks to her intervention, the country avoided the disintegration of its political and territorial unity. Still other women accessed political power through religion. In the fourteenth century, Lalla Aziza Seksawiya was a Sufi saint who enjoyed wide religious and political powers.[30] As such, she mediated and reconciled different tribal and intertribal groups in the Seksawa Valley. She also led a local resistance against Amir Ben Mohammed al-Hintati, who was both a Merinid general and the governor of Marrakesh. Lalla Aziza Seksawiya's tomb is a place of pilgrimage and prayers to this day.

Women were also governors. For instance, a woman named Zouhra became Hakimat Fez (Fez's governor) in 1464 and governed Fez for three years after the fall of Abd al-Haq, the last Merinid king.[31] Similarly, the famous As-sayyida al-hurra (the sovereign woman) served as Hakimat Tétouan (Tétouan's governor) from 1525 to 1542. As-sayyida al-hurra was the leader of pirates in the adjacent Northwestern Mediterranean Sea.[32] At the time, piracy was indistinguishable from politics: it was practiced not only for the immediate income it brought about but also as a way to continue the struggle against the Christian enemy. As the organizer of resistance against the Spaniards and the Portuguese's invasions, As-sayyida al-hurra built and repaired boats and developed a naval force in the port of Tetouan. In addition, she often ventured out of this port into the high seas, leading piracy in the

Mediterranean and giving orders to her captains to take whatever actions were needed to counter the foreign naval expansionist plans. During her reign, she effectively repelled the invasion projects of the Spaniards and the Portuguese and achieved important financial gains due to piracy, thereby bringing wealth and prosperity to her community.

Women were diplomats as well. An example is Sahaba er-Rahmania, who acted as an ambassador in the Ottoman court, one of the most powerful world empires in the sixteenth century.[33] Sahaba er-Rahmainia tactfully asked the Ottoman sultan Salim to militarily support her son Abd al-Malek in his struggle to regain his throne back. Her intervention not only enabled her son to regain power but ultimately led to making his reign one of the most prosperous eras in Moroccan history. In a similar fashion, princess Fatima played the role of a diplomat in the administration of her husband, Sultan Mohammed III, in the eighteenth century.[34] In this role, she corresponded with European princesses, negotiating the liberation of their respective prisoners as well as securing favorable alliances for the sultan. One princess she corresponded with was Louisa de Asturias.

Women were political advisers, too. In the eighth century, a woman named Kenza twice saved Moroccan political and territorial unity. First, she gave birth to a son, Idris II, who succeeded his father when the Idrisid monarchy had just been instituted in Morocco. Second, after Idris II's death, she convinced her grandson, Mohammed Ben Idris, to share governance over the kingdom with his brothers. By decentralizing the government, the Idrisid monarchy temporarily managed to maintain the nation's stability.[35] Consequently, the inhabitants of the Maghreb experienced a period of great prosperity, evidenced by the appearance of great fortunes, such as that of the family al-Fihri.[36] In the ninth century, the heir to one such fortune—Fatima al-Fihri—founded the University al-Qaraouiyine in Fez, a major educational and spiritual center in the Muslim world that contributed to a transfer of knowledge between the Orient and the West; it is today the oldest operating university in the world.[37] In the thirteenth century, the Almohad prince Abd al-Wahid al-Rachid became sultan as a result of the political ingenuity of his mother, Hababa.[38] After Idris al-Ma'mun, al-Rachid's father, died while traveling, Hababa convinced the military chiefs to temporarily hide his death and proclaim her fourteen-year-old son the Moroccan sultan. This was done in order to maintain unity against al-Ma'mun's nephew, Yahya, who had already taken over Marrakesh.

Women were also warriors. In the twelfth century, the Almoravid princess Fanu, Omar Ben Yintan's daughter, disguised herself as a man to courageously fight the Almohads during the takeover of Marrakesh in 1147.[39] She was believed to have fallen only once during the battle in which the Almohads were able to enter the Almoravid palace. Princess Fanu was not the only historically recorded female warrior. In the twelfth century, the daughter of the religious and political leader Mehdi ibn Tumart attacked her father on his way back home, and fought him, in order to prove to him that she could be a caliph, the highest political leadership in the Islamic world.[40]

Finally, with the advent of colonialism, women participated in the anti-colonial struggles,[41] some as leaders and others as ordinary women. At the end of the nineteenth century, a politically engaged poetess named Hadda Zaydia, better known as Kharbucha, encouraged her tribe to rise up against the tyrannical Aïssa Tamri Ben Omar. He was the neighboring tribe's chief and an ally of the French colonizers.[42] In the conflict that followed, Kharbucha was captured, tortured, and executed. Her poems are still historically relevant, as they inform historians about peasants' struggles against abusive central power. In the twentieth century, Malika al-Fassi was the only woman to have signed the manifesto of independence in 1944,[43] and Farida Hassan spied on the Spanish military camps during the Rif War.[44]

Can we consider these women pioneers of feminism? For now, the question remains without an answer because—apart from Malika al-Fassi—none of these political leaders left any written reflections about the status of women. Nevertheless, it is clear that these women did not consider their sex to be an obstacle to governing or participating in the political sphere. Rather, they found ways to transcend the social restrictions imposed upon their sex, often acting behind the scenes or through pathways open to women. For instance, Zaynab al-Nafzawiyya governed through her husband and Khnata Bent Bakkar governed through her son, thus transcending the masculine power structures. At the very least, then, these women should be considered resistors of the restrictions placed on women's roles by their own society.

*Women in the Moroccan Public Sphere*

Paralleling their political involvement, women from ancient Morocco to the colonial period participated in diverse sectors of the public sphere outside of politics. Indeed, the historical record includes numerous women whose consciousness, actions, stances, and way of life can be considered forms of resistance to gender discrimination. In this chapter, I will mention only a few such women. One was the thirteenth-century Moroccan explorer Oum al-Yamane.[45] She left Morocco in 1226, accomplished the pilgrimage to Mecca by foot, and spent four years in the Middle East. In 1235, she left again for other pilgrimages and explorations. However, she died on her way back to Morocco.[46] During the Merinid reign in Morocco, which spanned the thirteenth to fifteenth centuries, Aïcha Bent al-Jayyar was a doctor and a pharmacist who practiced in Ceuta.[47] In the fifteenth century, theologian Oum Hani Bint Mohamed al-Abdoussi was recognized by her peers as an authoritative *faqiha*, or legal expert.[48] In the seventeenth century, Sayyida Aïcha al-Adawiya was a Sufi religious leader who had numerous disciples.[49] She was also known by the nickname "Ariyatra's" (the naked head), because she did not wear a veil. To this day, her tomb is an area of pilgrimage and refuge in Meknes. In the eighteenth century, Ftatime Bint Abd Slam was famous for her expertise in making plaster and healing broken arms and legs.[50] In the nineteenth century, Aïcha Dhaljbel was a *majduba* (woman shaman) in Tetouan.[51] And in the twentieth century, Touria Chaoui was the first woman pilot in Morocco.[52]

Even though these women left no written reflections on women's status, their ways of life attest to their belief that their sex did not condemn them to limit their activities to the private sphere.

There is also evidence of women from medieval Morocco—immortalized through their writings—who demonstrated a stance that can be described as feminist. For example, the famous thirteenth-century Andalusian poetess Hafsa Bint al-Hajj Ar-Rakuniya, who lived during the rule of one of the grand empires of the Maghreb, led a life that negated all of the social gender constructions of proper womanly behavior.[53] Hafsa was a free woman who disdained any restriction upon her language and her body and was renowned for her sharp satires as well as for her famous lovers. Indeed, a substantial portion of her poetry praises love and sensuality. The great poetess Nazhun Bint al-Qila'i—who lived during the Maghreb grand empire of the twelfth century—likewise transcended social restrictions imposed on the feminine body and language.[54] Nazhun led such a libertine life that the famous satirist Abu Bakr al-Makhzumi labeled her a whore. Far from passively enduring the insult, she composed a satire in reply, ridiculing the latter's own sexual practices. At the end of the satire, she stated:

> I replied to a poem by the other,
> so tell me, who is more poetic?
> If the creation made me a woman,
> my poetry is masculine.[55]

In this way, Nazhun proved to her audience that even though she was a woman, and thus a subordinate person in accordance with the social construction of the sexes of her time, her poetry belongs to a superior genre. Indeed, some literary critics count Nazhun among the greatest feminists in the world,[56] thus calling into question the dominant belief that Venetian Christine de Pizan was the first woman to write in defense of her sex.

Evidence such as Nazhun's writings demonstrates a long history of resistance to gender that set the stage for modern Moroccan feminism in the twentieth century. However, as discussed in the next section, the modern Moroccan feminists also aptly integrated the great ideas of their time into their responses to women's conditions in society. These ideas included socialist and Marxist orthodoxies as well as the concepts of democracy and human rights.

## Modern Moroccan Feminism

Rabea Naciri, Fatima Saddiqi, and Abdelssamad Dialmy, experts in modern Moroccan feminism, locate the genesis of this feminism in the first half of the twentieth century.[57] Perhaps its first expression came in 1935, when Malika al-Fassi wrote an article, published by *al-Maghreb* magazine, advocating women's right to education.[58] Al-Fassi thus became the first female journalist in Morocco.[59] A few years later, Rhimou al-Madani published similar articles in the Tetouanian press.[60] Unfortunately, she has been ignored by contemporary historians. As a result, not much is known about her writings and her activities. Malika al-Fassi, however, emerged as the pioneer of modern Moroccan feminism. Indeed, from 1935 to 1943, al-Fassi wrote a series of articles advocating women's progress, with a focus on education.[61] She also operated in the political sphere. In 1946 al-Fassi founded Akhawat al-Safaa (Sisters of Purity), a women's movement within al-Istiqlal (Party of Independence), whose main function was the study of the status of women.[62] During the first assembly of the Akhawat al-Safaa organization on May 23, 1947, in Fez, Habiba Guessouss, another feminist who has regrettably sunk into historical oblivion, gave a speech to celebrate the occasion:

> Honorable ladies,
>
> On this happy day, we want to thank all of you, on behalf of the association, for your presence in this General Assembly.... We are full of hope that we will succeed in the near future. We believe that we will overcome backward traditions with determination, patience, and wisdom. Today, many Moroccans accept the idea of promoting women's rights. This is why we believe that creating a woman's association composed of qualified women would help to fulfill our mission and thus contribute further to women's emancipation.[63]

Soon after, the organization formulated a series of demands, among which were women's right to education and legal reforms, especially advocating the abolition of polygamy.[64]

Not all of the first generation of modern Moroccan feminists were women.[65] Rather, the feminism of this era was produced by both men and women. However, even though male feminists and female feminists pursued the same goal—women's emancipation—the two feminisms differed from one another. When male feminists advocated women's liberation, the targeted goal was not women's progress per se but, rather, women's progress in the context of achieving national progress and advancement.[66] By contrast, women's feminism advocated women's liberation, with the specific aim of improving women's lives.[67] This difference can be explained by the fact that male feminism was stimulated by the European encounter, whereas female feminism derives its origins from Moroccan social reality. In other words, even though modern Moroccan feminism emerged during the colonial period, this feminism was not a western product, and even less a colonial one. On the contrary, women were reacting to local social constructions of inequalities between the sexes, as well as participating in the social and political debates of its time, including such issues as power relations among nations, national development and social inequalities.

The next generation of feminists involved women who'd had true access to education, partly owing to the actions of the first generation of modern Moroccan feminists. Thus by the 1960s, a decade after achieving independence, Morocco had its first women jurists, doctors, pharmacists, and academics.[68] Indeed, they were both literally and figuratively the authors of the feminist ideas that emerged in newspapers and academic reviews of this period.[69] This generation of feminists, while advocating the liberation of women and the development of their human potential, also highlighted women's domestic roles. In short, they sought to improve women's lives, although without questioning patriarchal norms and values. Zakia Daoud and Leila Abouzeid were two of the journalists in this feminist generation.[70]

In the 1970s, Moroccan women such as the novelist Khnata Bennouna began to write novels and sociological studies questioning the validity of patriarchal structures.[71] At the same time, along with the development of journalistic, literary, and academic writing, partisan feminism emerged in Morocco. Various feminist groups were formed within socialist-leaning political parties such as the Socialist Union of Popular Forces (SUPF) and the Party of Progress and Socialism (PPS).[72] The paradigm of these feminists was "insufficiency," by which they meant to criticize the insufficiency of women's rights. Thus many of these feminists called for equality between adult women and men in terms of the legal treatment they received.[73] Among their first demands was the abolition of a series of legal discriminations against women, mainly in the private sphere. These included the abolition of the obligation for an adult woman to have a male guardian, the abolition of the requirement for a male to legally support his wife (which resulted in the exclusion of women from the job market and the public sphere), the abolition of polygamy, and the transformation of the marriage dissolution process into a judicial divorce.[74] Moreover, in 1977, the women of the national congress of SUPF connected the reform of the private sphere to the wider project of socialism. However, the male elites of SUPF did not share this position. According to them, feminism was a bourgeois ideology and therefore only the abolition of capitalism would bring about women's liberation.[75] As a result, the SUPF's parliamentary group did not retain the women's requests within their party platform.[76]

Following this event, these feminists operating within socialist-leaning parties realized that women's issues transcended class struggles and the limitations of socialist and Marxist orthodoxies.[77] From that point on, they described the discriminations faced by women in terms of power relations between the genders, locating these concerns within the broader issues of democracy and human rights. In addition, they realized that the political parties did not adequately represent women. Tired of being marginalized within "male political clubs," they decided to found autonomous associations whose objective was the advancement of women's rights. This "associative" feminism, which began in the 1980s, entailed the formation of various feminist and feminine autonomous associations, only some of which kept a strong link to a specific political party. These associations included the Democratic Association of Moroccan women, founded in 1985; the Union of the Feminine Action, founded in 1987; and the Moroccan Association of Women's rights, founded in 1992. Among other issues, they advocated the implementation of rights for women that were already legally recognized, the abolition of legal discriminations against women, the end of women's poverty, the eradication of women's illiteracy, and the elimination of all forms of violence against women such as domestic violence and sexual harassment.[78] This feminist generation produced feminists who became well-respected public figures—namely, Latifa Jbabdi, Nouzha Skalli, Amina Lemrini, and Latifa Smires Bennani.[79]

It is in the context of associative feminism that Latifa Jbabdi, founder and president of the Union of Feminine Action, organized the "One Million Signatures" campaign in 1992.[80] This campaign aimed at gathering a million signatures in an effort to pressure the ruling elites to change the *Mudawana* (the Moroccan family code) so as to eradicate a series of legal discriminations against women. The text of the petition was sent to King Hassan II, to members of the parliament, and to the main newspapers in the country. This petition constitutes a major document in the history of Moroccan feminism. For the first time, women were mobilizing *en masse* around common demands and directly expressing their demands to the concerned authorities. The text of the petition is reprinted below:

> We, the undersigned, declare that we strongly believe that only a democratization of relations within the family and society in general can lead to the construction of a real democracy. The Personal Status Law articles are in utter contradiction to the Moroccan Constitution, which explicitly guarantees equality between men and women. The present Personal Status Law is out of date and its articles are unjust toward women, as they cause unnecessary family crises and social tragedies. We, here, demand to change its articles according to the following principles:
>
> Consider the family as a Unit based on equity, equality, and mutual respect.
>
> Consider women, in the same way as men, legally recognized as soon as they reach majority age.
>
> A woman who reaches majority should be able to marry without a legal guardian.
>
> Both husband and wife should have the same rights and duties.
>
> Divorce should be judicial, and both husband and wife should have an equal right to file for divorce.
>
> Polygamy should be abolished.
>
> Mothers should have parental rights in the same way as fathers.
>
> Work and education should be considered women's pre-eminent rights; husbands should have no prerogative to deprive their wives of these rights.[81]

In response to this initiative, the government changed the "family code." Although the legal modifications were minor, they accomplished a major shift in the spirit of the law: because people came to recognize that *Mu-*

*dawana* was a human product able to be abrogated, it lost its status as a supposedly sacred text with immutable provisions. Moreover, the petition stimulated deep social debates that contributed to publicizing discriminations faced by women.

Yet even while feminism was gaining additional rights for Moroccan women, it faced a backlash with the emergence of Islamism as early as the 1980s.[82] Although it utilizes a religious discourse, Islamism is in fact a political movement—and its objective is to legitimize patriarchal norms and values. As such, it targets illiterate women and marginalized social classes, advocating the veil and women's seclusion. To confront this threat, feminists—while publically affirming their spiritual ties to Islam—have requested that contextual readings of the Quran elicit more liberal interpretations of religious texts.[83]

Currently, in the context of the Arab Spring, women's organizations demand that the constitution guarantee a quota of 50 percent for women in all spheres of activity, including every level of decision making. Thus, the feminist movement represents one of the main actors promoting democratization in the Moroccan political scene.[84] Feminist associations are more accessible to women than political parties and, for this reason, represent, express, and channel women's demands to a greater extent.

At present, there are two types of feminist associations in Morocco. The first seeks to fill the state's social deficiency toward women and children, providing legal support and material assistance to single mothers, housing to homeless children, and shelter to victims of domestic violence. The second works to bring about a society that does not discriminate against women. Given the extent and diversity of their activities, the women's associations developing today have a wide-ranging network of alliances both with Moroccan civil society and with numerous international governmental and nongovernmental organizations.

This brief history of modern Moroccan feminism deserves some reflection. During its various stages of evolution, Moroccan feminists made use of key concepts such as national development, socialism, Marxism, class struggles, gender, democracy, and human rights. But these are not examples of the mere importation of western concepts. Indeed, as intellectual productions they have become the inheritance of all humanity. In the case of Moroccan feminists, defining women's issues in terms of democracy and human rights has been a strategic choice—one that reflects the social and political struggles of their time: they have chosen the most favorable concepts for the advancement of women's rights in their society. This explains why Moroccan feminism has successively adapted socialist and Marxist orthodoxies, a democracy and human rights discourse, and the recognition of Islam as spirituality. In short, when the dominant feminist historiography perceives nonwestern feminism as a product of "indigenous" Occidentalized elites, it denies nonwestern feminists their ability to rethink and adapt according to their individuality ideas of their time to the needs of their society.

To summarize thus far: Whereas women's resistance to social constructions of inequalities between the sexes has existed in Moroccan society since ancient times, modern feminism was born in Morocco in the first half of the twentieth century. Since then, feminists have mobilized around a twofold objective: the promotion of women's rights and the elimination of all forms of discrimination against women. With a plurality of voices, they have claimed such rights as the right to education, the right to vote, access to employment, democratization of the private sphere, and criminalization of violence against women—demands that are similar to those of feminists in the West and elsewhere. Moreover, most of these feminists and women's organizations have exchanged their experiences and knowledge with western feminists, western women's groups, and human rights NGOs through a tightly woven network of international solidarity. In a sense, then, Moroccan feminists have been engaged in a universal feminist dialogue—one that concerns issues and interests facing *all* women. Facilitation of this dialogue requires the abolition of categories that divide women within cultural, religious, and national identities.

## AFRICAN EXPERIENCES IN FEMINISM: MOROCCAN FEMINIST VOICES

So that we can better understand this history of modern Moroccan feminism, the next section features three different feminist voices expressing their views of women's issues: Mririda N'Ayt Atiq, who represents a precolonial feminist consciousness; Malika al-Fassi, who represents a conservative feminism; and Hakima Chaoui, whose poetry employs both religious and antireligious themes.

*Mririda N'Ayt Atiq: A Precolonial Feminist Consciousness*

Mririda N'Ayt Atiq's work is a perfect example of a home-grown precolonial feminist consciousness.[85] The illiterate poetess Mririda was born sometime before the end of the nineteenth century in Magdaz, in the Tassaut Valley beneath the Atlas Mountains. At that time, Tassaut Valley was so remote as to be completely sheltered from western influences. Since Moroccan society favored oral tradition, Mririda's work would probably have remained unpublished if she had not meet René Euloge, a French teacher in Morocco and the first westerner to set foot in Magdaz. Mririda's poems reached us thanks to Euloge, who recorded them in 1927, translated them into French, and published them in 1959.[86]

Mririda's songs and poems were as much her own individual creation as they were a part of the Berbers' oral tradition. Their distinguishing feature is that they vividly convey the voice of a woman who bitterly contested the inequalities between the sexes in her own society. Yet Mririda's songs and poems inform us not only about women's status in Morocco at the beginning of the twentieth century but also about her way of life. For example, we learn that Mririda chose to be a prostitute:

> THE BAD LOVER
> Leave me, soldier without sense or manners!
> I can see that you are full of contempt,
> Your hand raised, insults on your lips,
> Now that you've had what you want from me.
> And you leave, calling me a dog!
> Sated with my pleasures,
> You'd have me blush for my trade,
> But you, were you ashamed

When you pushed gently at my door,
Up like a bull?
Were you coming to play cards?
You turned yourself into something humble,
Agreeing right off to my demands,
To losing all your pay in advance.
And the more your eyes undressed me,
The more your rough desire put you in my power.

When you finally took off my clothes
I could have had your soul for the asking!
I could have cursed your mother
And your father, and their ancestors!
Toward what paradise were you flying?

But now that you've calmed down,
You're back on earth,
Arrogant, rough and coarse as your *djellaba*
[traditional long unisex outer robe].

Guest of mine for the moment, my slave,
Don't you feel my disgust and hate?
One of these days
The memory of tonight will bring you back to me
Conquered and submissive again.
You'll leave your pride at the door
And I'll laugh at your glances and your wishes.
But you'll have to pay three times the price next time!
This will be the cost of your insults and pride.

I'll no more notice your clutching
Than the river notices a drop of rain.[87]

As a prostitute, Mririda considered any social condemnation of prostitutes to be hypocritical. She further argued that if such condemnation has to exist, then it surely should be extended to the prostitute's customers as well. In so saying, she reminded the client in the poem—and, by extension, any other man who frequented prostitutes—that he has no lesson to give her concerning her "sex work," since he is the one who knocked on her door. Some of Mririda's poems also indicate that instead of getting married, she deliberately chose prostitution, a job that enabled her to maintain her autonomy and freedom:

POOR NAÏVE MAN

Poor naïve young man, stop bothering me.
I've come to see my parents,
Not to look for a husband. God help me!
And I'll soon return to Azilal, if God wishes it.
One night with me has made you crazy—
Without laughing you ask me to be your wife!
I know how long that would last. . . .
What can you give me for my liberty?
But first of all, don't take this reproachful air
To shame me for my trade,
This trade that's given you pleasure.
What other could please me more?
And you beg me to be yours only!
Do you have something to give me?
Tell me, naïve young man.—Days without meat?
Without sugar and song?
Sweat and painful work?
The dung of the stable, stinking clothes
And the thick air of the smoky kitchen
While you're off dancing the *adersi* [traditional dance]?
And no doubt you'd want a household of sons.
Can't you see this isn't for me?
Let me return to the market of Azilal.
You are wasting your time and your begging tires me.
Why would I want to work
When I'm covered with silver and precious gifts?

> I'm like a flower with an intoxicating perfume
> Which has only the agreeable worry of opening itself
> To receive, at its wish—each night, each day—
> The freshness of the dew, the caress of the sun.[88]

Mririda's rejection of marriage may have stemmed from a belief that, in a society in which men were in charge of the family, marriage disempowered women. She believed that it not only dispossessed women of their personal freedom but also enslaved them in domestic work and childbirth—preferably, giving birth to sons. Although Mririda was illiterate, she perceived with clarity the institutions, such as marriage, that perpetuated these social patriarchal structures.

Similarly, there is an instance in which she resorted to an illegal abortion—enabling her to maintain control over her body and, correspondingly, over her sexuality:

### SISTER

> Sister, don't scold me.
> I know I shouldn't have slept in the *azib* [remote pasture].
> You know, sister, what can happen in a sheepfold
> On a warm night, close to a young man. . . .
> Am I the only girl to give in
> To the wishes of a young man?
> How could I know that this night
> Would bring a heavy stomach?
> Sister, keep my secret!
> Old Tamoucha knows the virtues of plants,
> Of plants that will quickly deliver me.
> Sister, you know well that afterwards
> There won't be a trace.
> Tamoucha has the alum and resin ready
> To restore my virginity.
> She has even promised to mention marriage
> (Is it possible?) to our dear cousin. . . .
> Tell me, sister, will he make a good husband?[89]

When Mririda speaks about a marriage with a cousin, it is to ridicule the patriarchs who think they are able to control women's bodies and sexuality, requiring that women should be virgins and be "given" to their cousins. Mririda wanted to be no one's wife. In fact, given the social constructions of inequalities between sexes that are unfavorable to women, what Mririda wanted were some fleeting moments of joy and pleasure:

> What do you want? . . .
> You make me laugh, son of the high pasture.
> I don't care about money or a scarf,
> and even less about marriage.
> I expect from you
> what you expect from me.
> And satisfied, we will leave each other.
> What I want, strong son of the high pasture,
> what I want is the shelter of this bush
> where you will lie on my breasts—which I hold
> out to you—and in a moment
> happiness sweeter than milk,
> while my eyes lose themselves in the sky.[90]

After all, Mririda's way of life is a bitter scream of rebellion against the social constructions of inequalities between the sexes. Having refused the institution of marriage, the poetess's choice to engage in prostitution and illegal abortion does appear to have allowed her some measure of independence.

### Malika al-Fassi: A Conservative Feminism

Like Mririda, Malika al-Fassi was conscious of the ways that the society in which she lived created inequalities between the sexes, and of the resulting unfavorable impact on women's lives.[91] However, al-Fassi's feminism differed significantly from that of the rebellious poetess. Whereas Mririda's feminist consciousness was expressed through an individual rebellious way of life, al-Fassi's joined with other feminist voices to create the shared movement of modern Moroccan feminism. These different pathways may have been related to the disparity in their socioeconomic backgrounds: whereas Mririda was poor and illiterate, al-Fassi led a privileged life. In fact, al-Fassi was born into one of the wealthiest and most erudite families in Morocco. She also benefited from the beliefs of her father, al-Cadi al-Fassi, who considered education to be a civic obligation and thus ensured that she received a proper education.

As a child, Malika al-Fassi did not understand why her teachers came to her house while her brothers and male cousins went school. Eventually, however, she realized that there was no school for girls in Morocco at that time—and that women in general were excluded from national education. Accordingly, at the young age of fifteen, she wrote an article advocating women's right to education. The article, published by *al-Maghreb* magazine in 1935, was signed "al-Fatate" (the young girl). Hers was the first feminine voice to have made its way into the national press:

> When I consider the situation of women in Morocco, I find an abundance of ignorance and backward-looking traditions, which have nothing to do with Islam. Islam refutes these traditions. I devote this article to women because they live in decadence and inertia. I call upon you to rescue and free women from the chains of ignorance and illiteracy and provide them with a proper education.
>
> Let us ignore the talk of egoists who underestimate women and undervalue their purpose, and let us consider the problems of this task, hoping that we will reach a solution. Whoever has studied the past or present of civilized nations, and has witnessed the culture and advantages that women enjoy, will realize that women are essential in all human societies, that women form the cornerstones of rebuilding a nation. They are the first teachers of children and bear responsibility for the future generation. Therefore, we must first ask how this generation should grow and what objectives it should attain. Should our children acquire cowardice, a mean spirit, and useless traditions, which will prove harmful to any nation? Or should they acquire virtue and self-reliance? The answer is self-evident. The education of young girls should then be compulsory, and only dull minds would resist this on the grounds that girls' education is an outrage. Women are considered by many to be ig-

norant and feeble-minded, higher in status only than animals. Yet, one cannot deny that many women are strong, well educated, and tactful, albeit in a few limited circles.

That is why I feel sad about the present state of Moroccan women. And therefore, I have thought of a solution: I call on all Moroccans to open the doors to girls' education so that they may acquire religious and literary knowledge in the Arabic language, so as to develop noble skills and wisdom.[92]

Malika al-Fassi's feminism was rooted directly in the real repercussions of the inequalities between sexes in Moroccan society: women's illiteracy and their exclusion from the educational system. In denouncing this woeful situation at age fifteen, al-Fassi set herself on a feminist pathway to which she remained faithful over the years. Her first article was followed by several more published between 1935 and 1943, all advocating women's right to education. These articles may not have yielded significant results in terms of women's right to education, but they did initiate deep social debates about women's status in society. Some of al-Fassi's readers opposed women's rights on the pretense that these rights were western imports threatening national culture and religion. They reacted by writing their own articles, but Al-Fassi proved willing to enter into dialogue with her dissenters, writing this in 1935:

I was sad to read an article in *al-Maghrib* [*al-Maghreb*] magazine with faulty ideas which called women's progress "Western," and claimed that it would only lead women to separate from their religion and to lose their values. . . . I didn't think that such ideas could be published [anymore], ideas that set back girls' progress, and postpone their education. . . . I was afraid of the influence that such an article might have; I, who cling to our language and religion and to those of our traditions that do not harm Islam or Moroccan civilization. I wanted to answer that article, but for various reasons I restrained myself. But now I think that I must write a word on the subject.

It is no secret that the Moroccan woman's life is stillness and languor. Why not, since she only leaves her mother to go to the handicraft mistress' house. And when she finishes there with skill in some craft, she becomes a prisoner in the house. All she knows of the secrets of life is what her grandmother and some old women tell her, such as stories about *djinn* [wicked spirits, imps] and the *baraka* [blessing, holiness] of saints: Sidi so-and-so, he who swears by him becomes blind; Sidi so-and-so, he who spends time in his shrine will be healthy, rich and vigorous . . . and so forth and so forth.

Is it fair that the young Moroccan girl remains the way she has always been, in an era of science and knowledge? Is it good for her to stay the way she was, when her sisters in the Middle East have already gained a significant amount of knowledge? Is it good for her to stay the way she was, when a number of the most talented Moroccan youth have scattered to Eastern and Western countries to get knowledge and high culture; when the Qaraouiyine University is wide open and training students every year; when schools are full of boys; when the Middle East is sending us torrents of books, and papers and magazines, written by the region's best scholars; when knowledge is rapidly spreading throughout Morocco? Yet the young Moroccan girl knows nothing of all this, and gains nothing from it. How can educated youth accept as a wife and be comfortable with her, and give her the reins in socializing their children, when the youth have dealt with knowledge and formulated ideas, and gained enough learning to make them despise an ignorant woman?

This situation may lead to disaster: either marrying a foreign woman—and we have seen the signs of that, and the Middle Easterners have known its calamities and write about it—or it may lead to celibacy, which is a second calamity that destroys even civilized nations, let alone underdeveloped countries. It is possible to avoid these two calamities, since there is a way out: Giving girls a good education that will raise their level of culture and lead to the happiness of both man and wife.[93]

In 1946, Malika al-Fassi made a decision that ensured that the call for women's access to education would be widely heard: she founded Akhawat al-Safaa (Sisters of Purity), a women's association within the political party Istiqlal (The Independence). Akhawat al-Safaa's objective was the promotion of women's rights. The first issue that al-Fassi promoted within this organization was the necessity to establish secondary schools for girls. The Akhawat al-Safaa association eventually led to the creation of classrooms for girls in schools and was also a factor in the birth of the modern feminist movement in Morocco.

Malika al-Fassi campaigned for women's access to education until her death in 2007. However, she advocated education for women only through the secondary-school level:

> But will this education be primary, or secondary, or superior? I think that what is appropriate for girls is secondary education, because the primary level alone will be incomplete. . . . As for superior education, it is usually used to obtain a career, and careers are men's duty because of the life responsibilities that are imposed on them. . . . We know the social harm caused by women's work from Westerners' experience and from Middle Easterners who have imitated them. For when a woman works outside the house, she who is responsible for the housework and the socialization and welfare of the children, it does nothing but take men's work and tear apart the family bonds because of the clashes that it causes.[94]

Al-Fassi's feminism did not significantly differ from the feminism of many of her male colleagues. Both were fostered by the nationalist reformist current during the beginning of the twentieth century. In this sense, al-Fassi's feminism has roots in exchanges with Europe. Nonetheless, she sought to dissociate herself from the West and to reject some aspects of western feminism:

> The word "equality," which is thundering now in the West and the Middle East, is nothing but a fraud. I don't understand woman's imitation of man, by working and taking on rights that are not hers, thus neglecting her home responsibility and all the burdens related to it. Is earning money man's only virtue? Are there not other social virtues equally or more important than earning money? Isn't the socialization of children and the managing of the house a great and gracious accomplishment? . . . Men and women were created to cooperate, to confront the difficulties of life together. Man works hard outside the home, and woman inside, and it is through this association and cooperation that they reach equality, not in doing the same work.[95]

We can see form these quotations that Malika al-Fassi's feminism did not question the basic social patriarchal structures of Moroccan society at the time. In fact, al-Fassi rejected the principle of equality between the sexes, preferring instead to emphasize the complimentary nature of the sexes. In the name of this latter principle, al-Fassi considered it women's primary role to remain as mothers and wives. It was for this reason that she advocated a limited level of education for women; according to her, women did not need a PhD in order to be good mothers and good wives. We can thus conclude that al-Fassi's feminism was a conservative feminism.

### Hakima Chaoui: A Religious and Antireligious Feminism

Unlike Malika al-Fassi's feminism, Hakima Chaoui's completely rejected the patriarchal structures of Moroccan society, including the religious beliefs that legitimated them. The context of this poetess's feminism was the increasing delegitimization of Moroccan feminism by Islamists in the 1980s. These Islamists exploited religion in order to promote women's subordination, using Islam as a justification for their advocacy of veiling, women's exclusion from the workplace, women's seclusion, and the glorification of women's roles solely as mothers and wives. Writing in response, Chaoui utilized a religious discourse—precisely in order to bring into question not only the degrading images of women produced by religious fundamentalists but also their patriarchal norms and values. This discourse resulted in a feminist message that was paradoxically both religious and antireligious:

> YOU [in the feminine form]
> Bright you are my lady
> Like a sun
> And the sun rises every day
> From your eyes
> Majestic you are
> Like a palm tree
> And under your feet the moon
> Crawls

And the stars multiply
In your hands
Enflamed you are my lady
As the flames of revolution
And many revolutions
Learnt from you . . .
Cursed is he my lady
Who said
You were created from a crooked rib
Cursed is he my lady
Who named you
The sign of assent is silence
Cursed from the origins of creation
He who said
You were a pudenda
From your voice to your toes
Cursed
He who speaks poorly of you . . .
Dignified, you are my lady
And this present is igniting
To burn yesterday's books
And to write your forgotten history
Cursed is he who betrays your sex
When you are the progeny of mankind
Of the moon
Of the sun.[96]

Chaoui's attempts to restore women's dignity through her poetry resulted in harassment and death threats. On March 8, 2001, International
Women's Day, she read the poem transcribed above to a radio audience.
The Islamists' reaction was immediate. Accused of blaspheming against the
Prophet, the poetess was excommunicated by the fundamentalist newspaper *Attajdid*.[97] Though undoubtedly stressful for Chaoui, this episode nevertheless contributed to greater publicity for her poems. But an inescapable

question remains: How many women have been silenced over the centuries, and how many more are still silent out of fear of reprisals?

## QUESTIONS

1. According to most mainstream histories of feminism, where and when did feminism emerge? Based on the information provided in this chapter, do you agree or disagree? Why?

2. Consider the popular conceptions of African women described in the "Global Context" section of the chapter. How does Moroccan feminists' activism compare with these conceptions?

3. What does Mririda's poem "Sister" suggest about precolonial Moroccan women's control of their reproductive lives?

4. Malika al-Fassi opposed the principle of equality between the sexes, instead favoring that of complementarity between the sexes. Can women attain equality of rights while claiming difference?

5. Compare Hakima Chaoui's poems to the images conveyed by western media regarding the veil and Muslim women.

6. Compare and contrast the feminisms of Mririda, al-Fassi, and Chaoui.

7. French philosopher Michel Foucault asserted that power and knowledge are often intertwined. Can this statement be applied to our knowledge about the history of feminism?

## FURTHER READINGS

Baker, Alison. *Voices of Resistance: Oral Histories of Moroccan Women.* New York: State University Press of New York, 1998.

Brodkin, Karen. *Sisters and Wives: The Past and Future of Sexual Equality.* Westport, CT: Greenwood Press, 1979.

Eisenstein, Zillah. *Against Empire, Feminisms, Racism, and the West.* New York: Zed Books, 2004.

Mohanty, Chandra Talpade, Ann Russo, and Lourdes Torres, eds. *Third World Women and the Politics of Feminism.* Bloomington: Indiana University Press, 1991.

Narayan, Uma. *Dislocating Cultures, Identities, Traditions, and Third-World Feminism.* New York: Routledge, 1997.

Oyewumi, Oyeonke. *The Invention of Women: Making an African Sense of Western Gender*. Minneapolis: University of Minnesota Press, 1997.

Pennell, C. R. "Women and Resistance to Colonialism in Morocco: The Rif 1916–1926," *Journal of African History* 28, no. 1 (1987): 107–118.

Sadiqi, Fatima, Amira Nowaira, Azza el-Kholy, and Moha Ennaji, eds. *Women Writing Africa: The Northern Region*. New York: The Feminist Press, 2009.

Tazi, Abd al-Hadi. *Al-Mar'ah fi tarikh al-gharb al-islami*. Casablanca: Fennec, 1993.

## NOTES

1. Miriam Schneir, ed., *Feminism: The Essential Historical Writings* (New York: Random House, 1972), p. xii; Estelle B. Freedman, ed., *The Essential Feminist Reader* (New York: The Modern Library, 2007), p. xv; Eliane Gubin, Catherine Jacques, and Florence Rochefort, *Le siècle des féminismes* (Paris: Les Éditions de l'Atelier, 2004), p. 15.

2. Schneir, *Feminism: The Essential Historical Writings*, p. xiv.

3. Ibid.

4. Freedman, *The Essential Feminist Reader*, p. xii; Gubin, Jacques, and Rochefort, *Le siècle des féminismes*, p. 15.

5. Chandra Talpade Mohanty, Ann Russo, and Lourdes Torres, eds., *Third World Women and the Politics of Feminism* (Bloomington: Indiana University Press, 1991), p. 3. In the introduction to the book, Mohanty opposes the feminist historiography of Western countries with that of "developing nations." In order to avoid confusion due to multiple terminological referents, the concept of "developing nations" has been replaced by that of "the rest of the world."

6. Schneir, *Feminism: The Essential Historical Writings*, ed., op. cit., p. xii.

7. Simone de Beauvoir, translated and edited by H. M. Parshley, *The Second Sex* (New York: Vintage Books, 1989), p. 105.

8. Schneir, *Feminism: The Essential Historical Writings*, p. xii; Maggie Humm, ed., *Modern Feminisms: Political, Literary, Cultural* (New York: Columbia University Press, 1992), p. 4.

9. Janet S. Chafetz and Anthony Gary Dworkin, *Female Revolt: Women's Movements in World and Historical Perspective* (Totowa, NJ: Rowman & Allanheld, 1986), p. 103.

10. Schneir, *Feminism: The Essential Historical Writings*, pp. xiv–xv.

11. Humm, *Modern Feminisms*, p. 2.

12. Chafetz and Dworkin, *Female Revolt*, p. 163.

13. The first slogan is Simone de Beauvoir's, in *The Second Sex*; the second slogan is Carol Hanisch's, in Theresa Man Ling Lee, "Rethinking the Personal and the Political: Feminist Activism and Civic Engagement," *Hypatia* 22, no. 4 (2007): 163.

14. De Beauvoir, *The Second Sex*; Betty Friedan, *The Feminine Mystique* (New York: Norton, 1962); Kate Millett, *Sexual Politics* (Garden City: Doubleday, 1970); Shulamith Firestone, *The Dialectic of Sex: The Case of Feminist Revolution* (New York: Morrow, 1970).

15. Susan Faludi, *Backlash: The Undeclared War Against American Women* (New York: Anchor Book, 1992), pp. ix–xxiii, 454–460; Drucilla Cornell, *At the Heart of Freedom, Feminism, Sex and Equality* (Princeton: Princeton University Press, 1998); Leslie Heywood and Jennifer Drake, eds., *Third Wave Agenda, Being Feminist, Doing Feminism* (Minneapolis: University of Minnesota Press, 1997).

16. Chilla Bulbeck, *Re-orienting Western Feminisms: Women's Diversity in a Postcolonial World* (Cambridge: Cambridge University Press, 1998), pp. 2–10.

17. Chandra Mohanty, "Under Western Eyes, Feminist Scholarship and Colonial Discourse," in Chandra Mohanty, Ann Russo and Lourdes Torres, eds., *Third World Women and the Politics of Feminism* (Bloomington: Indiana University Press, 1991), p. 56.

18. Ibid., p. 55.

19. Ibid., p. 56.

20. Ibid.

21. Gubin, Jacques, and Rochefort, *Le siècle des féminismes*, p. 15.

22. Chafetz and Dworkin, *Female Revolt*, p. 191.

23. Freedman, *The Essential Feminist Reader*, p. xii; Gubin, Jacques, Rochefort, *Le siècle des féminismes*, pp. 15–16; Alison Baker, *Voices of Resistance: Oral Histories of Moroccan Women* (New York: State University Press of New York, 1998), p. 19.

24. Bulbeck, *Re-orienting Western Feminisms*, p. 18.

25. Ifi Amadiume, *Male Daughters, Female Husbands: Gender and Sex in an African Society* (London: Zed Books, 1987); Oyeronke Oyewumi, *The Invention of Women* (Minneapolis: University of Minnesota Press, 1997).

26. Count Byron de Prorok, *In Quest of Lost Worlds* (London: Frederick Muller, 1935), pp. 3–56.

27. David Sweetman, *Women Leaders in African History* (London: Heinemann, 1984), pp. 17–21.

28. H. T. Norris, *The Berbers in Arabic Literature* (Beirut: Librairie du Liban, 1982), pp. 131–140.

29. Fatima Sadiqi, Amira Nowaira, Azza el-Kholy, and Moha Ennaji, eds., *Women Writing Africa: The Northern Region* (New York: The Feminist Press, 2009), pp. 98–100.

30. Ibn Qunfudh, *Uns al-faqir wa-izz al-haqir* (Rabat: Éditions techniques Nord-Africaines, 1965), pp. 86–87.

31. Abd al-Hadi Tazi, *al-Mar'ah fi tarikh al-gharb al-islami* (Casablanca: Fennec, 1993), pp. 218–219.

32. Chantal de la Véronne, *Sida el-Horra, la noble dame* (Paris: Hespéris-Tamuda, 1956), pp. 222–225.

33. Mohamed Saleh al-Amrani Benkhaldoun, *Sab' Sayiddate Morakouchiyyate bistihqaq* (Morakouch: Manchourate Jaridat al-afaq al-marghebiya, 2009), pp. 99–111.

34. Tazi, *al-Mar'ah fi tarikh al-gharb al-islami*, pp. 248–249.

35. William Spencer, *A Historical Dictionary of Morocco* (Metuchen, NJ: Scarecrow Press, 1980), p. 67.

36. Mahmud Ismail, *Al-adarisah* (Cairo: Maktabat madbuli, 1991), pp. 63–80.

37. Hezreen Abdul Rashid, "Fatima al-Fihri, Founder of the Oldest University in the World," available online at http://theurbanmuslimwomen.wordpress.com/2008/08/04/fatima-al-fihri-founder-of-the-oldest-university-in-the-world/ (accessed on August 3, 2010).

38. Gaston Deverdun, *Marrakesh des origines à 1912*, vol. 1 (Rabat: Éditions techniques Nord-Africaines, 1959), pp. 18–19, 292.

39. Ibid., p. 160.

40. Abd al-Aziz ibn Abd Allah, *Mazahir al-hadarah al-maghribiyah*, vol. 2 (Dar al-Bayda: Dar al-Sulami lil-ta'lif wa-al-Nashr, 1597–1958), p. 127.

41. C. R. Pennell, "Women and Resistance to Colonialism in Morocco: The Rif 1916–1926," *Journal of African History* 28, no. 1 (1987): 107–118.

42. *Maalamat al-Maghrib/L'encyclopédie du Maroc* (Salé: Association des auteurs marocains pour la publication, 2005), pp. 3642–3643, 3685–3686.

43. Baker, *Voices of Resistance*, pp. 63–78.

44. *Maalamat al-Maghrib/L'encyclopédie du Maroc*, p. 7068.

45. Tazi, *al-Mar'ah fi tarikh al-gharb al-islami*, p. 167.

46. Ibid.

47. Ibid., p. 127.

48. Ibid., pp. 96–97.

49. Mohamed Qadiri, *Nachr al-Mathani, Archives marocaines*, vol. 24 (Paris: Maison Esnest Leroux, 1917), pp. 202–203.

50. Mohammed Ibn Azzuz Hakim, *Tatawiniyat fi dhakirat at-tarikh* (Tétouan: Matbaat al-Khalij alArabi, 2001), p. 37.

51. Ibid., p. 50.

52. Osire Glacier, *Political Women in Morocco, Then and Now* (Trenton, NJ: Africa World Press, 2013).

53. Jennifer Heath, *The Scimitar and the Veil: Extraordinary Women of Islam* (New Jersey: Hidden Spring, 2004), pp. 418–419.

54. Marlé Hammond, "'He Said, She Said': Narrations of Women's Verse in Classical Arabic Literature. A Case Study: Nazhun's Hija' of Abu Bakr al-Makhzumi," *Arabic Middle Eastern Literatures* 6, no. 1 (2003): 3–18.

55. I provided this translation, which can be found in Abd Muhanna, *Mu'jam al-nisa ah-shairate fi al-jahiliya wa l-islam* (Beyruth: Dar al-kutub al-ilmiya, 1990), p. 251.

56. Teresa Garulo, *Diwan de las poetisas de Al-Andalus* (Madrid: Hiperion, 1986), pp. 110–120.

57. Rabéa Naciri, "The Women's Movement and Political Discourse in Morocco," *Occasional Paper* 8 (1998): 1–28; Fatima Sadiqi, "The Central Role of the Family Law in the Moroccan Feminist Movement," *British Journal of Middle Eastern Studies* 35 (2008): 325–337; and Abdessamad Dialmy, *Le féminisme au Maroc* (Casablanca: Éditions Toubkal, 2008).

58. *Al-Mujahida al-Marhuma Lalla Malika al-Fassiya* (Rabat: Mandoubiyat samiya li-Qudama' al-muqawimine wa aadha' jaysh at-tahrire, 2008), pp. 58–60.

59. *Al-Mujahida al-Marhuma Lalla Malika al-Fassiya*, pp. 56–57.

60. Latifa Akharbach and Narjis Rerhaye, *Femmes et politique* (Casablanca: Le Fennec, 1992), p. 20.

61. *Al-Mujahida al-Marhuma Lalla Malika al-Fassiya*, pp. 56–70.

62. Sadiqi, Nowaira, el-Kholy, and Ennaji, *Women Writing Africa*, p. 161.

63. Ibid., p. 174.

64. Sadiqi, "The Central Role of the Family Law in the Moroccan Feminist Movement," p. 325.

65. Ibid.

66. Ibid.

67. Ibid.

68. Ibid., p. 327.

69. Ibid.

70. Ibid.

71. Ibid.

72. Ibid.

73. Ibid.

74. Ibid.

75. Ibid., pp. 125–126.

76. Ibid., p. 126.

77. Ibid., Naciri, pp. 7–8.

78. Ibid.

79. Ibid.

80. Sadiqi, Nowaira, el-Kholy, and Ennaji, *Women Writing Africa*, pp. 277–278.

81. Ibid., p. 278.

82. Sadiqi, "The Central Role of the Family Law in the Moroccan Feminist Movement," p. 330.

83. Ibid.

84. Ibid., p. 332.

85. Mririda N'Ayt Atiq (Mririda N'Aït Attik), *Songs of Mririda, Courtesan of the High Atlas*, translated by Daniel Halpern and Paula Paley (Greensboro, NC: Unicorn Press, 1974).

86. Mririda N'Ayt Atiq (Mririda n'Aït Attik), *Les chants de Tassaout*, translated by René Euloge (Marrakech: Éditions de la Tighermt, 1959).

87. Mririda, *Songs of Mririda, Courtesan of the High Atlas*, pp. 15–16.

88. Ibid., p. 17.

89. Ibid., p. 19.

90. Ibid., p. 18.

91. *Al-Mujahida al-Marhuma Lalla Malika al-Fassiya.*

92. Sadiqi, Nowaira, el-Kholy, and Ennaji, *Women Writing Africa*, p. 145.

93. Baker, op.cit., p. 64.

94. Ibid.

95. Ibid.

96. Hakima Chaoui, *Ishraqat al-jorh wa al-ishq* (Rabat: Imperial, 2001), pp. 47–49. Here, too, I provided the translation.

97. Ibid.

# Index